Who gets what in the city? Why do some people receive more city services than others? What are the rules that guide urban bureaucratic behavior? How can city agencies better achieve their goals?

The authors of URBAN OUTCOMES address these questions through an intensive study of three agencies in Oakland, California: the Oakland Public Schools, the Oakland Street Department, and the Oakland Public Library. Within each agency the authors describe how administrators acquire and budget their funds and how they allocate their outputs to different sections of the city.

Frank S. Levy teaches in the Department of Economics at Berkeley. Arnold J. Meltsner is a member of the faculty of Graduate School of Public Policy at Berkeley. Aaron Wildavsky is Dean of the Graduate School of Public Policy and Professor of Political Science at Berkeley.

Urban Outcomes

This volume is sponsored by the
OAKLAND PROJECT
University of California, Berkeley

Urban Outcomes

Schools, Streets, and Libraries

Frank Levy
Arnold J. Meltsner
Aaron Wildavsky

UNIVERSITY OF CALIFORNIA PRESS
BERKELEY, LOS ANGELES, LONDON

University of California Press
Berkeley and Los Angeles, California
University of California Press, Ltd.
London, England
Copyright © 1974, by
The Regents of the University of California
ISBN: 0-520-02546-6
Library of Congress Catalog Card Number: 73-83054
Printed in the United States of America

The Oakland Project

At a time when much is said but little is done about the university's relationship to urban problems, it may be useful for those who are looking for ways of relating the university to the city to take a brief look at the Oakland Project of the University of California, which combined policy analysis, service to city officials and community groups, action in implementing proposals, training of graduate students, teaching new undergraduate courses, and scholarly studies of urban politics. The "university" is an abstraction, and as such it exists only for direct educational functions, not for the purpose of doing work within cities. Yet there are faculty members and students who are willing to devote large portions of their time and energy to investigating urban problems and to making small contributions toward resolving them. Our cities, however, do not need an invasion of unskilled students and professors. There is no point in hurtling into the urban crisis unless one has some special talent to contribute. After all, there are many people in city government—and even more on street corners—who are less inept than untrained academics. University people must offer the cities the talent and resources which they need and which they could not get otherwise.

In 1966 a group of graduate students and faculty members at the University of California at Berkeley became involved in a program of policy research and action in the neighboring city of

Oakland. As members of the Oakland Project, they tried to meet some of the city's most pressing analytical needs and also to make suggestions that could be implemented.

Members of the project made substantial time commitments (usually about two years) to working in a particular Oakland city agency. Normal working time was two days a week, although special crisis situations in the city sometimes necessitated much larger blocks of time. Since project members worked with city officials and remained in the city to help implement the suggestions they made, they avoided the "hit-and-run" stigma that members of city agencies often attach to outsiders. By attempting first to deal with problems as city officials understand them, project members developed the necessary confidence to be asked to undertake studies with broader implications.

The Oakland Project became a point of communication for individuals and groups in the city of Oakland and throughout the University of California. Its focus expanded from a concentration on city budgeting to a wide range of substantive policies and questions of political process; for example, revenue, police, personnel, federal aid, education, libraries, and the institutionalization of policy analysis. The Project provided assistance to governmental (mayor, city manager, chief of police, head of civil service, superintendent of schools) and nongovernmental (community group) actors. In order to transmit the knowledge gained, Oakland Project members taught courses—open to both undergraduate and graduate students—dealing with urban problems and policies. The Project's scholarly objective is to improve policy analysis by providing new ways of understanding decisions and outcomes that affect cities. Its members have based numerous research essays on their experience in the city. It is hoped that the books in this series will be another means of transmitting what they have learned to a wider audience.

AARON WILDAVSKY

Contents

Acknowledgments

We owe a number of debts both individually and collectively. Financial support for our early research efforts came from the Urban Institute, particularly for the school chapter, for which the Institute's support permitted Levy to work for a year within the Oakland Public Schools both as a teacher's aide and as a member of the business office staff. Without the cooperation of the business office, the district administration, and a number of elementary school teachers and principals, the research for the school chapter would have been impossible. Additional thanks for careful reading and comments on earlier drafts must go to Marty Levin, Jesse McCorry, and Jeffrey Pressman. In particular, the section on budgetary behavior of school officials benefited from McCorry's comments and his unpublished manuscript on Oakland's budgeting. The calculations in the section in chapter 1 on the schools' distribution of resources were performed by Donald Sant and Greg Duncan.

Meltsner wishes to express his indebtedness to Professor Judith May of the Oakland Project, who studied the budgeting process in the Oakland Street and Engineering Department in 1966, and to his research assistant Suzanne B. Haas, who conducted many interviews and contributed considerably to the writing of the street chapter. Once again city officials saved us from making many mistakes.

City Manager Jerry Keithley's request for an evaluation provided the first stimulus for our interest in the Oakland Library. The initial work, including most of the interviews with library personnel, was conducted by Fred Deyo, then a graduate student in the Sociology Department of the University of California. Wildavsky made extensive use of a report Deyo wrote on the budgetary process in the Library. Later on, Michael Teitz, a professor in the City Planning Department, had his students do a systems analysis of the library system, and Wildavsky used parts of it. Susan Choy helped summarize the major findings of Professor Teitz and his students.

A number of our colleagues had the perseverance to read and give us comments on the entire manuscript. Besides our friends at the Graduate School of Public Policy, we wish to thank Professors Victor P. Goldberg, Norton Long, Dale Marshall, and James Q. Wilson. In an enterprise of this sort, a number of secretaries are involved in typing numerous drafts and changes, but we particularly want to thank Dorothy Grupp, who coordinated three busy and sometimes distracted authors. We also want to express our appreciation to Professor Melvin Webber, of the University of California's Center for Planning and Development Research, who with his quiet support has made many of the books of the Oakland Project series possible. Without his encouragement and the provision of indispensable amounts of financial support, the Oakland Project, and the books that stem from it, would not have prospered.

F.L.
A.J.M.
A.W.

Introduction

Outcomes are the "so-what" of politics. They are the judgments by which citizens evaluate their government. If outputs are what governments produce, outcomes are the grand design which citizens see behind those outputs.

The distinction is delicate enough to deserve an example. The Parks Department produces an output—to wit, parks. For any period of time we can discuss the distribution of that output: the Maple Street playground received new swings; the Downtown War Memorial received new flowers and a repainting. But often, citizens are not satisfied with such a discussion. They (and we) want to go further to characterize and judge the distribution: the Park Department favors the poor, or it discriminates against black neighborhoods, or it spends too much money for what it produces. When we move into the realm of evaluation, we are talking about outcomes.

This book concentrates on the government's distribution of goods and services to the citizens of Oakland, California. We want to find out how such agencies as schools, libraries, and streets allocate their outputs among groups in the city, and what makes the agency allocate its outputs as it does. We ask how the distribution of agency outputs produces outcomes affecting different kinds of people, and how to alter outputs so as to change outcomes. But before doing so we must distinguish between decisions, outputs, outcomes, and impacts of public organizations.

Consider government as a mechanism that makes decisions about what it should do. The decisions result in the production of outputs. Officials dispense these outputs to citizens in such a way that we talk about a distribution of outputs or discern a pattern of resource allocation. When anyone evaluates this distribution or pattern, we refer to outcomes. To inquire about the impact of an outcome is to ask how the lives of individual citizens are altered by governmental action in the future.

Decisions are choices among alternative courses of action; they can be studied in terms of their causes or consequences. Who made the decision and how was it made? We can try to understand why one particular choice was made and others were not, focusing on the officials who make decisions and the processes which result in their choices. Or our attention may shift from decision to outputs—from organizational choice to organizational production. The question then is: What do these choices lead the organization to produce?

This concern leads naturally to identifying outputs, that is, goods and services that the organization produces: the number of books available or taken out, students who graduate with high school degrees, miles of city streets resurfaced. Outputs, then, represent the way to classify goods and services supplied by a public agency and received by (or directed at) the public. Thus one can be reasonably objective about outputs. People may disagree about which ones are important, but there should be widespread agreement on what a particular output is, how it is measured, and what the quantities are (within a reasonable margin of error).

This is all on firm, traditional ground in the study of organizations. Decisions are made, outputs are identified and, it is hoped, accounted for. This book can (and does) ask how organizational decisions lead to particular outputs. But our investigation goes further, to the uncharted territory of outcomes. We turn away from producing organization, strictly conceived, and instead focus on the citizen-consumers of its goods and services.

Our concept of outcomes includes a subjective element of evaluation because it involves human preferences—likes and dislikes, pain and pleasure. In this book we are the evaluators, and we study the distribution of outputs precisely in order to make normative judgments. Should outputs be distributed in other ways or in different proportions? Are their consequences good (or bad) for various people differently situated? Ought people who are worse off be made better off? The appearance of "should" or "ought" words signals going beyond "facts" into the realm of "values." We will try to make our criteria for judgment as clear and explicit as possible, and to argue in their favor as persuasively as we know how, but there is (and must be) plenty of room for disagreement; applying other criteria could result in different valuations. Or the applicability of several criteria to the same distribution of outputs might lead to different appraisals of how their combined consequences should be evaluated.

If we are on less than objective ground, we share that ground with others, most notably the courts. In recent years, judges have begun to apply the guarantees of the Fourteenth Amendment's equal protection clause to the provision of public services. Several public school finance cases, beginning with *Serrano* v. *Priest*,[1] have overturned state legislation which, in the words of the court, "makes education a function of [local] wealth." In *Hawkins* v. *Shaw*,[2] the Fifth Circuit Court of Appeals found unconstitutional racial discrimination in the provision of such public services as streets and lighting, and required equalization of those services. While these decisions suggest that gross and irrational inequalities with respect to the provision of public services will not be tolerated by the courts, they are less specific in defining appropriate remedies; the school finance decisions have placed on state legislatures the burden of formulating a constitutionally acceptable allocation formula.[3] Before this task can be done well, more will have to be known about outcomes.

Our book is about immediate outcomes, not distant impacts.

1. *Serrano* v. *Priest*, 5 Cal 3rd 584, 487 P 2d 1241 (1971).
2. *Hawkins* v. *Shaw*, 437 Federal Reporter (Second Series) 1286. For a decision which requires strict *intra*-district equality of school resources, see *Hobson* v. *Hansen*, 327 F. Supp. 844 (1971).
3. To discuss these decisions in this way does not mean we disagree with all of them. In *Hawkins*, for example, the town of Shaw, Mississippi had for years restricted its public works activities to white neighborhoods; white areas had paved streets and street lights while black neighborhoods had none. It was a case where most people would agree that discrimination was present. Precisely because the case was so clear cut, it offers little guidance for the situations more commonly encountered in many cities.

Who knows what the final consequences of schooling are for individuals? We don't and, so Jencks et al. inform us, neither does anyone else.[4] The ramifications of freeways, for instance, are so diverse—employment, social interaction, racial conflict, agricultural and industrial production—no one can project them in the distant future, let alone separate these consequences from others with different causes. One blanches at the very thought. No, we shall be more than satisfied with discerning and discussing just a few prominent, immediate outcomes.

Neither have we studied (nor do we know) how school, library, and street outputs affect specific individuals. The best we can do is talk about outcomes for social groups designated by income, race, and neighborhood. There are, moreover, so many forces working on these groups that it is usually impossible to separate the consequences of the outputs one has in mind from all the others. Hence we look for the most immediate outcomes so as to know which groups get more good outputs and less bad ones. Maybe futurologists now and historians later can predict or assess the ultimate impacts of governmental activity.

Just as outcomes are seen as the near consequences of outputs, so also do we want to explain outcomes by their most immediate causes. We cling to close causation partly because more distant causes are difficult to disentangle. Our other main interest is to suggest how outcomes might be altered. Organizational change demands that active participants be able to manipulate variables within their control. The variables should be on hand and available in the present. For the same reason, we note, but find irrelevant, causal factors that are beyond anyone's immediate control, or that are too "lumpy" or highly aggregated for anyone to manipulate. The basic idea is to make the study of outcomes relevant to potential change in public policy.

OUTPUTS, OUTCOMES, AND IMPACTS

We are not first. Others before us have also tried to distinguish among outputs, outcomes, and impacts. It may help the reader's perspective if we distinguish between our efforts and theirs. The most important difference, perhaps, is our central concern with

4. Christopher Jencks et al., *Inequality: A Reassessment of the Effect of Family and Schooling in America* (New York: Basic Books, 1972).

outcomes; thus we are interested in more extensive discussion and more precise delineation, while other authors deal with the concept of outcomes in passing as a very small part of a much larger problem.

Because outcomes have not been at the center of scholarly attention, the term has so far no standard meaning and it is often hard to know what a particular author means when he uses it. "What are our values?" Karl Deutsch asks rhetorically. "What outcomes do we desire?" [5] By "outcomes" does he mean views about the goods and services governments should produce, or the goals or objectives citizens wish governments to accomplish, or some desired choices among policy alternatives currently being considered?

It could be easily shown (without swamping the reader with examples) that most writers, including these authors in other works, use the term "outcome" casually to mean the result of a disputed action. Thus everyone refers to "electoral outcomes," signifying who won, or "policy outcomes," meaning which alternative has been chosen—a convenient synonym to designate winners and losers.[6] As such we have no quarrel with the usage; difficulties arise only with the need for more precise meaning. Thus, an intuitive notion of outcomes is of something at the end of a complicated process rather than at the beginning—an effect rather than a cause.[7] Heinz Eulau and Robert Eyestone find outcomes "the concrete manifestations of policy—revenues, expenditures, regulations, court decisions, the exertion of police power and so on." [8] In our terms, they are talking about outputs; they focus not on what people get but on what government does.

5. Karl W. Deutsch, *The Nerves of Government* (New York: Free Press, 1963), p. xiii.
6. See Michael Lipsky, *Protest in City Politics* (Chicago: Rand McNally, 1970), pp. 4, 15, 200. Another example are the political scientists who look at what happens to legal outcomes after a court decision. See, for example, Richard M. Johnson, *The Dynamics of Compliance: Supreme Court Decision-Making from a New Perspective* (Evanston: Northwestern University Press, 1967), and Theodore L. Becker, ed., *The Impact of Supreme Court Decisions* (New York: Oxford University Press, 1969).
7. Thomas R. Dye, *Politics, Economics, and the Public: Policy Outcomes in the American States* (Chicago: Rand McNally, 1966), pp. 1–3.
8. Heinz Eulau and Robert Eyestone, "Policy Maps of City Councils and Policy Outcomes, a Development Analysis," *American Political Science Review* 62 (March 1968): 126.

According to Bryan Fry and Richard Winters, "the distribution of benefits or sanctions" are not outcomes but "the most significant output dimension for political scientists, since much of the conflict preceding adoption of a program is not about whether it should be embarked upon, but who will pay and who will benefit." What, then, are outcomes? To learn that "political variables will have a stronger influence on policy outcomes than will socio-economic variables" or that "the political analyst may have to look beyond levels of taxes and expenditures to find politics having an independent or dominant influence on policy outcomes in the state" [9] does not help clarify whether outputs are what government produces, or how its products benefit or deprive citizens. The point is not to criticize these authors—their uses of the term may be sufficiently precise for the purposes they have in mind— but to illustrate the variety of usages surrounding the meaning of "outcomes."

Taking a cue from David Easton, we would like to show the importance of distinguishing outputs and impacts from outcomes. "Failure to do this," as he puts it, "would lead us to consider the infinite chain of effects that might flow from an authoritative allocation as part and parcel of the allocation. We might even be driven ultimately to consider all social behavior as part of the output of the authorities." [10] How can we make these distinctions?

Let us begin by adopting one of the common definitions of outputs as goods and services produced by government. This usage is consistent with Robert Lineberry and Edmund Fowler when they speak of treating "two policy outputs, taxation and expenditure levels of cities, as dependent variables" or write that "region proved to be a more important predictor of . . . policy outputs like urban renewal expenditures than did the socio-economic composition of the population." [11] The same is true of Ira Sharkansky and Richard Hofferbert when they refer to " 'outputs'

9. Brian Fry and Richard Winters, "The Politics of Redistribution," *American Political Science Review* 64 (June 1970): 508, 510.

10. David Easton, *A Systems Analysis of Political Life* (New York: John Wiley and Sons, 1965), p. 351.

11. Robert L. Lineberry and Edmund P. Fowler, "Reformism and Public Policies in American Cities," *American Political Science Review* 61 (September 1967): 701, 702.

expressed as service actually rendered" or say that "the highway outputs measures recorded the mileage of various types of state roads in relation to population." [12]

Roland Pennock's distinction between outputs and outcomes comes closest to our own. Pennock asks whether it can be said that one goal is as good as another or whether states are to "be judged partly by the goals they select." At that point Pennock pauses to

note that we are no longer discussing only outputs, in the sense of binding policies and decisions; rather, we are considering *outcomes*. We are talking about the consequences of outputs—consequences for the people, for the society as a whole or for some subset other than the polity, as, for instance, the economy or the family. We are indeed still dealing with the attainment of political goals, but the focus of attention is upon those goals that satisfy "needs"—not just needs of the state as such, that will enable it to persist, but human needs whose fulfillment makes the polity valuable to man and gives it its justification.[13]

Later, in a footnote, Pennock alludes to "the *outcome* of these outputs" [14] precisely in the sense we intend.

Our use of outcomes is also compatible with John J. Kirlin's and Steven P. Erie's specification of "micro-outputs,"

defined as the actual services rendered to citizens and the manner (norms) of service providers. Thus, it is necessary not only to know that a particular percentage of a city budget goes to parks and recreation activities, but also to know what services are rendered (defined as the incidence of different types of services received by various groups of the city's citizens), and the behavioral norms of the service-rendering personnel (are they, for example, disdainful of the elderly, or surly to minorities?).[15]

Still, there can be too much of a good thing. Martin Levin argues that "policy analysts ought to evaluate the *impact* or *outcomes* of these policy outputs and thus attempt to discover their

12. Ira Sharkansky and Richard Hofferbert, "Dimensions of State Politics, Economics, and Public Policy," *American Political Science Review* 63 (September 1969): 872.

13. J. Roland Pennock, "Political Development, Political Systems, and Political Goods," *World Politics* 18 (April 1966): 420.

14. Ibid., p. 424.

15. John J. Kirlin and Stephen P. Erie, "Developments in Research, The Study of City Governance and Public Policy Making: A Critical Appraisal," *Public Administration Review* 32 (March, April, 1972): 180.

ultimate consequences for society." [16] Outcomes here refer to distant consequences for citizens. He recognizes the immense problems in figuring out what these consequences might ultimately be, but he does not cease speaking of them as "ultimate."

In our studies of schools, libraries, and streets, much of the discussion treats outputs of Oakland's government agencies: books ordered in different parts of the city; per pupil expenditures under the compensatory provisions of the Elementary and Secondary Education Act; miles of streets and highway construction. After describing them, we change our focus to "should" or "ought" questions: Should rich and poor he treated alike in pupil/teacher ratios, for example; should more attention be paid to transportation within the city rather than through it? Here, where values are placed on outputs—values based on how they affect citizens now—we are talking about outcomes.

WHO BENEFITS?

This book will move beyond the question of who causes outputs and will look instead at what kinds of outcomes outputs cause. It responds to a call in the political science literature (and even more to informal conversation among political scientists) for increased emphasis on the impact of government upon its citizens. These new studies, in James Q. Wilson's apt phrase, should go beyond asking "Who governs?" to the analysis of "What *difference* does it make who governs?" [17] Robert C. Fried spelled it out in a recent book review: "We need to know much more about the distribution of community services than about the *presumed* determinants of that distribution. We need to be able to tell what the performance of urban government is, measured both objectively and subjectively, in a range of groups and neighborhoods, in order to see how it relates to various community traits, including the distribution of influence." [18]

16. Martin A. Levin, "Policy Evaluation and Recidivism," *Law and Society Review* 6, no. 1 (August 1971): 18.
17. James Q. Wilson, "Problems in the Study of Urban Politics," in Edward H. Buehrig, ed., *Essays in Political Science* (Bloomington and London: Indiana University Press, 1964), p. 133.
18. Robert C. Fried's review of Delbert C. Miller's *International Community Power Structures: Comparative Studies of Four World Cities* in *Midwest Journal of Political Science* 15 (August 1971): 630–631.

The literature bulges with suggestions to work on the distribution of benefits, the major outcome which we study. In recommending this cause, Jacob and Lipsky point out that

even programs that apparently benefit most of the population—such as education and highway construction—have a variable incidence of benefits. Thus to understand the politics of education at the state level one must understand how grants-in-aid are distributed to school districts. To comprehend the bitter in-fighting about education in an urban community one needs measures of the inequalities in the distribution of schools, teachers, and teaching aids throughout the city.[19]

Agreed. Our study of education is concerned primarily with the issue of equality in distributing resources within a school district.

Economists join political scientists in this concern with the egalitarian distribution of benefits. Anthony Downs states that he takes "explicit account of redistribution effects in evaluating policy alternatives," and, as he puts it vigorously:

I reject the common assumption that all the costs and benefits of any policy are borne by the same people; so redistribution effects can be ignored. Economists in particular are fond of isolating the so-called "efficiency implications of a policy from its income redistribution implications." . . . True, efficiency and redistribution effects should often be separated analytically. But they must both be considered in designing policy recommendations, because congressmen and other real actors do not separate them when adopting policies. Moreover, in most cases, the redistribution impacts of a policy are vitally important in determining its desirability. This means most public policy decisions are strongly political in nature, and cannot be treated as purely economic or scientific.[20]

What then is to be distributed? Or, more accurately, how shall we characterize the outputs that are distributed? What level of analysis is best for dealing with outcomes?

19. Herbert Jacob and Michael Lipsky, "Outputs, Structure, and Power: An Assessment of Change in the Study of State and Local Politics," *Journal of Politics* 30 (May 1968): 515–516.

20. Anthony Downs, *Urban Problems and Prospects* (Chicago: Markham Publishing Company, 1970), pp. 4–5. Of course, other economists have focused on distribution effects. See, for example, W. Lee Hansen and Burton A. Weisbrod, *Benefits, Costs and Finance of Public Higher Education* (Chicago: Markham Publishing Company, 1969).

WHY THE AGGREGATIVE APPROACH IS NOT HELPFUL

Though a number of authors recently have focused on outputs of state and local governments, their studies have relied on a highly aggregative approach,[21] which may be useful for some purposes but obscures questions of distribution and changes in policy.

The aggregative approach to municipal resource allocation tries to build an empirical theory of the determinants of municipal expenditure, most often using multiple regression analysis. To the extent that it is articulated, the theory lies in choosing independent variables which are used to explain the variation in governmental expenditure from city to city. A few studies seek to describe a full theoretical model,[22] but most assume that independent variables, like community income, are translated into dependent variables, like dollars of police expenditure, by something called "the political process."

We find these aggregative studies deficient in two respects. First, they say little about the allocation process itself and, therefore, do not identify particular levers which might be used to alter policy outcomes. Clark's fine analysis of fifty-one American com-

21. For example, see: Richard E. Dawson and James A. Robinson, "Inter-Party Competition, Economic Variables and Welfare Policies in the American States," *Journal of Politics* 25 (May 1963): 265–289; Glenn W. Fisher, "Interstate Variation in State and Local Government Expenditure," *National Tax Journal* 17 (March 1964): 57–74; Richard I. Hofferbert, "The Relation Between Public Policy and Some Structural and Environmental Variables in the American States," *American Political Science Review* 60 (March 1966): 273–282; Ira Sharkansky, *Spending in the American States* (Chicago: Rand McNally, 1968), pp. 54–77 and 110–130; Ira Sharkansky and Richard I. Hofferbert, "Dimensions of State Politics, Economics, and Public Policy," *American Political Science Review* 63 (September 1969): 867–879; Brian R. Fry and Richard F. Winters, "The Politics of Redistribution," *American Political Science Review* 64 (June 1970): 508–522. There is also a large literature that focuses on cities, counties, and metropolitan areas. See, for example, Henry J. Schmandt and G. Ross Stephens, "Local Government Expenditure Patterns in the United States," *Land Economics* 39 (November 1963): 397–406; Alan K. Campbell and Seymour Sacks, *Metropolitan America: Fiscal Patterns and Governmental Systems* (New York: Free Press, 1967); John C. Weicher, "Determinants of Central City Expenditures: Some Overlooked Factors and Problems," *National Tax Journal* 23 (December 1970): 379–396.

22. One example is Robert L. Lineberry and Edmund P. Fowler, "Reformism and Public Policies in American Cities," *American Political Science Review* 61 (September 1967): 701–716.

munities investigates (among other things) the effect of several independent variables on a dependent variable which used general budget expenditures as a measure of policy output. His most "influential" explanatory variable was the percentage of the city's population who were Catholic, particularly Irish Catholic.[23] From a policy perspective, if a community wants to increase its budget, should one suggest that it import Catholics from Ireland and solve two problems with one recommendation? Or, would proselytizing Jews and Protestants help? Many of the more prosaic findings, such as the relationship between city expenditure and citizen median income, display a similar lack of policy direction. What good does it do for a mayor to know that if his city were richer it could spend more? This is not to suggest that demographic variables are unimportant in determining municipal outcomes, or that it is not essential to learn about the constraints that bind. Rather we say that, for purposes of policy, it is important to focus on those variables which are under the agency's (or at least someone's) control.

The second difficulty with aggregative studies is with their choice of output measures. Typically the studies define an output as per capita municipal expenditure, or per capita expenditure in a particular category such as education. Yet simple averages obscure information. Average dollars of education expenditure per child may hide substantial differences from school to school and leave unanswered many questions of distribution.

Moreover, there is no simple way to translate dollars of expenditure into benefits. In our library study, for example, dollars spent on salaries for personnel must be distinguished from dollars spent on acquiring new books. Such differences are significant to the citizen; he can take out books every day, but what does he do with librarians? Yet both categories are obscured by simple per capita dollar expenditure measures.

Whatever level of aggregation one decides to use—many cities or just one, neighborhoods and income levels rather than citywide averages—focusing on outcomes rather than outputs decisively

23. Terry N. Clark, "Community Structure, Decision-Making, Budget Expenditures, and Urban Renewal in 51 American Communities," in Charles M. Bojean, Terry N. Clark, Robert L. Lineberry, eds., *Community Politics: A Behavioral Approach* (New York: Free Press, 1971), pp. 293–313.

changes the nature of analysis. Outputs are neutral; outcomes are always judgmental. According to which criteria, then, shall we judge?

The standards of efficiency, responsiveness, and equity come to mind. Most of the time bureaucrats try to allocate resources efficiently, and most of the time observers point out their inefficiencies; this book is no exception. Yet responsiveness and equity are more interesting and difficult to gauge than is efficiency.

One problem in evaluating an agency's responsiveness is time. Policies stay constant from year to year, but neighborhoods change, beneficiaries move, tastes alter, and new needs emerge. A good idea ten years ago is unfair treatment today. Bureaucrats thus are often accused of not being responsive. A bureaucrat unresponsive to citizens' wishes is somehow venal. But he who interviews and works closely with officials of the street department, the library, and the school district finds them hardworking, well-intentioned, honest citizens. Somehow the stereotype of the entrenched bureaucracy doesn't mesh with our picture of Oakland's officials, partly because the official may be responsive, though unfortunately to yesterday's demands.

Take the pattern of allocation of street construction funds. In chapter 2 we describe the way in which large portions of street funds go to the "select" street system (that of heavily traveled arterials) while neighborhood streets are virtually ignored. To criticize street engineers for such an allocation pattern is to chide them for not keeping up with the times. No doubt, several decades ago, motorists wanted an efficient traffic circulation for getting around the city quickly. Even today that desire exists, but it has met head on with an opposite feeling. People begin to see the automobile as a mixed blessing; they want neighborhoods to stay in, rather than to drive through. Tastes have shifted, and the engineers appear unresponsive.

It is easy enough to say that outcomes ought to accord with citizen preferences. But how could those preferences be determined in regard to individual areas of policy such as streets, libraries, and education? While it is plausible to argue that citizens who had fierce objections to the patterns of allocations would make their will felt through the electoral process, there are some practical difficulties.

The truly fierce objections are few and far between. While citizens often judge distribution patterns—the hills have better streets than the flatlands—few are moved to concerted political action. Where citizen protests occur they are usually the response of a small minority concerning a tiny portion of existing allocations, such as the closure of a single branch library or the reduction of hours for certain high school grades. Indeed, far more substantial reallocations have taken place in schools and libraries without any change in elected representation or any visible election issue. One reason citizens do not know is that the bureaucrats and politicians don't know either, because they are not used to thinking in these terms. Another reason is that acquiring and interpreting the data is costly in time and complex in thought. Most citizens aren't informed on distributional issues most of the time because it does not pay them, compared with alternative uses of their energies, to learn about seemingly endless numbers of policies.[24]

The problem is further complicated by the nature of the electoral process. With a few exceptions—school tax elections come to mind—citizens rarely vote on policy. All they can do directly is to vote in or out different candidates. If few citizens are vitally concerned about reallocations, few politicians will risk enemies by campaigning on clearly stated allocation issues, and such issues will disappear from the electoral scene.[25]

Thus there is ordinarily no public opinion to which one can appeal in disputes about what is a proper allocation of effort. Few care and even less know. If the question is expanded to include alternative allocations within the same policy area (how much for the central versus the branch libraries) or among different areas

24. Citizens might hold officials accountable if there were readily accessible measures of outcomes and simply interpretable impacts. Test scores in reading and mathematics might serve the purpose even though the ultimate consequences of education are not well understood. See Aaron Wildavsky, "A Program of Accountability for Elementary Schools," *Phi Delta Kappan* 52, no. 4 (December 1970): 212–216.

25. For the sad story of Mr. and Mrs. Model Citizen who followed the civic injunction to be interested and active in almost everything, see Aaron Wildavsky, "A Strategy of Political Participation," *Leadership in a Small Town* (Totowa, N.J.: Bedminster Press, 1964), pp. 353–360.

(streets versus schools versus libraries), it is difficult to imagine what an intelligible answer would be like. Officials or researchers could, of course, try a sample survey every few years if they could afford it. Any reply, however, would likely be an artifact of the survey and not, with rare exceptions, a considered response. The number of permutations and combinations would be so large as to require not one but a series of lengthy questionnaires. To be realistic, of course, preference on allocations would also have to be gauged against willingness to pay taxes. And not one electorate but four—city, school, state, and nation—would have to be consulted because, as we shall see, all these levels control significant financial levers. Even if these electorates were consulted, it is not likely that citizen preferences for expenditures would be consistent with their desire to pay taxes.[26]

Despite these difficulties, some might argue that we should have undertaken a survey to assist us in judging outcomes. Using students the Oakland Project did conduct an open-ended, man-on-the-street survey.[27] We interviewed young and old, black and white in different areas of the city. While one could get a measure of affect toward the city (for many the city meant San Francisco), we did not see an expression of specific policy preferences about resource allocation. Which is to say that they had feelings about whether they were satisfied with transportation in general but few clues about possible reallocations.

Let us consider schools as a case where citizens have opinions. Most citizens were unhappy with the schools—"they are all incompetent." Everyone wanted changes in the schools, but there was no agreement on what kinds of changes. Besides vague references to racial tension, citizens frequently transferred their unhappiness to personnel or official bodies: "Unless there's a more responsive superintendent, the schools will get worse"; or "The city government and the Board of Education are simply not responding to people needs"; or "The teachers keep order; that's all." Citizens with children in the public schools asked primarily

26. For the importance of the connection between taxes and services, see Arnold J. Meltsner, *The Politics of City Revenue* (Berkeley and Los Angeles: University of California Press, 1971), pp. 189–196.

27. The results were written up by Mari Malvey and Aaron Wildavsky in a forthcoming publication of the Oakland Project, *Coping with the Environment*.

for changes in curricula toward greater "relevancy," "meaningful-ness," or "catching up with today's problems." Older Oaklanders, particularly those over sixty-five, had different complaints about the school system: "The schools are too extravagant today. When I was in grammar school, nothing at all was wasted." "Nowadays teachers give the kids too much latitude."

There was some differentiation by geographic area. The hill schools were the best. They are "newer and get top quality teach-ers." Hill residents liked their own neighborhood school but dis-liked the rest of them: "Miller [a hill school] is a good school but the rest of them are bad, bad, bad"; or "The schools are poorly administered and good in some areas, depending on how good the PTA is and how good the home is at supplementing the school." Flatland residents thought all the schools were bad but usually expressed their concern in terms of their children: "The children don't care about learning. . . . They aren't interested"; or "The children don't pay attention."

Thus it is not that citizens do not have opinions, but rather that they are unlikely to go beyond generalities and do not have the knowledge to suggest specific resource allocations. If citizens were not aware of the compensatory actions going on in flatland schools, what can we expect in technical and complex areas such as streets? The responsibility for evaluating the outcomes of the policy pro-cess cannot be fobbed off on the general citizenry. Except for helping set the broad constraints, such as tax rates, and the minor complaints, such as bad streets, citizens are not so much sources of advice as in need of it.

Program evaluation is talked about a lot, but seldom made.[28] Officials are so busy running programs that they seldom check on whether these programs do what is desirable. Or they assume, in the absence of the public outcry, that whatever they are doing must be what was wanted or they would hear about it.

Since citizens are not often agitated, angry, and active, Oak-land officials understandably are not always alive to clues about shifting tastes and perceived needs; they rely instead on profes-

28. See Aaron Wildavsky, "The Self-Evaluating Organization," *Public Administration Review* 32 (September/October 1972): 509–520, and Jeanne Nienaber and Aaron Wildavsky, *The Budgeting and Evaluation of Federal Recreation Programs or Money Doesn't Grow on Trees* (New York: Basic Books, Inc., 1973).

sional standards and values. Thus the library has so many professionals that frequently it costs more to circulate a book than to buy
it, and street engineers keep building major streets while ignoring
neighborhood potholes.

Even when officials do see a need for additional services, the
money is not there. State school officials, concerned about local
educators spreading compensatory education funds too thin for
visible results, concentrate the money on fewer students. But
federal compensatory educational funds are insufficient for
Oakland's large poor population; the money goes to schools with
the poorest children. The schools with students just a little less
poor live without. Similarly, street engineers know that some of
Oakland's poor neighborhoods need curbs, sidewalks, and street
construction, but there is little money at their disposal for such
uses. Library personnel are reluctant to spend more to increase
circulation at the same time that officials economize by cutting
out some branch libraries.

Having discussed responsiveness in a preliminary way, we turn
now to consider the standard of equity. Usually, in America, what
is just and fair is equated with what is equal. Yet several previous comparative urban studies, involving traffic law enforcement and welfare administration, have shown that citizens were
not treated equally.[29] It seemed appropriate to us, therefore, to
investigate the question of differential treatment within one
city. We look at the level of resources received by whites compared with blacks, and by rich compared with poor neighborhoods—tests for discrimination which have a natural appeal in
today's politics.

Chapter 4 recognizes that equal opportunity—each citizen receiving the same dollar value of services—is just one of several
measures of equality by which to judge an agency. A second
standard is market equity—that an agency should give a citizen
benefits in proportion to the taxes he pays. A third standard is
equal results—that an agency should allocate its resources so that

29. See John A. Gardiner, "Police Enforcement of Traffic Laws: A
Comparative Analysis," and Martha Derthick, "Intercity Differences in
Administration of the Public Assistance Program: The Case of Massachu-
setts," in *City Politics and Public Policy*, James Q. Wilson, ed. (New York:
John Wiley and Sons, 1968), pp. 151–172, 243–266.

all people are in an equal condition after the money is spent. Applied to the street department, market equity limits a neighborhood's street repair to the taxes it pays. Equal opportunity requires the agency to spend the same amount to resurface streets in every neighborhood of equivalent population. Equal results demand that it recognize streets in poorer neighborhoods to be generally older and in worse condition; the department would have to concentrate resources in those neighborhoods until their streets were on a par with others in the city.

It is possible to array these standards on a rough scale—market equity, equal opportunity, and equal results—with each standard requiring more redistribution of revenues than the previous one. In chapter 4, we judge Oakland's pattern of distribution by these three standards and find that, by following the course of least resistance, local agencies reinforce a class bias—the more you have the more you get. Only when officials deliberately seek to redistribute resources so those most in need receive more do they approach equal opportunity. Thus, to illustrate, the schools, in 1970/71, have by determined action achieved a measure of equality in dollars spent per child on teachers' salaries from local resources.

OUR APPROACH AND ITS LIMITATIONS

Our research method, one of close causation, investigates decision rules which cause public agencies to produce particular outputs. Why is a certain budget request granted? Is it the result of a new decision or a repetition of one made in the past? Is it made because of local (state and federal) political pressure, or because of regulations governing outside sources of funds? Is it made because of professional norms? We try not to let the causal chain become so attenuated that policy changes can be neither suggested nor implemented.

To understand where the outputs go, we will rely heavily on the city's geography and neighborhoods. Correspondingly, it is important for the reader to have a picture of the city in mind. Oakland sits on the east side of San Francisco Bay, directly across from San Francisco itself. By the 1970 census, its population was 361,561, of whom 34% were black, 48% were white and the remainder Asian and Chicano. Its median family income was $9,626

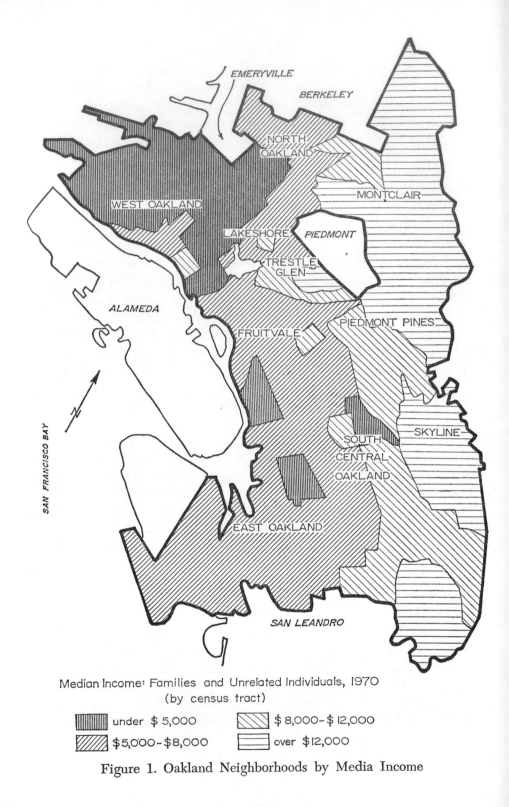

Median Income: Families and Unrelated Individuals, 1970
(by census tract)

under $5,000		$8,000-$12,000	
$5,000-$8,000		over $12,000	

Figure 1. Oakland Neighborhoods by Media Income

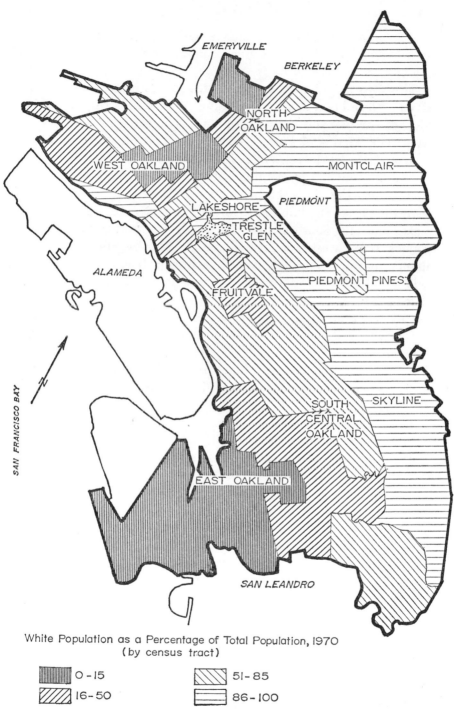

White Population as a Percentage of Total Population, 1970
(by census tract)

▓ 0 – 15	◪ 51 – 85
◩ 16 – 50	▤ 86 – 100

Figure 2. Oakland Neighborhoods by Racial Composition

and 22% of its families had income below the poverty standard. It is as close as California cities come to being a big city with big city problems.

The city's neighborhoods are illustrated in Figures 1 and 2. The city's eastern boundary lies in a range of low hills with a striking view of the bay and the Golden Gate. The areas in these hills—Montclair, Piedmont Pines, Trestle Glen and Skyline (Piedmont is a separate city)—contain neighborhoods which are uniformly high in income and predominantly white except for some integration toward the city's southeastern corner.

At the foot of the hills are the neighborhoods of North Oakland, Lakeshore and South Central Oakland. The lakeshore area surrounds Lake Merrit, a focal point of the city, and contains a number of upper middle-income apartments. The other areas contain middle-class and working-class neighborhoods with a fair degree of integration.

Closest to the bay and the island city of Alameda are the areas of West Oakland, Fruitvale and East Oakland. West Oakland is predominantly black and the poorest area in the city. East Oakland, too, is predominantly black but contains a wider mixture of income groups. Fruitvale contains the majority of the city's Chicano population.

By knowing the city's geography, we can trace the kinds of resources which go to each neighborhood. The location of a branch library, a school, or a street improvement project provides initial insights into the distribution of benefits to groups of Oakland's citizens. Our choice of agencies is helpful. Schools and libraries produce semiprivate goods; it is easy to associate the allocation of resources to a neighborhood school or branch library with a particular group of people. Our research also permits a fairly detailed analysis of different resources such as class size, teacher experience, and supplies in the schools, and expenditures on personnel and new acquisitions in the libraries. Attributing the benefits of streets is harder; a neighborhood may not benefit at all from a major street that passes through it. But, by separating neighborhood streets from major arterials and by using transportation study data, it is possible to impute street services to beneficiary groups.

Selecting outcomes is easier than measuring them. What benefits does a citizen get? What does he lose? What does he get compared with what he pays? Caught between a desire for objective indicators of equity and the citizen's subjective evaluation, it is not surprising that investigators choose measures that are not entirely satisfactory. Economists, for example, are not hiding covert interest in social stratification when they examine tax incidence in terms of income classes. They are looking for a convenient, somewhat objective, handle to get at outcomes. If every citizen is not adequately portrayed, that is the inevitable price of doing the analysis at all. When we examine the distribution of street resources between Oakland's rich hills and poor flatlands, student/teacher ratios by income and percent minority, and library expenditure by branch, we are doing the same thing. The alternative is silence.

Ideally, we would have liked to have a time stream of outcomes which could have been collapsed mechanically into a single measure, much like the economists' procedure for discounting costs and benefits. But this kind of work was beyond our scope. Though past reasons for current outcomes could be reconstructed, we could not tabulate past outcomes themselves. For the most part, the library and school studies focus on resource distributions for one or two years. The street study looked at a large number of construction projects that took many years to complete, but we could not handle the problem of shifting beneficiaries and benefits. To the extent that agency rules altered since these studies were originally written, we have tried to point out these changes.

No doubt some readers will wish our analysis had gone beyond outcomes, to impacts. They will say we should have looked at whether educational achievement over time improves with more money. Or, what is the eventual displacement of housing and air pollution outcomes when a freeway runs through you neighborhood? In self-defense, we would argue that the distribution of resources is an important policy question in its own right. And there is the fact of inadequate knowledge. There is no theory for relating educational resources to results, and we are just beginning to learn about the effects of air pollution. Moreover, as the study of impacts is pushed further down the chain of cause and effect, too many antecedents enter the picture, antecedents which we understand little and can control less.

Another problem is the generality of these studies. Outcomes do not stand still; they change as values change. We do believe these studies accurately portray the behavior of the three agencies at the time they were written. But who knows whether these studies will describe these agencies ten years from now (or similar agencies in other cities at any time)? In truth, we hope not. We believe these outcomes should be changed, and perhaps we can help make this a self-fulfilling prophecy.

AN OVERVIEW

The plan of the book is as follows. Chapter 1 describes the budgetary process and resulting allocations of the Oakland Unified School District. We examine forces shaping the budgetary process: restrictions governing outside (state and federal) sources of funds, and political requests including pressure from employee negotiations. Several distributions of benefits emerge from this process. One distribution shows that the well-to-do schools and the poorest schools receive relatively high levels of resources (though for different reasons) while schools between these extremes do less well.

Chapter 2 describes resource allocations in Oakland's Street and Engineering Department. We examine the forces which shape the agency's decisions: restrictions governing outside funds, and professional norms (the conceptions of the engineers themselves about how street funds should be spent). The resulting outcomes are not easy to characterize. Most resources go not to particular neighborhoods but to large arterial streets—the select street system. The automobile is the prime beneficiary of Oakland's street expenditures.

Chapter 3 describes the budgetary process in the Oakland libraries. Again the dominant force shaping allocations is clearly the professional norms of the personnel, especially the former chief librarian. Their outputs lead to outcomes that rank employees above patrons, the central library above branches, and salaries above books. Neither rich nor poor do as well as they might, but the poor end up worse because they start with less.

In the last chapter, which compares findings across libraries, schools, and streets, we look at several factors that, in varying combinations, shape the distribution of agency outputs: profes-

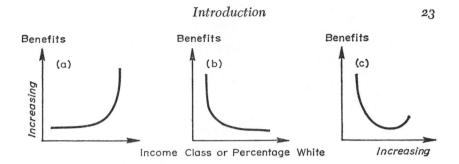

Figure 3. Alternative Distributions of Benefits by Income Class

sional and bureaucratic norms, citizen initiative, and the effects of outside funds. In our studies we found a number of distribution patterns. To indicate these patterns we have drawn three graphs in figure 3. Benefits (teachers per student, dollars of street repaving funds per neighborhood) are placed on the vertical axis, and income class or percent white (of the school or of neighborhood residents) are placed on the horizontal axis.

Some output distributions benefit mostly the rich—the J shape of figure 3 (a); some benefit primarily the poor—the L shape of figure 3 (b); and some benefit both the rich and the poor but not the people in between—the U shape of 3 (c). A general discussion follows of how these distributions of outputs can be judged, and then we address the question raised by Karl Deutsch in his presidential address to the American Political Science Association: "How and to what extent could this distribution of outcomes be changed by a change in any of those of its surrounding conditions over which we have some control?" [30]

30. Karl W. Deutsch, "On Political Theory and Political Action," *American Political Science Review* 65 (March 1971): 25.

1

Schools

How much money should we spend on public education? How should we allocate the money we spend? If we have no clear answers to these questions, we should not be surprised. Public attitudes toward education have gone through enormous fluctuations in the last fifteen years and anyone with the slightest memory will have trouble recalling what he believes on the subject.

The cycle began in 1957 with the launch of Sputnik and the national drive to surpass the Russians in space. In 1956 we spent $388 per child in our elementary and high schools. By 1964 that figure (corrected for inflation) had risen to $493.

At the same time schools became a focus of the civil rights revolution. We believed that education could provide equal opportunity for everyone if it were adequately funded. That idea became crystallized in the Elementary and Secondary Education Act of 1965, a bill which at once established the federal role in public education and the idea of compensatory education programs for the disadvantaged. By the end of 1965, Sputnik and the civil rights movement together were generating public support for schools at a level which educators would have thought impossible ten years before.

The wave crested shortly thereafter and the reasons were not all bad. We had built up the schools, in part, to beat the Russians to the moon, and we beat the Russians to the moon. When that job was accomplished, it was not surprising that some people wanted to turn to other priorities.

As enthusiasm waned the commitment to equal opportunity became increasingly muddled. We found that compensatory education programs could not raise low achievement levels as quickly as we had first supposed. Moreover, the programs did not significantly cool Negro demands for more integration. In the North, like the South before it, public school policy became centered on race, and this caused an additional falling away of support.

The concern with race created a heightened interest in the distribution of resources within districts: how much Negro schools were receiving vis-à-vis white schools. Race (together with the successful moon shots) also played a part in the taxpayers' revolt, the refusal of taxpayers to approve increased expenditures even when their refusal meant program reductions. The taxpayers' revolt, in turn, helped motivate the recent court cases challenging the local property tax as a basis for school finance. And combined with all these events was the new militancy of teachers' unions.

If most districts have seen one or two of these conflicts, the Oakland Unified School District has seen them all. In 1969 the district was charged with the misuse of Elementary and Secondary Education Act funds, and questions of anti-Negro and anti-Mexican discrimination still hang in the air. The district is short on money but the voters have consistently refused to increase the property tax rate. The district has two teachers' organizations, and both have become active in demanding larger salaries and benefits. The first major school finance decision, *Serrano* v. *Priest*,[1] occurred in California, and Oakland now faces a recalculation of its state educational aid.

The conflicts are all important in their own right, but for our purposes they are particularly important since they all influence the way in which the district allocates its resources among programs and distributes its programs among different groups in the city. In this chapter we will describe the process of allocation and distribution, beginning with a discussion of the Oakland district's

1. *Serrano* v. *Priest*, 5 Cal 3rd 584, 487 P 2d 1241 (1971). Other, later decisions include *Rodriguez* v. *San Antonio Independent School District* 337 F. Supp. 280 (W. D. Texas 1971) (currently under consideration by the Supreme Court), *Van Dusartz* v. *Hatfield*, 334 F. Supp. 870 (D. Minn., 1971), and *Robinson* v. *Cahill*, 118 N.J. Super. 223, 287 A. 2d 187 (1972).

financial environment—the varied sources from which it raises its revenues. The single most important source is the local property tax, and our discussion of the tax leads naturally into a discussion of the *Serrano* decision.[2] We will also show how restrictions governing both the property tax and many smaller sources of revenue critically influence the district's selection of programs. This discussion is contained in the first section.

Next we will describe the budgetary behavior of district officials. The officials work within the financial environment and pursue an incremental strategy, never reviewing the budget as a whole. Rather they take the budgetary base as a constant and make small program and distributional adjustments within an overall budget constraint. This incremental behavior has been described in a number of contexts,[3] but in Oakland it has several distinguishing features. One is the degree to which program decisions must adjust to district-wide salary settlements. Another is the combination of state and county procedures which forces many budget decisions to be made in a short and confusing time span.

In the following section we describe the distribution of resources among Oakland's sixty-three elementary schools. We chose elementary schools for examination because each school serves a small neighborhood population. Using the schools, it is possible to estimate the number of teachers and amount of supplies going to each racial and income group. The evidence runs against most preconceptions. For 1969/70 resources followed a U-shaped distribution: high-income and low-income schools both received relatively large resources. Schools in between these extremes did not do as well. (A similar relationship held when the schools were classified by percentage of minority students rather than income.) In 1970 the district hired a new superintendent whose policies moderated the resources going to the upper-income schools. The resulting distribution favored the poorest schools even more.

2. Since this chapter was originally written, the Supreme Court overturned a lower court decision in *Rodriguez* v. *San Antonio School Board,* a Texas school finance case similar to *Serrano. Serrano,* however, was decided largely in terms of the California State Constitution, and so the decision—technically a requirement that a lower state court rehear arguments in the case—is still in effect.

3. See n. 26 below.

The choice of a new superintendent, the district's first black superintendent, represented the decision of the district's board of education to pay more attention to the schools' large minority population. The superintendent has accomplished some redistribution of resources toward minorities and this redistribution may continue, but we suggest, in the final section, that the overall level of resources in the system is unlikely to change in the near future. Groups who favor greater spending—parents and teachers—have only limited power in the electorate. A more likely source of change is the new state-aid formula required by *Serrano*, but even this change is likely to be a small one. The court wants a formula that is "wealth free," a formula that allows a district to raise property tax revenue as if its property tax base per child were equal to the average tax base per child in the state. But Oakland's tax base per child is already very close to the state average, and so under the court's logic, school financing in Oakland is not in need of remedy. It may be, however, that when the state develops a new aid formula, it will change other aid regulations, which will force Oakland to change its distribution of resources. We will discuss these potential changes in detail.

THE FINANCIAL ENVIRONMENT

Allocation begins with the acquisition of money. Our description of this process emphasizes one major theme: The district must obtain its money from a number of different sources, each with its own restrictions, and together these restrictions exert a substantial influence on allocations.

THE SCHOOLS AND THE CITY

We can get a first sense of the school district's budget by comparing it with the budget of the city. The Oakland Unified School District and the City of Oakland have budgets of roughly equal size. The 1969/70 municipal budget was $65.1 million, a figure that included police and fire services, public works, libraries, parks, and sanitation as its principal items. The school budget for that year was $65.8 million and included normal educational expenses as well as certain cafeteria, preschool, and recreation services.

The school budget has more revenue sources that are restricted to specific uses. For 1969/70, only 66 percent of budgetary funds were under complete administrative discretion; the corresponding figure for the municipal budget was 80 percent. The remainder of the school budget consisted of state funds for the mentally retarded, federal funds for compensatory education, property override taxes for preschool programs, and other restricted items.

The two organizations differ in their ability to raise discretionary monies. Legally, the city council can set the municipal property tax rate at any level. The board of education sets the general school tax rate only within a maximum limit, a limit whose increase requires direct voter approval. We will argue below that this combination of tight general monies together with many sources of restricted funding gives the board of education a peculiarly liberal attitude on questions of spending, an attitude that also sets it apart from the city council.

THE SOURCES OF FUNDING

In discussing sources of funding, it will be convenient to use a typology based on three criteria: (1) Can funds from the source be used for any purpose, or must they be used for some particular purpose? (2) Does the source have an upper limit or is it open-ended? (3) Do funds for the source come from the federal, the state, or the local level? We use the first two criteria to classify the major sources of funding for 1969/70 in table 1-1. We group the sources for discussion, using the third criteria.

Local revenue—was approximately 68 percent of the total 1969/70 expenditures of $61 million.[4]

Local Revenue Means the Property Tax

The principal revenue sources are local and all of them involve the property tax. An Oakland homeowner receives a school tax bill that contains two parts: the general monies tax rate of $2.855 per $100 of assessed valuation and a set of eighteen override taxes that are earmarked for special purposes such as adult education, teachers' retirement funds, and fire and earthquake safety alter-

4. The budget had beginning and ending balances of about $5 million. Most of this money was contained in various restricted-purpose accounts. Thus expenditures for 1969/70 were only $61 million while the budget was $65.8 million.

TABLE 1-1: Classification of Sources of Funding by Purpose and Limit [a]

	Closed-ended	*Open-ended*
General [b] Monies	General monies property tax	7th-and-8th-grade property override tax
	State basic equalization, and class-size bonus aid	
	Federal aid under P.L. 874	
	$39 million, 66% of total expenditure	$2.2 million, 3.3% of total expenditure
Special Monies	Federal compensatory aid under the Elementary and Secondary Education Act	State aid to special classes, educationally handi-capped, etc.
	State compensatory and preschool aid under AB 1331, SB 28	Certain property override taxes like teachers' retire-ment fund, health insur-ance, mentally retarded
	Certain property override taxes like adult education, community services, opportunity schools	
	$5.9 million, 8.9% of total expenditure	$18.2 million, 21.7% of total expenditure

SOURCE: *Statistical and Financial Data, 1969/70 and Preliminary Estimates of General Fund Revenues & Expenditures for the Fiscal Year, 1970/71.* Both published by the Oakland Unified School District.

[a] Figures are based on the 1969/70 school year. Total expenditures for this year were approximately $65.1 million. This figure includes a total beginning and ending balance for all accounts of about $5 million. In computing percentage figures, the expenditure base was corrected for this balance.

[b] "General Monies" as used here refers to monies which can legally be allocated to any purpose by the board of education. The definition differs from the official school definition of the General Purpose Fund, which includes state payments for special classes for the physically handicapped, mentally retarded, and so on.

ations. In 1969/70 the override taxes totaled $1.676 per $100 of assessed valuation.[5]

The general monies tax is at its legal maximum. Like most California school districts, Oakland is fiscally independent and the maximum can be raised only by direct voter approval. The last approval was in 1958. Since then the board of education has placed five different tax increases on the ballot, all of which have failed.[6]

These failures and similar failures in other communities are something of an irony. The fiscally independent district was supposed to free education from politics. Voters and school boards were to deal directly without the intervention of mayors, city councilmen and other politicians. But fiscal independence had an unintended result: it made education the only public service under direct voter control. When citizens felt the pressure of increases in the overall tax load, they voted down school taxes, not so much out of dislike for the schools but because school taxes were the only part of the tax bill which they could control. In Oakland the process was hastened because the electorate was largely white and without young children, and the children in the schools were largely black.[7]

With the general tax rate fixed, increases in general revenues are limited to increases in Oakland's assessed valuation, a figure that runs about 3 percent per year. In 1969/70 the general monies tax rate raised about $27 million, or about 44 percent of all expenditures.[8]

5. In 1968 all California counties were required to begin standardizing their assessments at 25 percent of market value, and to complete it by 1971. For a discussion of the effects of this requirement upon the district's revenues, see the section that begins on p. 52 and f. 46, p. 60.

6. Technically, the maximum approved by the voters was $2.77 per $100. In 1968 the state excluded personal property estimates (e.g., furniture) from property tax rolls. To compensate school districts for this loss, the state permitted a percentage increase in the maximum tax limit beginning in 1969. In Oakland, this increase raised the maximum from $2.77 to $2.855.

7. Preliminary 1970 census figures showed Oakland's population to be 34 percent black and about 48 percent white. The remainder were Spanish surname and Asian. By contrast, the schools were 59 percent black and 25 percent white. Though whites do not make up a majority of the population, their higher average age and higher rates of registration give them a majority in the electorate.

8. A final problem with the property tax seems to occur in periods of inflation. The district believes that wages and salaries should rise as fast as

Override Taxes Are an Escape Valve

Unlike the general monies property tax, many override property taxes do not have upper limits. These taxes can be regarded as a substitute for state aid: the state legislature passes a bill that allows local boards of education to invoke, at their option, a property override tax for a particular purpose. The adoption of an override is not subject to direct voter approval.

Theoretically, the board is free to reject an override tax, but in fact almost all of the overrides are adopted.[9] The taxes cover two different types of expenses. One is an expense which the schools would have even if there were no override tax. The set of four taxes that finance the district's contribution to employee pension and health insurance funds is an example. These taxes are close to state aid because they release a portion of general monies, but the state legislature can pass the overrides without bearing the onus for increased taxes—a distinct advantage from its point of view.

Override taxes also finance projects which, given the district's limited resources, would not be undertaken if the override were unavailable. An example is the override tax for the two Opportunity Schools, which offer special curricula to students who otherwise would be dropouts. These overrides do not release general monies but they are useful in helping the district and the Oakland Board of Education acquire additional resources to distribute.

This goal—acquiring resources to distribute—is not as common as it first appears. It is a normal goal for an agency that does not

the overall rate of inflation in the economy. Salary items make up about 85 percent of operating expenses, and so general monies expenditures will rise with the price level. For the district's budget to stay in balance, it follows that assessed valuation in the district must also rise as fast as the price level. This may not happen, however; if federal authorities choose to fight inflation through tight money policies, mortgage interest rates may be driven up substantially. These high mortgage rates will be capitalized into housing prices, thus slowing their growth. This appears to have happened in 1969/70 when the cost of living rose by 5.2 percent but assessed valuation in the district rose only by 3 percent.

9. Oakland has not adopted several override taxes for programs for which there would be very little demand—e.g. a tax to maintain classrooms in hospitals. The remainder of the unadopted overrides are taxes which Oakland is ineligible to use. An example is the override to finance high school tuition payments of students in those districts that have no high schools.

raise its own revenues, say a federal agency that depends upon congressional appropriations. But when an agency raises its own revenues, it may be concerned about tax rates as well as spending. In *The Politics of City Revenue,* Meltsner shows that the Oakland city manager's principal goal is to hold the line on city taxes, a goal shared by the city council. The council and the manager pursue the goal even when this requires making program cuts.

The school district and the city government differ in their outlooks because they differ in their taxing powers. The city council has the power to set its own tax rate at any level and it feels (with justification) that citizens hold it responsible for the level of taxes. Councilmen are constantly threatened by adverse opinion which may result in anything from a defeat at the polls to the movement of business and middle-class citizens out of the city. The council responds to this threat by holding the line on taxes.

The fiscally independent board of education must go to the voters for a tax increase. Because voters seem to control spending policy directly, tax issues are removed from board elections. There is no need for board members to fear political competition from "low school tax" insurgents. But the story does not end there. The board puts a tax increase on the ballot because it is convinced that more resources are needed for proper operation of the schools. The defeat of the tax increase does not change that feeling. When the board has a chance to obtain a new program—a program it had not intended to fund—it will accept the program even if it means enacting an override. The board will substitute the programs it *can* finance for the program it *wants to* finance.

The board's outlook is reinforced by its contact with constituents. The board deals with people in the school system—parents, teachers, and students—who want more resources rather than lower taxes. Board members come into contact with "the whole community" only at tax election time. Their view is much more selective than the view of city councilmen, who regularly see both people who want more services and people who want lower taxes.

If the board of education had the power to set its own general monies tax rate, it might hesitate to adopt some of the overrides. Under current circumstances, adoption of these overrides is almost automatic.

Override Taxes Shape Priorities

Since almost all overrides are adopted, it follows that specific overrides permitted by the legislature exert a strong influence on the allocation of resources in the system. An example of this influence occurs in wage negotiations. The school district's contributions to employee pension and health insurance funds—fringe benefits—are financed through override taxes, but salary increases are financed from general monies. When general monies are tight, the school department will be more willing to negotiate increases in fringe benefits than negotiate increases in salary per se.

Overrides also affect allocation through the seventh and eighth grade tax. The tax was originally introduced by the legislature to aid districts in the state-mandated transition from seventh and eighth grades taught as elementary grades (one teacher per class teaching all subjects) to seventh and eighth grades taught as high school grades. The tax is open-ended. It is set each year to cover the extra expense which the district incurs in organizing the two grades in a multiple-teacher format. This expense can be written as follows: To calculate the seventh and eighth grade tax:

1. Estimate the cost of the seventh and eighth grades for the coming year. This cost includes all teachers' and principals' salaries, supply costs, and an assigned portion of administrative costs.
2. Estimate the costs of seventh and eighth grades as if they were run on an elementary school format by multiplying projected per student costs in grades 1–6 by the projected seventh and eighth grade enrollment.
3. Set the seventh and eighth grade tax rate to raise an amount of revenue equal to (1) minus (2).

The unintended result of this tax is to place a high priority on seventh and eighth grade expenditures. If general monies are tight, there is no point in cutting expenditures in the seventh and eighth grades since their excess costs are financed by the restricted tax. In 1969/70, a year in which many programs were cut, the seventh and eighth grades received a $160,000 increase in their counseling program; a $270,000 reading and mathematics program was adopted for 1970/71 under similar tight circumstances.

State revenue—approximately 23 percent of the total 1969/70 expenditures of $61 million.

The State Aid Formula Has Its Problems

State aid, like property tax revenues, comes both in general and in specific forms. The largest is the state contribution to general monies, formally known as "basic and equalization aid." The determination of this contribution was one concern of the California Supreme Court in *Serrano* v. *Priest*. The aid is computed by a formula that depends on two constants: a foundation rate and a basic rate. For a simplified calculation of state aid per student: [10]

1. Take as a foundation rate $375 per unit of average daily attendance (ADA).[11]
2. Subtract 1 percent x (assessed valuation of the community per ADA).
3. Call the difference "computed state aid."
4. Basic state aid equals $125.
5. Actual state aid equals "computed state aid" *or* basic state aid, whichever is *larger*.

The court in *Serrano* was concerned with the extent to which state aid freed a local district's expenditure from dependence on its local tax base.[12] Some evidence on this point is contained in

10. Actual calculations are more complicated in several ways. First, separate calculations are required for grades K–8 and 9–12. The assessed valuation of the district is apportioned between the two calculations on the basis of the students enrolled in each group of grades. The assessed valuation itself is standardized by the state's determination of the ratio of assessed valuation to market value in the district's county (after 1971 all counties will be required to assess at 25 percent of market value and this will no longer be a factor). The foundation rate of $375 is for grades K–8. The corresponding figure for 9–12 is $508. Similarly the 1 percent figure (2) is for the K–8 calculation. The corresponding figure for 9–12 is .8 percent. Finally, actual calculations subtract from line (1) not only a proportion of the assessed valuation but other items including county and city payments in lieu of taxes (e.g., from the airport) and Aid to Federally Impacted Areas (P.L. 874).

11. Average Daily Attendance is the unit upon which all state aid calculations are based. It refers to the number of children attending classes on an average day during the year. As is explained later in this section, the use of this statistic in aid formulas is occasionally altered to influence school department decisions.

12. In a two-step argument the court attacked this dependence of a district's expenditure upon its property tax base. First, it argued that education was a particularly important service of government. As such it was subject to special scrutiny under the equal protection clause of the California

TABLE 1-2: Tax Base and Tax Rate Data for Oakland and
Four Neighboring Communities (1968)

	(1) Assessed Value per Person	(2) Assessed Value per ADA	(3) General Monies School Tax Rate [a]	(4) Tax Revenue per ADA
Oakland	$ 2,146	$12,008	$2.77/$100	$ 332.62
Fremont	1,917	5,245	4.25/100	222.91
Hayward	1,793	5,747	3.477/100	199.92
Piedmont	3,476	11,718	4.844/100	567.62
Emeryville	20,752	95,122	1.65/100	1,569.51

	(5) Approximate State Aid per ADA [b]	(6) Total of (4) and (5)	(7) Tax Rate for Municipal Services
Oakland	$254.92	$ 587.54	$3.06
Fremont	322.55	545.46	1.38
Hayward	317.53	517.45	1.57
Piedmont	257.82	825.44	2.41
Emeryville	125.00	1,694.51	.78

SOURCE: *Annual Report of Financial Transactions Concerning School Districts of California, 1968–69, Sacramento, Office of the State Controller, 1970; Annual Report of Financial Transactions Concerning the Cities of California, 1968–69, Sacramento, Office of State Controller, 1970.*

[a] All tax rates are listed at levels prior to the adjustment for the removal of personal property from the assessment rolls. See footnote 6.

[b] Calculations are made using the simplified formula reported on p. 34.

table 1-2. Table 1-2 presents approximate tax and state aid data for Oakland and four neighboring communities. Fremont and Hayward are mixed residential-industrial communities. Both are south of Oakland and have populations of 100,000. Piedmont is a high-income residential enclave of 11,000 surrounded on all sides

State Constitution. Like the corresponding clause in the U.S. Constitution, this clause sets out the duty of government to treat all citizens equally or, in the absence of strict equality, not to pursue policies which discriminate among groups on criteria like race, sex, and in some instances, wealth. The court then argued that because school districts are creatures of the state, they do not possess any special judicial standing (as opposed to, say, the state boundaries, which do have such standing). The existing structure of school finance is based largely on the boundaries of these local districts. If the districts did have special standing, the financial structure might be justified on that ground alone. In the absence of such standing, the court could rule that any advantages of the structure were outweighed by its violation of the equal protection clause.

by Oakland. Logically it should be part of Oakland, but it has managed to retain political independence. Emeryville is an industrial enclave, a tax shelter, also carved out of Oakland.

The basis of the court's concern can be seen by comparing Emeryville and Hayward. Column (2) shows that the two communities have radically different amounts of tax base per child. Emeryville's tax base per child is almost twenty times that of Hayward's. The remainder of table 1-2 shows that existing state aid does little to redress this imbalance. Column (3) shows that Emeryville taxes its property at a rate of about one-half of Hayward's. But column (6) shows that even after this low tax rate and state aid have been taken into account, Emeryville is able to spend three times as much per child as Hayward.[13]

The court noted several reasons for this result. The amount of aid distributed by the state is relatively small. In 1969/70 state aid was 35 percent of the average school district's expenditure, and the figure has been declining over time; in 1959/60 it had been 41 percent.[14] This low amount of aid limits, a priori, the extent to which the state can equalize differences in district tax bases.

The equalization process is limited further by the way in which the state aid formula is constructed. The limit on equalization

13. There is, however, a counter argument due to Robert Reischauer. It is based on the idea that the benefits of a community are capitalized into its housing prices. In Beverly Hills, a homeowner can obtain a high-cost school system at a low tax rate. The capitalization argument holds that this makes Beverly Hills a more desirable place to live and so the homeowner pays more for his house than he would if the same physical structure were located in a community without these tax advantages. If the market works perfectly and capitalization is complete, the increased cost of housing will just equal the size of the tax savings. A rich community will have an elaborate school system because it has more money to spend, not because it can get the system at a low price.

The truth of this argument depends on how well community benefits are capitalized in housing prices. Even if they are the state may still want to take a more active role in redistributing educational aid. But the redistribution should be undertaken because the public decides it is a good thing to do—not because people in communities with a high tax base are "getting away with murder."

14. *Public School Finance, Part 1: Expenditures for Education*, four-part mimeographed publication of the Office of the Legislative Analyst, Sacramento, California, November 12, 1970.

occurs in line (5). Under lines (1)–(3), the greater a district's assessed valuation the less aid it receives. Using these lines alone, a district like Emeryville or Beverly Hills would not qualify for any state aid. But line (5) guarantees that a district's aid cannot fall below $125 per child no matter how much tax base it has.

The California legislative analyst estimates that about one-half of state general monies aid is in the form of the $125 payment. This leaves only the other half—an amount equal to about 17 percent of all district current expenditures—to be used for equalization.

To highlight the other problems in the state aid formula above, we can describe what an "ideal" formula should accomplish. As indicated by the court, an ideal formula should be redistributive; it should require wealthier communities to pay a greater share of their costs than poor communities. The formula should also reward educational spending by granting more aid to communities which, other things being equal, tax themselves at higher rates. Finally, the formula should take into account any inherent differences in district costs.

The existing state formula presents problems on each of these counts. The formula attempts to adjust for a district's wealth by reducing the foundation payment by 1 percent of the district's assessed valuation per child—line (2). Actually, this use of assessed valuation per child confuses wealth and tax effort.

Column (2) of table 1-2 shows that Oakland and Piedmont have approximately equal assessed valuation per child. According to the state aid formula, the two communities are equally wealthy and should be expected to produce an equal amount of revenue on their own. But a comparison of column (2) with column (1) shows that Oakland and Piedmont derive their high assessed valuations in different ways. Piedmont is a rich community with an average proportion of children in the population. Oakland is a community of average wealth with a very low proportion of children in its population.

In the context of the fiscally independent school district, these communities should produce different amounts of local revenue. The average voter in Oakland has less income than the average voter in Piedmont; he is also less likely to have children in the schools. To him a school tax of a given rate will represent greater financial hardship [15] and smaller direct benefit. For both reasons, he will not be as willing to vote for large school taxes as the Piedmont voter. By focusing on assessed valuation per child as its only measure of wealth, the state formula ignores these differences.

A district's tax efforts does not even enter into the state formula. The 1 percent figure in line (2) indicates that the formula treats the assessed valuation of every district as if it were being taxed at $1/$100 of assessed valuation.

On grounds of equity, we might argue that a district which taxes itself higher (lower) than this $1/$100 rate should be rewarded (penalized) accordingly. By this argument, Oakland should receive less state aid than any other community in table 1-2 except Emeryville. This argument has its problems, however. The relatively low proportion of children in Oakland may imply a higher level of "effort" than the tax rate alone would indicate. In addition, a discussion of tax effort should consider more than just school taxes. Column (7) in table 1-2 shows municipal tax rates for the five communities. The data in column (7) shows that Oakland's municipal tax rate is substantially higher than the rates of the other four communities. A homeowner in Fremont pays much higher school taxes than does a homeowner in Oakland, but his total tax rate (schools and municipal) is $5.63. The Oakland homeowner's combined rate is $5.83.[16]

If Oakland's high municipal tax rate resulted in the provision of public services at an elaborate level, comparisons of Oakland's municipal tax rate with those of other communities would be illegitimate. Actually, Oakland's high municipal rate reflects the high cost of providing normal services in a large city with a substantial low-income population.[17] There is a sense, then, in which

15. This statement assumes some diminishing marginal utility of income.

16. These figures ignore both county taxes and school override taxes. When overrides are included, the taxes for 1968 become $6.30 for Fremont and $7.27 for Oakland. This argument in turn must be modified to the extent that taxes are capitalized in lower house prices.

17. For a fuller discussion of these points, see: Frank Levy, "Revenue Sharing, the Tiebout Hypothesis, and the Urban Crisis," Working Paper No. 10 of the Department of Economics, University of California at Berkeley, April 1971.

Oakland's tax effort is higher than either Fremont's or Hayward's (though perhaps not as high as Piedmont's).

A final problem in the formula concerns its treatment of costs. The use of a standard foundation rate—line (1)—for all districts implies that normal educational costs [18] per student should be the same in all districts. In fact, urban districts experience higher normal costs than rural districts, which arise from such sources as increased vandalism, higher insurance premiums, higher labor costs and other factors. The cost differences suggest that the foundation rate should be set at different levels for different types of districts.

These formula problems are serious, and none are unique to California. They exist in most state formulas for the computation of school aid. Proposals for reform will be discussed in the final section.

State Aid Also Shapes Priorities

In addition to state basic and equalization aid there is a third state contribution to general monies, the class-size bonus. The district receives a $30 bonus for each child in grades 1–3 who is in a class of less than thirty-one pupils. This aid incentive, like the override taxes described above, has influenced local policy decisions.

During the middle 1960s the district allocated teachers to schools in a compensatory fashion. Class size was determined by a formula based on the percentage of children in the school with IQs below ninety. Average class size was to be thirty-four when that percentage was 15 or less, declining to twenty-nine when the percentage was 40 or more.[19] The state's implementation of the class-size bonus meant there would be a net loss of general revenue if any class was larger than thirty-one, and so the larger classes were eliminated. This was, of course, the intention of the bonus.

In 1969/70, and again in 1970/71, the district's preliminary budget was in deficit and the board of education had to consider program cuts. One major program cut considered (but not made)

18. As distinct from compensatory programs.
19. Memorandum from the Assistant Superintendent of Schools, dated July 1, 1965.

was the reduction of the high school day from six periods to five. Under the proposed cut, high school students would take one elective—music, science, a language—instead of two. The saving to the district would come through the reduction in teaching staff.[20]

Proposal of this particular cut was indirectly due to the class-size bonus. Saving salaries in grades 1–3 would mean raising class size in these grades, but the increased class size would wipe out the bonus and thus fail to increase general monies. A roughly similar situation governed grades 4–6. In grades 7–8 comparable salary savings would involve reducing the number of periods in the day. But this saving would not increase general monies since the excess costs of grades seven and eight are covered already by the seventh and eighth grade override tax. The state defined a standard high school day as five periods. The high school day could be cut from six periods to five without loss of state aid. It was this combination of incentives which produced the proposal for cutting the high school day.

Ultimately, the budget was cut in the areas of supplies and maintenance. These cuts could have been avoided by increasing the size of the brightest elementary classes to thirty-three or thirty-four, and many administrators would have preferred this alternative, but the class-size bonus took the decision out of their hands.

A final example of state influence occurred in the scheduling of kindergarten classes. Through 1966/67 Oakland (and many other districts) scheduled kindergarten in double session: one teacher teaches a 165-minute session in the morning, takes a lunch break, and teaches a 155-minute session in the afternoon. During this time the state defined the full kindergarten day as 180 minutes. For purposes of computing state aid, kindergarten ADAs were calculated on a proportional basis: a child enrolled in the morning session would be counted as 165/180 units of ADA, and so on.

In 1967/68 the state offered a bonus for districts to convert to single-session kindergarten—that is, two 180-minute sessions. A bonus was appropriate because single sessions eliminate the time for a lunch break and so require twice the number of teachers, one for the morning and another for the afternoon. For each child enrolled in a 180-minute session, the district received credit

20. For a discussion of why this saving was not adopted, see p. 58.

for one and one-half units of ADA. This represented a bonus of one-half a unit or about $80, and while the amount did not cover expenses completely, it was a sufficient incentive for Oakland to make the conversion. By the end of 1967 half of the district's kindergartens were on single sessions.

At that point the state switched from the carrot to the stick. In the spring of 1968, it announced that there would be no single-session bonus for 1968/69. In the spring of 1969 it announced that double-session kindergartens would be penalized in the calculation of state aid: in February 1970 ADAs generated in double-session kindergartens would be multiplied by .75, in July 1970 they would be multiplied by .417, and in July 1971 they would not be counted at all.

The district was in a tight financial situation and it responded in ways that could conserve general monies. For 1968/69 the department managed to find funds to keep single sessions in schools which had them, but attempted no further expansion. In 1969/70 the first-stage penalty for double session was insufficient to offset its increased cost; all single-session kindergartens were dropped. In 1970/71 the second-stage penalty for double session was greater than the cost saving, and so all kindergartens went on single session. The district's criticism of the state's method was intense.

In addition to general aid, the state also offers funds for specific programs. These programs are classified in table 1-1 as open-ended, but their open-endedness is spurious. Most of the programs are per-class allowances for the blind, the mentally retarded, and the physically handicapped. The classes have well-defined standards for admission, and there is no incentive for an unqualified child to enter the class. There is little danger that expenses for these programs will get out of control.

Before 1969/70 the state program for the educationally handicapped did not fit this description. The educationally handicapped program provided a substantial per-class allowance ($13,360 when first instituted) for eligible students, but unlike the other programs, the criteria for admission to the program were vague, based on the presence of learning problems rather than "objective" measures like IQ tests or scores on vision tests. The official definition of an educationally handicapped child reads: "Educationally Handicapped minors are minors, other than physically handicapped minors [as officially defined] or mentally retarded minors [as officially defined] who, by reason of marked learning or behavioral problems or a combination thereof, cannot receive the reasonable benefit of ordinary education facilities." [21]

Given the vague entrance definition and the large per-class allowance, children in a poor school district could obtain real benefits in an educationally handicapped class. As a result, the line between educationally handicapped classes and compensatory programs (especially in those schools which did not have funds for compensatory programs) became more blurred than the state had intended.

The state had anticipated this problem by stipulating that a district could have no more than 2 percent of its students defined as educationally handicapped. But as enrollment in the program climbed, even this standard required more money than the state wanted to pay. In 1969 the state amended the regulations so that the number of educationally handicapped children in a district could not increase by more than 20 percent a year unless the State Department of Education gave specific approval.

The state also funds two compensatory education programs. AB 1331 gives allowances for pre-school classes established in low-income areas. SB 28 gives money to hire extra elementary teachers to reduce class sizes to twenty-five in "tension areas." [22]

Unlike special-class funds, compensatory funds are closed-ended and, until 1970, were funded at relatively low levels. The legislature appropriates a certain aggregate amount for each program. The funds are then allocated by the State Department of Education to eligible districts, which make the funds go as far as they can. In Oakland there are seventeen "target area" elementary schools—schools that have equally low reading scores, equally high numbers of children whose families are on welfare, and so on. Oakland's share of SB 28 funds allowed only eleven out of seventeen schools to be covered in 1969/70. [23] In 1970/71, the state increased the program's funding to cover all schools.

21. California State Education Code at 6750.
22. The phase "tension area" is contained in the bill itself. AB stands for assembly bill (i.e., the bill was initiated in the California State Assembly). SB stands for (state) senate bill.
23. Four more were covered by ESEA funds leaving two schools uncovered by any compensatory program.

In addition to monetary aid, the state also supplies free textbooks to all elementary pupils. Every four years, the State Department of Education selects a slate of twenty-four books (six grades, four reading levels within a grade). In the spring of the selection year, each teacher orders from this slate for the following year. The allotment is one book per student.[24]

Federal revenue—approximately 9 percent of the total 1969/ 70 expenditures of $61 million.

The two largest elements of federal revenue have been the compensatory education funds received under Title I of the Elementary and Secondary Education Act of 1965 (ESEA), and a contribution to general monies received under P.L. 874, the program to aid federally impacted areas. In 1969/70 the ESEA funds totaled about 6 percent of all expenditures, and P.L. 874 funds about 1.6 percent.

ESEA Is a Source of Controversy

Title I funds under ESEA can be spent for a variety of purposes: teacher aides, support personnel including psychologists and reading specialists, extra supplies, and other items such as student trips. This flexibility makes the program more desirable than the state compensatory funds (SB 28), which can be used only to hire additional teachers to reduce class size. In the spring of 1969 a review team from the State Department of Education wrote a report charging Oakland with a gross misspending of ESEA funds. Their report accused the district of using some funds to benefit ineligible (rich) children. Further, the report examined the ESEA program that was reaching eligible children and found it badly motivated and designed. While these allegations were

24. This system has its proponents and detractors. The proponents argue that the system permits a greater ability to enforce standards and offers cost savings due to economies of scale. The economies are in part realized because the state can negotiate large orders with publishers for the book rights and do the printing on their own presses. Detractors argue that the slate selected by the state is too limited. This criticism was particularly intense during the last selection when the State Board of Education at the behest of the then state superintendent of public instruction overrode the selections made by the panel of teachers appointed by the state board. The detractors also point to the serious delays in book delivery which have resulted from problems in the state printing operation.

not entirely correct (the second was far more accurate than the first), they made ESEA funds a point of substantial conflict. The charges will be discussed in detail in a later section.

P.L. 874 Is Uncertain

P.L. 874, too, has been the subject of controversy, but the controversy has been at the federal level. The program was designed originally to compensate school districts for the loss of tax revenues from federally owned housing other than public housing—for example, housing on an army base. As it was first conceived, the program paid a district for any of its students who lived on federal property. Later, the program was extended to include payments for children whose parents worked on federal property but lived in private housing. On economic grounds, this extension was hard to justify, since these families paid property taxes like any family with a private employer. Moreover, much of the extension often financed payments to the "wrong" district—for example, the Virginia and Maryland districts which received large aid payments because many of their residents worked for the federal government in the District of Columbia.

As part of an economy drive in early 1969, the president proposed returning to the original program. For Oakland this would have meant a reduction in aid from about $1 million to $50,000. Congress opposed this reduction, and the conflict was not resolved until well into the 1969/70 school year, a factor which posed special problems for the district's budget office.

As a summary of our discussion, table 1-3 lists sources of revenue along with their relative importance. The behavior of school officials in allocating this revenue will be discussed in the next section.

THE BUDGETARY BEHAVIOR OF SCHOOL OFFICIALS

In this section we describe how the school district administration allocates funds to various uses.[25] The behavior we discuss takes place within the funding restrictions described in the previous section. The combination of restrictions and budgetary

25. This section has benefited substantially from the comments and unpublished manuscript of Jesse McCorry.

TABLE 1-3: The Sources of Funding and Their Relative Importance:
1969–70

Name of Source *	Dollar Amount	Approximate Percentage of Expenditure ($61 million for 1969/70)
Local Sources:		
General monies property tax	28 million	46
16 override taxes (7th-and-8th-grade, also included in the 16 above)	13.2 million (1.7 million)	22 (3)
State Sources:		
Basic aid plus equalization aid plus grades 1–3 class-size bonus	10.1 million	17
Special class allowances, etc.	2.9 million	5
SB 28	0.3 million	0.4
Federal Sources:		
Compensatory funds under Title I of ESEA	3.4 million	6
P.L. 874	0.95 million	1.6

* Only major sources are listed. As was noted in table 1-1, the budget lists total expenditures of $65.8 million, but this figure includes beginning and ending balances of $5 million.

decisions determines the resources that are received by the child in the classroom. We will illustrate our discussion with examples from the 1969/70 district budget.

Budgetary Behavior Is Incremental Behavior

A discussion of budgetary behavior in public organizations can draw upon well-developed literature, which begins with budgeting at the federal level; later literature includes computer simulations of municipal budgeting and school district budgeting.[26]

26. For budgeting at the federal level, see Aaron Wildavsky, *The Politics of the Budgetary Process* (Boston: Little, Brown, 1964); Otto A. Davis,

The theme of these works—and the principle which facilitates computer simulation—is stability: stability over time of the budgetary process and the allocations which it generates. We find in Davis, Dempster, and Wildavsky what might be called the "principle of constancy":

Participants in budgeting deal with their overwhelming burdens by adopting aids to calculation. By far the most important aid to calculation is the incremental method. Budgets are never actively reviewed as a whole in the sense of considering at once the value of all existing programs as compared to all possible alternatives. Instead, this year's budget is based on last year's budget, with special attention given to a narrow range of increases or decreases. (Pp. 529–530)

Note that the reference is to the constancy of programs, rather than constancy of cost. This principle, when applied to schools, would refer to allocation of personnel but not to salaries paid those personnel.[27]

To adequately describe budgeting behavior in the Oakland schools, this principle of constancy needs to be supplemented with four other principles. (1) Because of the institutional arrangements of California school finance, most of Oakland's important budgeting decisions have to be made in a relatively short period of time. (2) The key budgetary decisions are the district-wide wage and salary negotiations. (3) The scrutiny accorded a request for a new program depends on the availability of *its* source of funds. Programs which are funded from override taxes or open-ended state funds are not budgeted in the regular sense but are allowed to grow at the will of their administrators. (4) Budget changes are asymmetrical. A general monies deficit is covered by cutting programs of low visibility (as distinguished

M. A. H. Dempster, and Aaron Wildavsky, "A Theory of the Budgetary Process," *American Political Science Review* 60 (1966): 529–547. For budgeting at a municipal level, see John P. Crecine, *Government Problem Solving: A Computer Simulation of Municipal Budgeting* (Chicago: Rand McNally, 1969). For budgeting at the school district level, see Donald Gerwin, *Budgeting Public Funds: The Decision Process in an Urban School District* (Madison: University of Wisconsin Press, 1969).

27. It appears that this incremental style has changed to a degree since the period when data for this chapter was collected. In the summer of 1970, the district hired a new superintendent. One of his first jobs was a full review of all general monies expenditure items. Nonetheless, this review did not result in substantial changes.

from low educational importance). A general monies surplus is disposed of by funding programs of high visibility.

Budgeting Begins in the Winter

The district's budget document, covering expenditures for one fiscal year, is constructed over a period of nine months. The period begins in December, when the district superintendent sends out his letter of budget instructions. It ends on August 15, when the budget document must be officially approved by the Oakland Board of Education and filed with Alameda County school officials.

The superintendent's letter outlines financial constraints for the coming year; he asks for program requests that can fit realistically within those constraints. He asks also for additional requests should unforeseen revenues become available. The letter goes to department heads and the various assistant superintendents, who in turn transmit the call to the principals.

The Size of the Request Depends on the Source of the Money

Program requests are submitted in January. An administrator's request will depend in part on where his funds come from. It has been suggested that a lower limit for an administrator's request is his current year's allocation; [28] for administrators of general monies programs this allocation is an upper limit as well.[29] Recent budget cuts have made these administrators so pessimistic that holding on to the current allocation is something of a victory.

The supervisor for secondary education felt that the system should be spending about $8.00 per student per year for the purchase of new high school textbooks. He could point to the early 1960s when $8.00 (corrected for inflation) was the actual amount spent. By 1968/69 the textbook allowance had been reduced to $2.79 per student, and it was the $2.79 figure that formed the basis of the supervisor's 1969/70 request. The elementary supervisor and the head librarian had similar problems.[30]

28. See Davis, Dempster, and Wildavsky.
29. This description abstracts from certain automatic program changes—for example, the increase in teachers due to increased enrollment.
30. Other comparisons: for supplementary elementary textbooks (e.g., workbooks and recorded material $.22 requested versus $1.75 desired; for instructional supplies (paper, pencils, art equipment) $3.60 requested versus $6.25 desired. All figures are for one elementary student for one year.

Administrators of programs funded from open-ended, restricted sources asked for much more. They operated under a different set of constraints or, more accurately, few constraints at all. Although they prepared some justification for their requests, they did not expect heavy scrutiny since their requests did not draw upon general monies. These administrators—for example, the principals of the dropout-prevention schools funded by overrides—had reputations of a decidedly entrepreneurial type, justified by substantial annual increases in both their personnel and materials.

An example in building maintenance highlights this contrast. Building maintenance has low visibility and it can be cut back without immediate consequences (unlike, say, a reduction in teachers). In 1969/70 a shortage of general monies caused a sharp cutback in general maintenance expenditures; that same year saw the two specially funded dropout-prevention schools ask for, and get, a complete repainting of their building in which each teacher could choose the color of his room. To the outside observer, these discrepancies represented district priorities; in fact, they represented the relative availability of funds and had little to do with priorities at all.[31]

A third, smaller group of requests came from administrators of programs funded from closed-ended, restricted sources. The adult education program is funded from an override tax with an upper limit of $.10/$100. In 1969/70 the administrator's budget reached that limit, and the business office staff warned him against any further expansion. The staff gave him estimates of how much the assessed valuation might rise (and how much his revenue would increase). He then had to decide how to adjust his program within the budget. Neither the administrator nor the staff seriously considered expanding the program through a transfer of general monies. Similarly, the ESEA compensatory education administrator has to adjust his program to the amount of money which the federal government (through the State Department of Education) makes available.

31. The dropout-prevention school was funded by an override tax. Because this tax and the other special sources of funding were passed by the state over time, without particular reference to each other, the observed availability of funds cannot even be said to represent priorities of the state.

Parents Make Requests Too

Another group of requests are initiated by parents or teachers in response to circumstances at a particular school. Throughout the late 1960s the junior and senior high schools saw an increasing number of violent incidents; most received press coverage, and each incident generated a number of phone calls from parents. In July 1969 a group of teachers in one high school asked the board to stop intramural sports until the safety of participating students could be guaranteed. In September 1969 two students in another high school were involved in a fight that ended in a shooting. Over several years this series of events caused the school department to increase its security forces substantially. From 1967 to 1969 the number of budgeted positions for security officers and campus control officers increased from 22.5 to 68. The positions were all funded from scarce general monies.

Another outside request concerned distribution of ESEA funds. In the spring of 1969 the State Department of Education instituted a guideline requiring ESEA funds to be concentrated; each child in the program had to receive $300 more than the normal district expenditure.[32] Until that time, Oakland had been distributing its ESEA funds evenly among seventeen "target area" elementary schools. The new regulation, together with limited amounts of ESEA funds, meant that eight of the schools had to be dropped from the program. The number of participating children fell from 12,200 to 5,800. One of the schools eliminated served a predominantly Mexican American neighborhood. The school had used ESEA funds to hire Spanish-speaking teacher aides from the community. When the eliminations were announced in June, parents and teachers from the school appeared before the board to protest the cuts. They requested $26,000 of district funds for creating an English-as-a-second-language program. The board was impressed with the proposal, but limited general monies stopped them from doing anything at the time. Later that summer it developed that revenues were higher than anticipated, and the request was approved.

A final example concerns the request of a middle-class parent

32. The circumstances which surround this new regulation are discussed beginning on p. 67.

group for additional school resources. In the spring of 1970 the board heard a presentation by a group of parents and teachers from an integrated, middle-class school who had worked out a revised curriculum. They wanted $20,000 to buy new instructional materials and to redesign several rooms and the school's library into open classrooms—rooms which could serve one large or several small groups. Again the board appeared impressed by the presentation, but funds were not available then nor over the remainder of the year; that project was not funded.

Earlier we described the goal of the school system as the acquisition of resources to distribute to constituents. The three requests just described illustrate this behavior. The board of education wanted to approve each request, withholding approval only when the administration could demonstrate a lack of funds. This behavior on the part of the board is understandable; it is made up of people who run for office. When faced with a highly visible request—a direct appeal from parents and teachers—they respond strongly.

The Preliminary Budget Is a Political Document

The superintendent, his administrators, and the business office staff evaluate budget requests during late winter. The superintendent and the business manager then prepare a preliminary version of the budget, which is published and transmitted to the board in May.

The general monies portion of the preliminary budget has in recent years been just in balance or has shown a deficit. Sometimes the deficit is real. At other times the deficit exists only because the business office has provided conservative revenue estimates. In either case, the preliminary deficit serves important political functions.

When budget cuts actually must be made, it is appropriate to demonstrate this fact to the voters by having the board make the cuts in public rather than have the administration do it in private. (This is appropriate strategy even if, as is usually so, the board cuts where the administration suggests cuts should be made.) When cuts are actually unnecessary, paper deficits still help maintain relations between the administration and its personnel. Several authors have shown how low revenue estimates reduce the possibilities for organizational conflict.[33] The estimates serve to increase the amount of formally uncommitted funds in the budget, funds which act as a hedge against uncertainty and increase administrative discretion. If the administration has underestimated revenues, it will have the pleasant job of disposing of a surplus. When it overestimates revenues, it has to bring the budget into balance by rescinding recently approved requests, a distasteful process, which causes hard feelings. The tendency toward low estimates is reinforced in Oakland because the estimates are used to begin district-wide wage and salary negotiations.

The Hard Work Comes in the Summer

Presentation of the preliminary budget marks the beginning of a period of intense activity.

End of May and June	The board brings the preliminary budget into balance making program cuts if necessary.
Early July	The state legislature passes the state budget, which includes the final figure for educational aid. Until the budget is passed, the amount of aid is uncertain. Proposals are made to increase the foundation rate. Other proposals are made to tighten the regulations on special classes. Most generally, the amount of aid depends on the overall size of the budget, and in recent years this has been a point of contention between the legislature and the governor. School districts are not sure of their entitlement until the governor actually signs the budget bill.[34]
Mid-July	The Alameda County Assessor's office releases firm estimates of assessed valuation in the district. These estimates enable the district to estimate its property tax revenue.

33. See Gerwin, p. 65; Richard M. Cyert and James G. March, *A Behavioral Theory of the Firm* (Englewood Cliffs, N.J., Prentice Hall, 1963), pp. 114–127; and Arnold J. Meltsner and Aaron Wildavsky, "Leave City Budgeting Alone!: A Survey, Case Study, and Recommendations for Reform" in John P. Crecine, ed., *Financing The Metropolis* (Beverly Hills, Sage Publications, Inc., 1970), pp. 328 ff.

34. Even the governor's signature may not end the uncertainty. In 1971 the governor signed a deficit budget. A deficit is unconstitutional in California, and the governor and legislature began work on new tax legislation

Mid-July and   When tax revenue and state aid figures are
early August   known, wage and salary negotiations begin in
        earnest. In recent years these negotiations
        have continued until the final budget is due.

August 15   The board is required by law to submit a
        final, balanced budget to the county superin-
        tendent of schools.

This scheduling is more the function of California institutions
than of general school district procedures. The midwest district
studied by Gerwin (pp. 18–19) receives firm notification of state
aid and regulations one year before they are to take effect, a procedure that would help Oakland substantially. Similarly, Oakland
would benefit from a longer period between the receipt of accurate assessed valuation figures and the budget due date. Even
one extra month between firm revenue estimates and the budget's
submission would result in a better budgetary process.

The Budget Evolves

The evolution of the 1969/70 budget can be seen in tables 1-4,
1-5, and 1-6. Table 1-4 presents general monies revenue estimates
for three budgets: the 1968/69 budget at the time the 1969/70
preliminary budget was issued; [35] the 1969/70 preliminary budget
itself, issued in May 1969; and the final 1969/70 budget, passed
in August of 1969.

The preliminary property tax estimate (column 2) was based
on the previous year's experience (column 1) and proved to be
very conservative. While the direction of the bias was predictable,
the size of the bias was due to unusual circumstances that year.
A 1968 state law required all counties to standardize property
assessments at 25 percent of market value by 1971. Like most
other counties, Alameda County (Oakland's county) was assess-

---

to bring the budget back into balance. The legislature had passed increased
educational aid, but the aid had been vetoed by the governor (who pos-
sesses the power of a line-item veto). The legislature countered with the
possibility of writing the educational aid as an unseparable provision of the
tax legislation. The issue was not resolved until October. The aid was not
passed.

35. Exact revenue figures do not become available until several months
after the fiscal year closes. This is due primarily to the collection of delin-
quent taxes over the year.

TABLE 1-4: General Monies Revenue Estimates for the 1969/70 Budget

	(1) Revenue Estimates for 1968/69 Budget at the Time the Preliminary 1969/70 Budget Was Prepared	(2) Revenue Estimates in the Preliminary 1969/70 Budget Dated May 3, 1969	(3) Revenue Estimates in the Official 1969/70 Budget Dated August 9, 1969
General monies property tax	$22,740,000	$23,670,000	$27,140,000
State basic and equalization aid and class-size bonus	10,035,000	10,300,000	10,210,000
P.L. 874	1,270,000	50,000	50,000 [a]

[a] The final resolution of P.L. 874 monies did not come until the spring of 1970. The final sum approved was $915,000.

ing substantially below the 25 percent standard. But unlike other counties, the Alameda assessor decided to complete the major part of the adjustment in the first year. Had school administrators been aware of the rapid adjustment, they could have planned on a large jump in tax revenues. In fact, they estimated an increase of only one million dollars, or 4.2 percent, the increase for a normal year.[36]

At the time the preliminary budget was prepared, the status of the federal P.L. 874 program, Aid to Federally Impacted Areas, also was in doubt. The president's redefinition of the program would have cut Oakland's share of aid to $50,000. There was evidence that congressional pressure might ultimately raise this figure, but again the preliminary budget worked from the minimum estimate.[37]

The preliminary budget did overestimate state educational aid.

36. There was an additional element of uncertainty in the estimate because, beginning in 1969, personal property estimates were to be excluded from the assessed valuation rolls. In compensation, the state mandated an increase in district general monies taxes. (For Oakland the increase was from $2.77 up to $2.855.) It was not entirely clear how these two factors would offset each other.
37. Oakland ultimately received $915,000 for 1969–70.

TABLE 1-5: Expenditure Estimates for the 1969/70 Budget by Major Expenditure Category

	(1) Estimates for the 1968/69 Budget at the Time the Preliminary 1969/70 Budget Was Prepared		(2) Estimates in the Preliminary 1969/70 Budget Dated May 3, 1969		(3) Estimates in the Official Budget Dated August 9, 1969	
	Dollars	Number of positions	Dollars	Number of positions	Dollars	Number of positions
Administration	1,246,300	108.8	1,219,700	108.1	1,336,300	108.4
Instruction	36,004,300	3,305.4	36,438,900	3,125.5	39,129,400	3,276.5
Health Services	650,100	56.8	638,700	57.4	647,400	53.6
Transportation	240,600		279,500		242,000	
Operation of Plant	4,273,200	416.0	4,408,500	421.5	4,497,800	400.3
Maintenance of Plant	1,412,000	11.3	1,515,700	11.0	1,516,400	11.0
Fixed Charges	4,350,400		4,885,300		5,331,700	
Food Services	475,000		475,400		500,000	
Community Services: Maintenance and Operation	656,000	36.8	705,000	38.4	797,700	38.4
Capital Outlay	202,100		173,000		209,800	
Capital Outlay (General)	2,744,000		3,463,200		3,944,377	

SOURCE: *Preliminary Estimates of General Fund* (May 3, 1969) and *General Fund Budget* (*Detailed*) (February 17, 1970). Budget as presented here does not include reserve and does not include federal-state special projects as defined in footnote 38.

The overestimate resulted from an overestimate of enrollment for 1969–70. The mistake was not serious, however. When enrollment projections were subsequently reduced, the need for teachers was also reduced and the net effect was a saving of district money.

Table 1-5 presents the expenditure side of the budget in a similar comparison. The regular budget includes all items except federal-state special projects.[38] Unfortunately, the budget's format does not permit an easy separation of general monies from special-class items as does the revenue format. Table 1-5 thus includes changes for both general monies and many special classes.[39] To correct for this problem, table 1-6 summarizes individually the major expenditure changes between the official 1968/69 and preliminary 1969/70 budgets, and it lists the source of funds for each change.

TABLE 1-6: Discussion of Major Changes in Expenditure Items from the Final Budget of 1968/69 to the Preliminary Budget of 1969/70, by Line Item Category. Funds Come from General Monies Unless Otherwise Noted

Administration
Increases: Automatic salary increments $ 19,000
Decreases: Reduction of one assistant superintendent
      position through attrition. (Salary) 19,000
      Exclusion of expenditure items for 1968/69
      school tax election 35,000
Instruction
Increases: Automatic salary increments (about $199,000
      from general monies) 258,000
      New principal and vice principal for school
      for mentally retarded (special funds) 22,000
      Six new teaching positions for Regional
      Occupational Centers (special funds) 54,000
      Five new teaching positions for Opportunity
      Schools (dropout prevention) (special funds) 45,000
      Seventeen new teaching positions for Educa-

38. These projects include federal funds from ESEA and the Vocational Education Act, SB 28 and AB 1331 funds, Neighborhood Youth Corps funds, and several other programs. Putting these programs in a separate budget seems to result from historical precedent rather than any objective differences with, for example, funds for the Educationally Handicapped program which is included in the regular budget.

39. That is, those special classes which are not classified as federal-state special projects. See footnote 38.

tionally Handicapped Program (special funds)	105,000
Nine new teaching positions for Adult Education (special funds)	45,000
Increase for testing materials to comply with new state regulations for standardized reading tests in all grades	23,000
Increase for supplies in Regional Occupation Centers (special funds)	57,000
Library book increase for elementary schools	6,500
Textbook increase for Regional Occupation Centers	14,000

Decreases: Net reduction of 34 elementary school positions, partly due to a state reduction of a program for reading specialists, partly due to a 1968/69 enrollment below projections. Eight of these positions were funded from general monies ..... 340,000 [a]

Reduction of 2 junior high school positions due to enrollment reduction 20,000

Health Services

Decreases: No major program changes, salaries adjusted downward because of changes in personnel who came in at lower salary schedule 12,000

Transportation

Increases: Increases for increased transportation of students in Physically Handicapped and Severely Mentally Retarded programs (special funds) 34,000

Operation of Plant

Increases: One custodian position added for Physically Handicapped Program (special funds) 6,000

Automatic salary increments 37,000

Addition of six positions for school security 34,000

Increased expenses for utilities (telephones, electricity, etc.) 33,000

Decreases: Reduction of 1.5 gardener positions 14,500

Maintenance of Plant

Increases: Increase due to fire damage to two school buildings 100,000

Fixed Charges

Increases: Increases in retirement and health benefits resulting from previous salary increases (override taxes) 232,000

Increase in insurance premiums 40,000

Increase in lease expenses for portable classrooms for Educationally Handicapped and other programs (special funds) 163,000

Food Services
   No changes in the program
Community Services
Increases: Salary increments (special funds)
    No other major program changes   35,000
Capital Outlay
Increases: Purchase of a site for a Regional Occupation
    Center and purchase of building to headquarter
    ROC, Educationally Handicapped and Oppor-
    tunity Schools programs (all special funds) 686,000 [b]
    Alteration expenditures to bring buildings in
    line with state earthquake safety codes (over-
    ride taxes)   648,000
Decreases: Reductions in alteration budget for fire safety
    improvements (override tax expires during the
    year)   210,000

---

[a] In addition to the listed reductions, there was a reduction of 40 positions due to the system's decision to return all kindergarten classes to double session (see pp. 40–41 for a further discussion). Through misunderstandings, the positions were not deleted from the budget, and state aid was calculated as if the 40 single-session classes were still in effect. The confusion was not cleared up until midway through 1969/70. By that time, unexpected increases in other district obligations—in particular the district's required contribution to the construction of a new school in a redevelopment area—had increased sufficiently to absorb the $300,000 of "found" money.

[b] Unlike other budget items, each site acquisition is a new item rather than an extension of an ongoing program (e.g., the purchase of new text books as part of the normal instructional program). The figure of $686,000 represents an increase in the acquisitions budget over 1968/69 of $233,000.

The budget changes shown in table 1-6 demonstrate the budgetary behavior just described. Changes were small in programs funded from general monies. The principal change was a decrease —a net reduction of eight elementary teaching positions. The decrease represented a downward revision of previous estimates of new students from scattered-site public housing. The only significant increases in general monies expenditures were increments to salaries of existing staff, that is, increases paid to staff who moved up the salary schedule through longer experience or earning a higher degree. The need for such increments can only be estimated, and are kept on the high side to increase budgetary slack.

In contrast, there were substantial changes in programs funded from special sources, including a new building site for a Regional Occupation Center (vocational education school), new portable

classroom leases for educationally handicapped and adult education classes, and thirty-five new academic positions. The programs
that grew were those which, through state and federal law, had
access to money.

The Budget Is Cut in Less Visible Areas

Despite the small increases in the general monies program, the
preliminary budget showed a $1.6 million deficit. By early June
several factors, most notably a revised estimate of assessed valuation, had reduced the deficit, but only to $827,000.[40] The board
of education had to make program cuts if the final budget were to
be balanced as required by law.

All cuts made were proposed to the board by the administration. Some were straightforward. In recent years, teacher needs
projections had become increasingly inaccurate. By basing the
budget on a projection of recent trends rather than the attendance
office projection, teacher needs could be cut by thirty-five positions, or $288,000.[41] Other cuts were not so painless. The admin-
istration proposed reductions in the maintenance, custodial, and
warehouse staffs; cuts in instructional supplies; and cuts in textbook allowances. In late June all were adopted.

These approved cuts contrasted with another proposed cut not
approved by the board: a reduction of the high school day from
six periods to five. The California State Department of Education
defines a full high school day as five periods. By eliminating the
sixth period, the district would not have lost state aid and would
have saved teacher salaries totaling $120,000. The penalty of the
cut would have fallen on high school students, who could have
taken only one elective (science, language, etc.) rather than
two.[42]

The reduction had first been seriously proposed in April. At

40. Superintendent's memo on changes from the *Preliminary to the
Tentative Budget* dated June 10, 1969.

41. These high projections were over and above projections related to
scattered-site public housing mentioned earlier. The attendance office based
its projections on forms filled out by principals who tended to be wildly
expansive when estimating their schools' future enrollments.

42. This was particularly important for children who intended to go on
to college. Most colleges required preparation that included two of the
electives.

that time the administration had sent a letter to parents of all pupils in the ninth through eleventh grades warning of the possible reduction for the coming year. The letter was supposed to mobilize community support for a school tax election to be held in June. But parental opposition to the reduction was so intense that when the tax election failed, the board voted to retain the sixth period nonetheless.[43]

The board was concerned with visibility. The sixth period was a highly visible item and ultimately it was retained. The cuts that were made were in far less visible areas like maintenance and warehouse staffs. But even these cuts can have repercussions. When the 1969/70 school year began, the understaffed warehouse had difficulty distributing books and supplies to schools. Many teachers complained about delays in getting needed materials.[44] In the end the aggregate effect of these delays may have been as educationally harmful as would have been the sixth-period reduction.[45]

Wage and Salary Negotiations Begin

By the end of July the administration realized that even the June revenue estimates had seriously understated the actual gain in assessed valuation. This, along with new information on state aid, and an original underestimate of the 1968/69 year-end balance, meant that the district would have approximately $3.1 mil-

43. The June 1969 election failed, as had four previous tax elections, for a number of reasons. This time, the district and the parents were involved in a controversy over the district's recent choice of a man to replace the retiring superintendent, a controversy so intense that the man eventually withdrew before he formally signed his contract.

44. The problem of delivery delays was serious enough that staff strength was returned to its former level in the next budget.

45. The visibility criterion may influence the skill mix of school personnel. Often the less visible positions are also the low-skilled positions—stock room men, clerks, office aides, custodians—while the visible positions including teachers have high entrance criteria. It follows that a period of budget cutting may fall particularly heavily on low-skilled individuals. Conversely the recent period of tight municipal and school budgets has created opportunities for a government-sponsored program of public service jobs directed at the low-skilled. For more discussion on these points, see Frank Levy and Michael Wiseman, "An Expanded Public Service Employment Program; Some Demand and Supply Considerations," Working Paper of the Department of Economics, University of California, Berkeley, August 1973.

lion more than had been estimated in the preliminary budget.[46] At this point serious salary negotiations began.

Gerwin (pp. 53–56) has described the comparison method by which employee groups like teachers use employee groups in other areas as a standard for wage demands. Oakland's comparison standards were the salaries paid in the seventeen other largest school districts in the state. It was an article of faith in the district that when possible the district's salary schedule should rank in the top quartile of the eighteen big districts (i.e., Oakland plus the others). A statement reflecting this attitude was issued by the previous superintendent in the preliminary 1968/69 budget, a document issued just before the June 1968 tax election:

[While this preliminary budget continues existing programs], it must be pointed out that at this time the budget forecast does not include any balance for either a cost of living adjustment (estimated at 4.8% in March 1968) or a salary increase. And yet, salaries must be improved. Labor union contracts require that we provide salary increases for our building trades personnel—we should not and cannot ignore the same needs for our other classified and certified personnel. The teachers and supporting staff are the key to a quality program. We must maintain competitive salaries in order to attract and to hold competent personnel.[47]

46. The increase in assessed valuation was due to the increase of the ratio of assessed valuation to market value, mandated by state law. The preliminary budget in May had projected an increase in assessed valuation of 4 percent. The revised estimate in June had projected a 15 percent increase. The assessor's firm estimate in July contained a 19 percent increase. This translated into a general monies tax revenue increase of $2.1 million.

The reassessment of property also affected state aid. Normally, an increase in a district's assessed valuation results in a decrease in state aid (see the formula on p. 34). All other things being equal, the $2.1 million increase in general monies tax revenue should have been offset by a $750,000 reduction in state equalization aid. But when the state calculates a district's aid, it standardizes the district's tax base for its ratio of assessment to market value. The state required all counties to set this ratio at 25 percent by 1971. Alameda County had completed the adjustment in 1969 when most other counties were still assessing at about 22½ percent. Since Alameda was assessing at 10 percent higher than the state average, its tax base was reduced by 10 percent for purposes of calculating state aid. Oakland, instead of losing $750,000 in state aid, received $180,000 additional state aid.

47. Statement of the superintendent in *Preliminary Estimates of the General Fund Revenues and Expenditures for 1968–69* (issued April 30, 1968), p. x.

Until the summer of 1969 these salary goals could be discussed at an abstract level. The upper quartile standard was subscribed to as an ideal, but all parties recognized that the money wasn't there. Actual salary negotiations were limited to figures near the increase in the cost of living. In the five years before 1969/70 all personnel had received annual increases (exclusive of earned increments) averaging 4.7 percent. These increases left Oakland eighth out of the eighteen districts in average salary paid, and sixteenth out of the eighteen in a combination of five salary checkpoints. In fringe benefits the district ranked third.[48]

With the windfall increase in assessed valuation and state aid, the context of negotiations changed sharply. The upper quartile standard was now within reach, and the district's two teachers' organizations became increasingly militant. One, the Oakland Chapter of the National Education Association, threatened the system with NEA sanction unless a sufficient increase was negotiated.[49]

Bargaining resulted in the resolution reproduced here, which specified that the $3.1 million of unanticipated revenue be disposed of in the following fashion: $2.46 million for a general salary increase of 7.5 percent; $500,000 to finance the district's contribution to a new school being built in an urban redevelopment area;[50] $35,000 to be placed in undistributed revenue; and $125,000 for various board-approved projects. Included in the $125,000 was $40,000 to replace Spanish language and compen-

48. The average salary for Oakland in 1968–69 was calculated at $9,971. The district with the highest average salary was San Bernardino with $10,876. The other comparison checkpoints included the starting and maximum salaries for teachers with various degree attainments. Source: *1968–69 Salary Bulletin No. 2*, memo written by the Director of Research of the Oakland Public Schools, April 29, 1969, and the California Teacher's Association *Bulletin No. 242*.

49. This militancy was due in part to competition between the already established NEA chapter and the small but rapidly growing AFT chapter. The AFT declined to take official part in the negotiating process since to do so they would have had to list their membership and reveal their numerical strength (still substantially less than the NEA group). They did, however, criticize everything negotiated by the NEA as being insufficient.

50. The board had entered into an agreement with the urban renewal agency to participate in this construction. Without the windfall it is not clear how the agreement could have been fulfilled.

satory personnel who had been removed from two schools when ESEA guidelines had been redefined.[51] Only $10,000 went toward restoring cuts made in June.

The board's resolution also contained an open-ended provision which provided that the first $820,000 of any additional general monies which the system might receive was to be applied to an additional 3 percent salary increase. This was directed at the possibility that Congress would pass a version of P.L. 874 substantially higher than that which the president had asked for. In fact, Congress did pass such a bill, and the full 10.5 percent salary increase was realized.

Resolution of the Board of Education
of the Oakland Unified School District, No. 22407

BE IT RESOLVED that the Oakland Unified School District Board of Education directs the Acting Superintendent to place the following items in the 1969/70 budget to be adopted August 9, 1969:

1. $2,460,000 to increase all certificated and classified salary schedule accounts to provide a salary increase of 7.5%.
2. $500,000 for transfer to the Special Reserve Fund to assist in financing complete construction of the Martin Luther King, Jr. Elementary School.
3. $125,000 to be used as follows:
   a. Human Relations Program $75,000
   b. English as a Second Language (ESL) at
      Lazear School 20,000
   c. Reading improvement program at
      Woodland School 20,000
   d. Restoration of elementary school librarian position .. 10,000
4. $35,000 to placed in the undistributed reserve.

BE IT FURTHER RESOLVED that as any "new" general purpose funds become available the Acting Superintendent is directed to allocate such funds as follows:

1. Up to $820,000 to further increase all certificated and classified salary schedule accounts to provide for an additional salary increase of three percent.
2. The next $255,000 shall be placed in the reserve for expenditures to be determined by the Board of Education.
3. Beyond $1,075,000 any remaining funds are to be utilized for further improvement of salaries up to the bottom of the top quarter of the 18 largest school districts or 16%, whatever is lower.

51. See p. 49 for a discussion of this request by parent groups.

BE IT FURTHER RESOLVED that "new" money shall be defined as follows— additional general purpose revenue estimated to be received during the year from state or federal sources—less any similarly estimated decrease in general purpose revenue, less the cost of financing any federal or state mandated programs requiring general purpose money, and less any emergency expenditures that must be financed from general purpose money, and less any emergency expenditures that must be financed from general purpose funds as determined by the Board of Education. BE IT FURTHER RESOLVED that the Acting Superintendent be directed to include a sum of $300,000 in the final budget for improvement of employee health and welfare benefits for all district employees.

Finally, salary negotiations produced a 6 percent increase in health and retirement benefits and a $120,000 increase in the counselor program for seventh and eighth grades. Both items were to be financed by increases in the override taxes.

As a result of the settlement, Oakland moved from eighth to sixth in average salary paid, sixteenth to eighth in the combination of salary schedule checkpoints, and third to first in average fringe benefits.

A Problem Is Posed for Educational Finance

By any standard the 1969 settlement was a large one. In 1970 negotiations returned to their normal pattern. Again revenues were tight. The negotiated salary increase was 4.5 percent, and the fringe benefit increase was 1.5 percent. Together they totaled 6 percent, approximately the national rate of inflation for the year.

If the 1969 settlement was unusual, it still poses a problem for educational finance: the design of proper constraints on any new, large grants of state or federal aid.

We have seen the problems that restrictions can create. Items like the seventh and eighth grade override tax and the Opportunity School override tax create spending "priorities" unrelated to the district's own preferences. Because these taxes and other restricted revenues are passed by different levels of government, over time and in a piecemeal fashion, they do not represent any coherent set of values.

If the presence of restrictions creates problems, their absence may create problems of a different sort. In a sense, the $3.1 million of unanticipated tax revenues (along with the P.L. 874 money, which was to come later) was an unrestricted grant. It could have been used for any purpose including salary increments, restoration of June budget cuts, and the addition of new programs.[52] In fact, 80 percent of the money was used for salary increments at a time when the budget had just been cut by more than $500,000 and items such as books and instructional materials were being supplied at very low levels.[53]

There were reasons for this allocation. One was the feeling that salaries in the system were low. Another was the willingness of the NEA to place sanctions on the system. But there is little to suggest that these factors were unique to 1969. The method of salary comparison with other districts almost always can generate reasons for salary increases. Similarly, the willingness of public employees to take strike actions will probably increase, not decrease, over time. Together these factors imply that an organization like the Oakland schools will be under continuing pressure to use unrestricted money for salary increments, even at the expense of program cuts.

Until recently, the schools could respond to this pressure by an appeal to "the realities." General monies were limited, and voters would not approve tax increases to expand them. Other sources of funds had restrictions that precluded their use for salary increases. School districts could argue, correctly, that the only real budgetary decisions were incremental: small changes in salaries and existing programs.

Precisely because this defense worked, it may have produced maladaptation. School officials could focus their allocative thinking on incremental decisions. They did not really learn to deal with employee organization pressure because they did not have to. If the amount of unrestricted funds was to increase sharply—perhaps through a one-time reformulation of state aid—schools

52. There was another potential use for such revenues: reduction of local taxes. Given Oakland's low school tax rate, however, it is understandable that the board and the administration never considered this possibility.

53. The allocation is all the more surprising given the volatile nature of the funds. Part of Oakland's bright revenue picture resulted from a temporary advantage in state aid—an advantage which arose because Alameda County was using a higher assessment ratio than were other counties in the state (see n. 46 above). By 1971, all counties would be required to assess at the higher ratio and so this advantage in state aid would be eliminated.

might not be able to resist pressure to put the new money into salary increases.

Labor negotiations in the public sector are hard enough in any context;[54] for an organization with little negotiating experience, they may be especially difficult. A redesign of educational financing that fails to take this into account may end up subverting its own goals.

THE SCHOOLS' DISTRIBUTION OF RESOURCES

We turn now to a principal outcome of the budgeting process— the schools' distribution of resources to different groups in the city. Oakland has large black and Mexican populations, and racial tensions are part of normal political life. General distributional questions translate into: "Do white children get more resources than minority children?" and "Do rich children get more resources than poor children?" There is also another, more specific question. In the spring of 1969, a review team from the California State Department of Education accused the district of misspending federal ESEA funds intended for poor children. Thus, the allocation of compensatory funds becomes a question in its own right.

Our interest in distributional questions comes in part from our limited understanding of education. When one child is in a smaller class than another, we assume he is "getting something extra." In terms of dollars per child, our assumption is correct. But suppose we defined the goal of education to be the child's performance on standardized reading tests, and suppose we had statistical evidence to show that this performance was *negatively* related to class size. Then the child would not be getting anything extra at all.

Such an analysis is, of course, impossible; we have no definition of the goals of education to which everyone subscribes, and in any event our understanding of the relationship between school resources and goal attainment is poor.[55]

54. See, for example, Harry H. Wellington and Ralph K. Winter, Jr., "The Limits of Collective Bargaining in Public Employment," *Yale Law Journal* 78, no. 7 (June 1969): 1107–1127.

55. See, for example, Marshall S. Smith, "Equality of Educational Opportunity: The Basic Findings Reconsidered," chapter 6 in Frederick Mosteller and Daniel P. Moynihan, eds., *On Equality of Educational Opportunity* (New York: Vintage Books, 1972).

Because we do not have this knowledge, we are forced to look at school resources not as means to an end but as ends in themselves. The outlook is far from ideal but it is a common language, shared by school administrators and parents. If no one can say with certainty what a child is receiving in relation to his needs, everyone can say how much a child gets, and how much he gets in relation to other children. And because everyone can say this, standards such as "equality of inputs" have a universal meaning.[56]

The Elementary Schools as a Test Case

We will base our analysis on data from Oakland's sixty-three elementary schools. These schools are small and because each draws its students from an immediate neighborhood, we can associate the resources in each school with a particular economic and racial group.

Our data are limited in several ways. The resources distributed among school buildings represent only part of the resources in the system. Certain funds—for example, the superintendent's salary—are spent on items which are not distributed among students in any meaningful sense. Other items, such as music teachers and principals, are distributed among individual schools, but they are either too small or their distribution is too uniform to merit detailed discussion.[57] For these reasons, we will limit our analysis to two important resources: teachers and instructional supplies.

We can analyze the distribution of teachers in some detail. Necessary data exists in central payroll listings which show for each school the number of teachers and each teacher's experience

56. What equality itself means is open to question. We will deal with this question more fully in chapter 4.

57. In the elementary schools in 1969–70, music instruction was offered on a limited basis, largely by instructors who worked in several schools. The student/teacher ratio was about 1,550:1, which permitted each student one period of music instruction every three weeks. There were several administrative formats, depending on school size. The three largest elementary schools (all over 1,150) had a principal, a vice-principal, and a head teacher (one-fourth of whose time was spent on administration). In these schools the student/administrator ratio was 576:1. The other sixty schools had various administrative combinations which varied from a head teacher and a part-time principal for the smallest schools (the principal covered two schools) to a full-time principal for the largest schools. Student/administrator ratios in these schools were in the range of 420–450:1, though a few were larger.

level, degree level, and source of funding (district funds or state or federal compensatory program). We will analyze these data for both 1969/70 and 1970/71.

There are no comparable listings of the distribution of supplies. We will, however, combine administrative bulletins and personal classroom observations to construct a qualitative picture of supply allocations.

A Look Ahead

We can provide a framework for the material which follows by summarizing our principal finding: For 1969/70 the distribution of dollar resources to income and racial groups has a U shape. Children in schools from the highest-income areas and children in schools from the lowest-income areas receive relatively high levels of resources (but for different reasons). Children from schools in between these extremes do not do as well. When we classify schools by the percentage of minority students, a similar result holds. For 1970/71, a new superintendent instituted policies that retained the extra resources in the poorest schools but reduced the extra resources in the richest schools. The resulting distribution assumed an L shape.

A *Preliminary Digression*

Before we discuss the distribution of resources, we will turn to the misspending of ESEA funds, the most dramatic of the distributional questions. In May of 1969 a review team from the California State Department of Education submitted a highly critical report of Oakland's ESEA program. The outgoing superintendent kept the report secret (even from the board of education) until a copy was leaked to the press in early August. A summary of the charges is contained in the following report.

Summary of Criticisms of Oakland's Use of ESEA Monies
Contained in Report of State Department of
Education Review Team, Dated May 1969

1. Children who participated in the program did not increase in achievement at rates above children who were not in the program.
2. Personnel in the program, particularly at the school level, were unfamiliar with the state guidelines for compensatory programs. Teachers seemed to view the program as one to motivate students

or improve their attitudes. Teachers seemed to be reluctant to focus on raising student achievement or to be held accountable for their work on the basis of standardized achievement tests.

3. There were too large a number of new teachers in schools receiving compensatory programs. These teachers were unfamiliar with the program's purposes and seemed to have low expectations for their students. In addition, principal turnover at the schools seemed high.

4. The resources given to each school were not sufficient to provide a complete compensatory program, as defined in the district's fund application, for every eligible child in the school. A complete program included remedial help, cultural enrichment, a full diagnosis of learning problems, etc.

5. Most schools were wasting money by serving children who were legally eligible for other special programs, in particular the Educationally Handicapped program.

6. The district's program had too large a proportion of administrative personnel and too few personnel assigned to individual schools.

7. It was not clear how children were selected to participate in the district's limited bussing program. Further, the district selected the receiving schools for this program on the basis of space available, a method which resulted in the selection of several schools which already had significant Negro student enrollments (other all white schools were selected as well).

8. Ineligible children in the integration receiving schools were being given resources which were intended for children who were bussed in.

9. Out of 477.1 positions discussed in the district's application, the review team could only account for 276.8. (The report, after presenting this figure, went on to say that part of the discrepancy was due to the method of counting: the district had proposed hiring 286 half-time aides which equaled 143 full-time positions of which the review team had found 142.5. This left the review team with a discrepancy of 51 positions rather than the 201 which the original figures suggest.)

The state charges were of two kinds: Points 1–7 heavily criticized the design of the district's program—inexperience of teachers, lack of diagnosis of learning problems, and so on.[58] Points 8 and 9 charged the district with direct misuse of funds—providing services to high income (presumably white) children who were

58. Even point 5, an apparent exception, refers not to ineligible recipients (rich children) but rather to eligible recipients who were also eligible for special classes and so should have been assigned to those classes to release more resources for other eligible children.

ineligible for the program under the law. Because these two charges were the most dramatic, they received the most public attention. A San Francisco *Chronicle* article of August 1 began:

Federal grants totalling $10 million aimed at helping 12,000 ghetto youngsters in the Oakland public schools were scattered throughout the district instead of going to 15 target schools, a State Department of Education evaluation team reported yesterday. . . . The misdirection of the funds, the report says, explains why the target area children made "no measurable academic gains"—a conclusion the district itself reached last year in a report to the department.[59]

The story went on to describe the 201 missing positions (point 9) though it ignored the state's qualification that the 201 missing positions might in fact be closer to 50.

The article, and others like it, provided a general disservice to the district and the district's parents. By focusing on the misspent funds, the articles discussed that part of the state report which ultimately proved weakest. Subsequent investigation showed the misspending charges to be dramatically overstated.[60] The articles ignored the strongest part of the report program—the bad design of the district's ESEA program.

Many of the design problems flowed from the district's goals. The administration and the board tried to be responsive to their constituents. Had they concentrated the ESEA funds in a few eligible schools, they would have been charged with unfair treatment by other eligible schools. To protect themselves, the district spread the ESEA funds thinly over all eligible children. The in-

59. San Francisco *Chronicle,* August 1, 1969. The $10 million figure refers to total ESEA grants over two years.

60. As was noted in point 9, the report itself qualified its charge of 201 missing positions and suggested that the true number might only be 51 missing positions (a fact ignored by the newspaper accounts). A further audit showed the actual number of missing positions to be something less than 10. Similarly, the magnitude of resources involved in point 8 was small. Each integration receiving school was assigned a half-time or full-time remedial reading teacher. This teacher would work with those bussed-in children who needed extra help as well as with those children who normally attended the school and required remedial work. In addition, each integration receiving school was paired with an ESEA school, and classes from both schools would go on joint trips to places like fire stations. Classes in the receiving schools averaged two such trips per year. Transportation costs came out of ESEA funds.

crease in resources was not very large in any particular school; each staff could feel justified in believing that their program was not sufficiently improved to obtain any particular educational goal.[61]

The State Department of Education responded to this problem (in Oakland and elsewhere) by developing additional ESEA guidelines. In the late spring of 1969, the state announced that district programs would have to concentrate on raising student achievement. Emphasis was to be placed on gains measured by standardized achievement tests. In addition, each child participating in an ESEA program had to receive at least $300 per year more in services than he would normally receive. This guideline forced Oakland to reduce the number of children participating in the program from 12,200 to 5,800.[62]

There was no guarantee that these new guidelines would make the program work. Contrary to the implication of the state report, no ESEA program in the state had produced dramatic gains in achievement. But at least the guidelines would allow a better determination of how ESEA funds were being spent. They would also force districts to generate data which could aid in investigating the relationship, if any, between extra resources and increased achievement.

DISTRIBUTION OF TEACHERS

We begin describing the resources in elementary schools by discussing the distribution of teachers. Teachers' salaries comprise the major portion of the annual budget as shown in table 1-7. There we present the relation of teachers' salaries to two cost definitions: the total budget, and the official definition of Current Operating Expense of Education.[63] The second statistic is the one commonly used in talking about "cost per student." Teacher costs

61. This behavior is not sufficient to cover all of the report's criticism, however. It does nothing to explain the top-heaviness of the program (point 6) or the rapid turnover of teachers and principals in ESEA schools.

62. The $300 did not have to come entirely from ESEA funds. Five of the nine schools enrolled in the program in 1969–70 made their concentration out of a combination of ESEA and SB 28 funds.

63. Current Operating Expense per student is a modification of the first figure. It removes from the budget food services, community services, reserves, capital accounts, and federal-state special projects.

TABLE 1-7: Average Cost per Student Figures, 1969/70 and
the Importance of Teachers' Salaries in Total Cost

	Aggregate Cost	Cost per ADA (total ADA = 63,343)
(1) Total 1969/70 budget	$65,753,284	$1,038
(2) Total teachers' salaries counted in (1) above	31,692,645	497
	(2)/(1) = 48%	
(3) Current operating expense of education [a]	52,852,000	834
(4) Teachers' salaries counted in (3) above	30,103,350	475
	(4)/(3) = 57%	

[a] Current operating expense of education equals the total budget minus the following items: food services, community services, capital outlay, reserves, and federal-state special projects.

are 48 percent of the total budget and 57 percent of Current Operating Expense.[64]

To discuss teacher distribution, we need several kinds of data. The first data are the student/teacher ratios when all teachers are counted: classroom teachers funded by the district, classroom teachers funded by the state through SB 28, and classroom and specialist teachers funded through ESEA.[65] In 1969/70, nine schools had either ESEA funds or a combination of ESEA and SB 28 funds. Six schools had SB 28 funds only.[66] In addition, five predominantly white schools served as receiving schools for the district's limited bussing program. Each of these schools received one and a fraction ESEA positions to provide remedial help for

64. The remainder of Current Operating Expense in Oakland for 1968–69 is as follows: administration, 3 percent; instructional expenses other than teachers (supplies, principals' salaries, testing and counselling personnel, etc.), 20 percent; health services, 1 percent; transportation, 1 percent; operation of plant, 8 percent; maintenance of plant, 3 percent; fixed charges, 8 percent. This breakdown is essentially the same for all large California districts.

65. For this analysis, students and teachers in educationally handicapped and other special programs (mentally retarded, etc.) are excluded.

66. As noted above, schools with ESEA funds could purchase extra supplies, hire teacher aides, and so on. SB 28 funds could be used only to hire extra classroom teachers to reduce average class size in the school to twenty-five.

bussed-in children. In 1970/71, an expansion of available funds enabled the district to increase the number of schools having compensatory programs. Fourteen schools had ESEA or a combination of ESEA and SB 28 funds while twelve had SB 28 funds only.

Our second set of data are the student/teacher ratios when only district-funded teachers are counted. We need this data to test for a more subtle form of misspending—funding substitution; the federal dollars go to eligible children, but the district reduces its own funds for those children. Here, we also look for changes between 1969/70 and 1970/71, when the new superintendent took office.

A third set of data are the average experience and degree levels of teachers in each school. The district's salary schedule is based on seniority and credentials paying extra salary increments for each of the first thirteen years on the job and each degree earned above B.A. In theory, experience and credentials both increase teaching ability. To the extent that this theory is correct, two schools can have equal student/teacher ratios but unequal resources because one school has experienced teachers with advanced degrees while the other does not.

Finally, we will examine data on average teacher-salary dollars per child in each school. We will use this statistic as a crude aggregating device by which we can compare, for example, a school with large classes and experienced teachers with a school with small classes and inexperienced teachers. These equations are very rough, and we cannot translate them into terms of educational effectiveness, but they do offer a gross measure of resource distribution.

An Examination of the Data

Table 1-8 presents student/teacher ratios when all teachers—district personnel and compensatory personnel—are counted. Part I of table 1-8 presents this data for 1969/70, and part II presents data for 1970/71. Within each part, schools are classified twice: once by the percentage of minority students and once by the median income of the surrounding census tract (1960 data).

The data show that gross discrimination was not present. When all personnel are counted, the lowest student/teacher ratios occur

TABLE 1-8: Ratios of Students to All Teachers (Including Compensatory Teachers) in Oakland Elementary Schools, 1969/70 and 1970/71

I. 1969/70

A. Schools classified by percentage of minority students

(1) Percent Minority (Negro and Mexican American)	0–10	11–50	51–90	91–100
(2) Number of Schools in Group	7	18	19	19
(3) Mean Ratio of Students to All Teachers in Group	31.3	30.6	29.0	25.8
(4) Standard Deviation of (3)	(1.81)	(3.24)	(3.46)	(4.15)

B. Schools classified by income of surrounding census tract (1960 income data)

(1) Income Class	9,000 & above	7,500–8,999	6,000–7,499	4,500–5,999	3,000–4,499
(2) Number of Schools in Group	8	9	21	18	7
(3) Mean Ratio of Students to All Teachers in Group	31.0	31.1	30.9	26.8	21.7
(4) Standard Deviation of (3)	(1.94)	(3.21)	(2.27)	(2.05)	(1.94)

II. 1970/71

A. Schools classified by percentage of minority students

(1) Percent Minority (Negro and Mexican American)	0–10	11–50	51–90	91–100
(2) Number of Schools in Group	7	18	19	19
(3) Mean Ratio of Students to All Teachers in Group	30.4	29.6	26.0	21.6
(4) Standard Deviation of (3)	(2.26)	(2.63)	(3.77)	(5.55)

B. Schools classified by income of surrounding census tract (1960 income data)

(1) Income Class	9,000 & above	7,500–8,999	6,000–7,499	4,500–5,999	3,000–4,499
(2) Number of Schools in Group	8	9	21	18	7
(3) Mean Ratio of Students to All Teachers in Group	31.2	29.3	28.5	23.0	18.1
(4) Standard Deviation of (3)	(2.65)	(1.93)	(2.07)	(5.45)	(1.68)

in the poorest, highest minority schools. In 1969/70, students in
the highest proportion minority schools had student/teacher
ratios of about 26:1 while students in the highest proportion white
schools had ratios of 31:1. For the same year, students in the
lowest-income class schools had ratios of 22:1 while students in
the highest-income class schools had ratios of 31:1. The results
for 1970/71 (table 1-8, part II) are similar. Note that for both
years, differences among schools are sharper when they are classified by income than when they are classified by race. The very
low class sizes are due to compensatory personnel, and these
programs were allocated on income rather than racial criteria.
While all of Oakland's poorest schools are predominantly Negro,
not all the predominantly Negro schools are very poor. In 1969/
70, there were seven schools in the lowest income class and all
were receiving compensatory funds. There were nineteen schools
with 91–100 percent minority student bodies, but only fifteen of
these nineteen had compensatory funds.

The ratios in table 1-8 are averages for each group of schools.
Within each group (e.g. 0–10 percent minority) there is school-
to-school variation around the average. If the within-group variations are sufficiently large, we may not be able to detect statisti-
cally significant differences between groups despite differences in
group averages. To investigate this possibility, we include in
table 1-8 the standard deviation around each ratio, and we include
in Appendix A student *t* statistics to test the hypothesis of significant differences. The tests confirm the discussion above.

The District's Own Personnel

The data in table 1-8 show the absence of gross discrimination
in resources: children in the poorest schools do not get less than
children in the richest schools, and in fact they get more. There
remains the possibility of funding substitution.

Compensatory funds are supposed to be pure supplements to
the normal district program. Funding substitution occurs if the
district cuts back its own personnel in those schools receiving
compensatory personnel. In this case, children in the compensatory schools may still be receiving more resources than other
children in the system, but they will not be receiving the amount
they are entitled to by law.

TABLE 1-9: Ratio of Students to Teachers Paid by the Oakland Public Schools (as Distinct from Teachers Paid by ESEA and SB 28 Compensatory Funds) 1969/70 and 1970/71

I. 1969/70

A. Schools classified by percentage of minority students

	0–10	11–50	51–90	91–100
(1) Percent Minority (Negro and Mexican American)	0–10	11–50	51–90	91–100
(2) Number of Schools in Group	7	18	19	19
(3) Mean Ratio of Students to O.P.S. Teachers in Group	31.3	31.1	30.2	29.8
(4) Standard Deviation of (3)	(1.81)	(2.80)	(2.28)	(2.94)

B. Schools classified by income of surrounding census tract (1960 income data)

	9,000 & above	7,500–8,999	6,000–7,499	4,500–5,999	3,000–4,499
(1) Income Class	9,000 & above	7,500–8,999	6,000–7,499	4,500–5,999	3,000–4,499
(2) Number of Schools in Group	8	9	21	18	7
(3) Mean Ratio of Students to O.P.S. Teachers in Group	31.2	32.0	30.9	29.2	29.6
(4) Standard Deviation of (3)	(2.75)	(1.73)	(2.28)	(2.60)	(3.10)

II. 1970/71

A. Schools classified by percentage of minority students

	0–10	11–50	51–90	91–100
(1) Percent Minority (Negro and Mexican American)	0–10	11–50	51–90	91–100
(2) Number of Schools in Group	7	18	19	19
(3) Mean Ratio of Students to O.P.S. Teachers in Group	30.8	30.5	28.8	27.4
(4) Standard Deviation of (3)	(2.30)	(2.57)	(3.01)	(4.66)

TABLE 1-9: (*continued*)

II. 1970/71

B. Schools classified by income of surrounding census tract (1960 income data)

	9,000 & above	7,500– 8,999	6,000– 7,499	4,500– 5,999	3,000– 4,499
(1) Income Class					
(2) Number of Schools in Group	8	9	21	18	7
(3) Mean Ratio of Students to O.P.S. Teachers in Group	31.2	30.7	29.4	27.3	28.3
(4) Standard Deviation of (3)	(2.65)	(1.63)	(2.16)	(5.20)	(3.58)

We investigate this possibility in table 1-9. Table 1-9 presents student/teacher ratios in a format similar to table 1-8 except that only teachers paid from regular district funds are counted. Compensatory teachers are excluded. The data in table 1-9 refute the idea of funding substitution and in fact show an opposite pattern. When only regular personnel are counted, the poorest schools (and highest minority schools) still have slightly *lower* student/teacher ratios than other schools in the system. This effect is particularly noticeable in 1970/71, when the new superintendent promoted some redistribution of the system's resources.

Together the data in tables 1-8 and 1-9 provide the following picture: The district assigned its own personnel to produce essentially equal student/teacher ratios in all schools (with a slight bias in favor of the poorest schools). The district then assigned personnel from compensatory programs to the poorest schools, where they were additions to, rather than substitutes for, district personnel.

The Distribution of Experience and Degree Levels

In table 1-10 we present the distribution of teachers by years of experience and by degree level held, for 1969/70. The district's salary schedule gives salary increments for each of the first thirteen years of experience. Correspondingly, teachers are listed in payroll records in one of thirteen experience categories ranging from first year to thirteen years and over. To simplify this data, table 1-10 contains experience categories for three years (e.g., first through third year, fourth through sixth, etc.).

TABLE 1-10: Distribution of Teachers' Experience and Educational
Attainment among Schools, 1970/71

	Teachers' Experience, All Schools (in percent)					
	1–3 yrs.	4–6 yrs.	7–9 yrs.	10–12 yrs.	13 yrs.+	Total
Classification						
All schools	21.1	14.5	11.5	29.9	23.0	100
By percent minority [a]						
0–10	6.7	3.0	9.7	33.0	47.6	100
11–50	13.8	11.0	9.2	36.0	29.9	100
51–90	27.6	16.5	15.1	22.7	18.2	100
91–100	23.2	17.6	10.4	31.2	17.5	100
By income class [b]						
$9,000 & above	9.7	5.3	10.6	31.6	42.9	100
7,500–8,999	9.1	10.0	8.3	39.6	33.1	100
6,000–7,499	24.2	12.3	13.1	27.9	22.5	100
4,500–5,999	24.9	17.5	10.5	29.3	17.7	100
3,000–4,499	17.4	22.4	12.4	29.2	18.6	100

	Educational Attainment, All Teachers in School (in percent)				
	4-yr. degree	4-yr. + 1-yr. credential	Master's degree	Ph.D. or equivalent	Total
Classification					
All schools	27.6	41.4	25.6	5.3	100
By percent minority [a]					
0–10	12.6	36.9	41.7	8.7	100
11–50	17.4	42.4	33.8	6.3	100
51–90	32.7	43.0	20.5	3.8	100
91–100	32.7	40.6	21.5	5.2	100
By income class [b]					
$9,000 & above	13.2	39.5	39.5	7.9	100
7,500–8,999	14.9	46.3	33.1	5.8	100
6,000–7,499	26.7	43.4	23.8	6.1	100
4,500–5,999	32.1	41.4	22.8	3.8	100
3,000–4,499	37.3	34.2	23.6	5.0	100

[a] Schools classified by percentage of minority students.
[b] Schools classified by income of surrounding census tract (1960 income data).

Similarly, the salary schedule recognizes four degree classifica-
tions: a four-year B.A. or B.S., a four-year degree together with a
one-year teaching credential, a master's degree, and a doctorate
degree or its equivalent in course units. The distribution of these
data also is contained in table 1-10.

The data in table 1-10 are for all teachers—teachers hired from
district funds and teachers hired from compensatory funds—and
their distribution shows a common pattern: white children and
children in rich schools have teachers with longer experience and
higher degree attainment. In schools with the greatest proportion
of white students, one out of every two teachers had thirteen or
more years of experience. In schools with the greatest proportion
of minority students, one out of five teachers had thirteen or more
years of experience, and one out of four teachers had less than
three years experience. The distribution of degree levels is similar
up through the master's degree (few teachers in any school have
Ph.D.s or equivalents).

We should not be surprised at the similar distributions of
teacher experience and degree level. Typically, a teacher will not
have advanced degrees when she begins to teach. She will earn
these degrees on the job, in part for educational purposes and in
part to increase her salary. She will complete her requirements by
taking night courses and summer courses stretching over a period
of years. A teacher who follows this pattern has to be on the job
a long time before she can earn an advanced degree.

How Things Got That Way

Why are the well-paid teachers concentrated in the upper-
income, white schools? The answer lies in a combination of
teacher preference for those schools and the district's transfer
policies. Until 1970/71, the district generally permitted teachers
with seniority to transfer freely within the system. (Beginning in
1970/71, the new superintendent cut back sharply on transfers
that were requested for "racial and economic" reasons.) [67] Most
teachers who wanted to transfer came from predominantly minority and poor schools; they wanted to move to what they perceived
as easier or more rewarding jobs in upper income schools.

Table 1-11 summarizes transfer data for 1969/70 when ninety-

67. There is also some evidence that transfer approval in 1969/70 was
tighter than it had been in previous years.

TABLE 1-11: Teacher Transfers Requested and Granted, 1969/70

	(A) *Transfers Requested*			
Percentage of minority students in present school	*Percentage of minority students in first choice*			
	0–10	*11–50*	*51–90*	*91–100*
0–10	0	0	1	0
11–50	0	0	3	0
51–90	6	7	6	3
91–100	5	11	15	14
(N = 71 total requests)				
	(B) *Transfers Granted*			
Percentage of minority students in school transferred from	*Percentage of minority students in school transferred to*			
	0–10	*11–50*	*51–90*	*91–100*
0–10	0	0	0	0
11–50	0	0	1	1
51–90	1	7	5	2
91–100	0	8	11	16
(N = 52 total approvals)				

one elementary teachers (representing about 8 percent of all those in the district) applied for a change of school. Twenty were general requests—"any school with a male principal" or "any junior high school"—and were eliminated from the sample. The remaining seventy-one transfer requests are shown in table 1-11 (A). The vertical axis of table 1-11 (A) represents the percentage of minority students in the teacher's school in 1969/70. The horizontal axis represents the percentage of minority students in the teacher's first choice of schools (teachers usually specified two or three choices).

Sixty-one percent of the first-choice requests were for schools with smaller minority populations than the teacher's then current school. Only 6 percent were for schools with higher minority populations. There were only four transfer requests from the twenty-one schools with over 50 percent white students.

Table 1-11 (B) presents similar data for the fifty-two requests that were granted; 52 percent were transfers from higher minority populations to lower ones. Eight percent were transfers from lower minority populations to higher ones.

To complete our story, the teachers whose transfers were approved had an average (mean) of eight years of teaching experience. We can surmise that the transfer pattern over a number of years provided the mechanism by which experienced teachers moved from the poorer, minority schools to richer, predominantly white schools. This accounts for the distributions shown in table 1-10.

What to Do?

The distributions of experience and education are disturbing, and an easy remedy is not apparent. Consider the distribution of experience. Beyond some point, a teacher's experience may be a disadvantage—she may become "hidebound"—but this process takes time. In the first years of a teacher's career, a lack of rigidity does not compensate for lack of experience on the job. We can argue, then, that the high proportion of teachers in minority schools with three or fewer years of experience is a cause for real concern.

The transfer patterns in table 1-11 suggest that one way to redress the imbalance of staff experience is to prohibit transfers. But the long-run impact of such a prohibition is unclear. We want experienced teachers for minority students, but we also want teachers with a positive attitude toward the students, an attitude probably lacking in teachers who want to transfer. Our goals of experience and proper attitude may well conflict.

Alternatively, we might allow transfers and try to better conditions in minority and low-income schools. If teachers do not now find these schools desirable, perhaps they can be attracted by smaller classes, more facilities, and other advantages. But we do not know how great an investment this would take. For several years before 1969/70, the poorest schools were receiving compensatory resources under ESEA and SB 28, but the data in table 1-11 suggest that there are still many requests for transfers out of these schools, while the data in table 1-10 show that their staff (including compensatory staff) have only slightly greater experience than the income class directly above it.

From these data we can conclude that the amounts currently

involved in compensatory programs either are too small or have been in existence too short a time to produce equality of conditions in teachers' eyes.[68]

The Distribution of Salary Dollars per Student

Tables 1-12 and 1-13 present data on the distribution of teacher-salary dollars per student for 1969/70 and 1970/71. The figures

TABLE 1-12: Distribution of Average Salary Dollars per Student among Schools, 1969/70

I. Salary Dollars per Student for All Teachers (District and Compensatory)				
A. Schools classified by percentage of minority students				
(1) Percent Minority (Negro and Mexican American)	0–10	11–50	51–90	91–100
(2) Number of Schools in Group	7	18	19	19
(3) Mean Salary Dollars of All Teachers per Student in Group	370.73	374.41	359.59	404.66
(4) Standard Deviation of (3)	(25.33)	(39.25)	(43.24)	(80.68)

B. Schools classified by income of surrounding census tract (1960 income data)					
(1) Income Class	9,000 & above	7,500– 8,999	6,000– 7,499	4,500– 5,999	3,000– 4,499
(2) Number of Schools in Group	8	9	21	18	7
(3) Mean Salary Dollars of All Teachers per Student in Group	383.09	372.76	349.62	373.38	481.79
(4) Standard Deviation of (3)	(40.08)	(28.07)	(36.09)	(50.45)	(60.58)

68. There are other possible conclusions to the argument. It may be that none of the teachers—new or old—have positive attitudes toward the students, and so nothing is lost by forcing the more experienced teachers to stay. On the other hand, it may be that career teachers in the system take initial assignments in poor and minority schools in the expectation that they will be able to move to a "better" school as they get seniority. If this option is not open, the teachers may simply choose a different school system. Finally, an additional conflict may arise between the goal of getting more minority teachers and getting more teachers with advanced degrees.

TABLE 1-12: (*continued*)

II. *Salary Dollars for Oakland Public School Teachers (Excludes Compensatory)*

A. *Schools classified by percentage of minority students*

---

(1) Percent Minority (Negro and Mexican American)	0–10	11–50	51–90	91–100
(2) Number of Schools in Group	7	18	19	19
(3) Mean Salary Dollars of O.P.S. Teachers per Student in Group	370.73	370.14	348.98	351.53
(4) Standard Deviation of (3)	(25.53)	(36.46)	(29.66)	(36.72)

B. *Schools classified by income of surrounding census tract (1960 income data)*

---

(1) Income Class	9,000 & above	7,500– 8,999	6,000– 7,499	4,500– 5,999	3,000– 4,999
(2) Number of Schools in Group	8	9	21	18	7
(3) Mean Salary Dollars of O.P.S. Teachers per Student in Group	378.92	361.34	348.83	353.40	368.31
(4) Standard Deviation of (3)	(31.51)	(26.30)	(36.10)	(27.76)	(46.82)

---

act as a rough summary of the data in tables 1-8 to 1-11 since they combine both salary per teacher (reflecting teacher experience and education) and student/teacher ratios.

The data reflect the patterns we have developed in the previous tables. We noted that in 1969/70 the district distributed its own personnel to produce relatively equal student/teacher ratios in all schools, with the teachers in the richer, predominantly white schools having greater experience and higher degree levels (table 1-9, part I, and table 1-10). The sum of these effects can be seen in part II of table 1-12. When only district personnel are counted, children in the highest proportion white schools received about $370 per student in teacher salaries, while children in the highest proportion minority schools received about $350 per student.

Part I of table 1-12 contains 1969/70 data when all personnel—district and compensatory—are counted. Here three effects are working: the equal distribution of district personnel, the concentration of high-salaried personnel in the richer, white schools,

and the concentration of compensatory personnel in the poorest
schools. As shown in part I of table 1-12, the salaries received by
the compensatory personnel more than outweigh the higher
salaries received by experienced teachers. When all personnel are
counted, children in the highest proportion white schools continue
to receive $370 per student, while children in the highest propor-
tion minority schools receive $404 per student.

For 1970/71, a slightly different pattern emerges. In that year,
the new superintendent allocated the district's own personnel
to produce smaller class sizes in the poorest schools. The effect of
this policy appears in part II of table 1-13: even before compensatory personnel are counted, children in the highest proportion
minority schools received $466 per student, while children in the
highest proportion white schools received $416 per student. When
compensatory personnel are added to these figures, the poorest
schools are favored even more (table 1-13, part I).

TABLE 1-13: Distribution of Average Salary Dollars per Student
among Schools, 1970/71

I. Salary Dollars per Student for All Teachers (District and Compensatory)

A. Schools classified by percentage of minority students

(1) Percent Minority (Negro and Mexican American)	0–10	11–50	51–90	91–100
(2) Number of Schools in Group	7	18	19	19
(3) Mean Salary Dollars of All Teachers per Student in Group	421.02	425.53	429.12	617.66
(4) Standard Deviation of (3)	(38.92)	(44.45)	(72.14)	(344.63)

B. Schools classified by income of surrounding census tract (1960 income data)

(1) Income Class	9,000 & above	7,500–8,999	6,000–7,499	4,500–5,999	3,000–4,499
(2) Number of Schools in Group	8	9	21	18	7
(3) Mean Salary Dollars of All Teachers per Student in Group	411.22	436.63	405.31	576.14	672.23
(4) Standard Deviation of (3)	(38.18)	(38.38)	(41.04)	(358.57)	(54.84)

TABLE 1-13: (*continued*)

II. *Salary Dollars for Oakland Public School Teachers (Excludes Compensatory)*

A. *Schools classified by percentage of minority students*

(1) Percent Minority (Negro and Mexican American)	0–10	11–50	51–90	91–100
(2) Number of Schools in Group	7	18	19	19
(3) Mean Salary Dollars of O.P.S. Teachers per Student in Group	416.10	415.49	385.56	466.23
(4) Standard Deviation of (3)	(46.00)	(49.47)	(48.14)	(226.03)

B. *Schools classified by income of surrounding census tract (1960 income data)*

(1) Income Class	9,000 & above	7,500– 8,999	6,000– 7,499	4,500– 5,999	3,000– 4,499
(2) Number of Schools in Group	8	9	21	18	7
(3) Mean Salary Dollars of O.P.S. Teachers per Student in Group	411.22	417.61	392.80	468.23	411.50
(4) Standard Deviation of (3)	(38.18)	(39.85)	(50.80)	(233.13)	(52.37)

The U-shaped Curve and the L-shaped Curve

If we were to construct a graph with salary dollars per student (benefits) on the vertical axis and income class or the percentage of minority students on the horizontal axis, the 1969/70 data would trace a U-shaped distribution. The richest schools had normal class sizes and teachers with long experience and high degree levels, so the average salary dollars per child in these schools were high. Children in the poorest schools had teachers with low experience and degree levels, but the addition of compensatory personnel drastically reduced student/teacher ratios. As a result, these schools also had high salary dollars per child.

Schools between these extremes—those lacking a concentration of either experienced teachers or compensatory personnel—did not do as well. Some differences were substantial. Children in schools in the third income class received about $24 less in salary dollars per child than children in the highest income class. For a classroom of thirty children, this is equivalent to $720 per year.

In 1970/71, the new superintendent reduced the relatively large salary resources going to schools in the highest income class by reallocating district personnel toward the poorer schools. Salary dollars per child were equalized across schools *before* compensatory personnel were counted. When compensatory personnel were added, the resulting distribution had a kind of L shape: children in the poorest schools received relatively large resources, while children in other schools received lower resources.

Our figures are for teachers only. Had we included other school-based personnel, the effects already noted would increase. Schools receiving ESEA funds would have shown such personnel as teacher aides, full-time nurses (most schools have part-time nurses), part-time psychologists, and full-time librarians. Occasionally, a high-income school would make up part of these services through volunteers—but only a part. Such a school may have had a volunteer librarian, and one or two classrooms may have had volunteer teacher aides. Any more than this was unusual.

THE SCHOOL'S DISTRIBUTION OF SUPPLIES

We turn now to distribution of classroom supplies. There is no central listing for supply allocations which corresponds to the central payroll listing for teacher assignments, but various bits and pieces of data are available.

An elementary school can get its supplies from three sources: the district's regular supply allocation, ESEA funds (if applicable), and direct parental contributions. The district handles its own supplies in a decentralized fashion. In the spring, each principal receives an estimated per-pupil supply allowance to cover all classroom materials for the following year: paper, pencils, arts and crafts materials, and so on. He receives a second allowance to cover books, workbooks, records, and other media material beyond the state-supplied textbooks. Each school's allowance is credited to the school's account at the district warehouse. In late spring the principal and his teachers forward supply orders, which are debited against the account. The items ordered are chosen from a supply catalog provided by the district.

Principals feel that the catalog's offerings are more than adequate: the problem is the small allowance per pupil. The budget cuts of June 1969 reduced an already tight preliminary supply budget. After the cuts, principals had $3.18 per student to spend for all instructional supplies for the year.

The administration was receiving reports by mid-autumn that no amount of scrimping could make that allowance last. In November, the board, at the request of the administration, transferred an additional $30,000 to the supply budget from unrestricted reserve. For elementary schools this meant an increase of the per-pupil figure from $3.18 to $3.60, still very meager. The supplementary book allowance for the year was $.12 per pupil— not enough to buy a single newspaper.

The nine ESEA schools had substantially larger budgets to work with. The total ESEA budget for the year for instructional supplies (including workbooks and other media material) was $77,260. The figure covered approximately 5,800 children, resulting in an average expenditure of $13.40 per child, an expenditure in addition to the regular district allowance.

Parent Contributions

If a school is located in a comfortable neighborhood (black or white), it can obtain resources from direct parental contributions, including such organizations as the Dads' Club and the PTA. As part of their yearly program, parent groups hold fund-raising events for the schools.

Two stories are illustrative: One principal described a school which began to experiment with a new kind of reading program that meant abandoning the state texts and purchasing other books. During the first two years the experiment was small: first one classroom and then two. Expenses were small and were picked up by the central administration, using supplementary funds. The program was so successful that in the third year the principal and teachers decided to expand it to all classrooms in the first three grades. The administration, however, said that they could not fund the expansion. At this point, parents decided to finance the program themselves. As the principal said, "They had bake sales, car washes, and God knows what else. I don't know how they did it, but each month we'd get another check for $100 or $120 to keep us going."

In another school the Dads' Club each year holds a two-night amateur show. This, together with PTA fund-raising activities, produces about $1,100 a year. The principal said that in previous years the money had gone for a Thermofax machine, a media center (slide viewers, records, etc.) and an opaque projector. In 1969/70 it went primarily for workbooks which the staff had requested. Every year a portion of the funds are allocated for extra supplies and books for the library.

Both groups of parents were raising about three dollars per child, an amount roughly equal to the district's own supply allocation. One school was predominantly white. The other was about two-thirds white and one-third black.

An Anecdotal Summary

After all the personnel and supply figures have been presented, it is appropriate for us to ask what they mean. During 1969/70, one of the authors spent time as a teacher's aide in three elementary schools: a middle-class, predominantly white school with an active parents' organization; a poor school that was receiving both ESEA and SB 28 funds; and a poor school that was receiving SB 28 funds only. The white school was an integration model school with black children, bussed in from other neighborhoods, comprising 10 percent of its enrollment.

The ESEA and middle-class schools differed primarily in their teaching staffs. Teachers in the middle-class school were older, had been in that particular school longer, and the entire staff (with the exception of the principal) was white. By contrast, many of the teachers in the ESEA school were in their first or second year and the staff was about one-third black.

There were also differences in staff size. The ESEA school had smaller class sizes as well as a full-time teacher's aide in each classroom, a full-time librarian, a full-time reading specialist, and a half-time nurse. The middle-class school had a volunteer librarian and one or two volunteer teacher's aides.

Though the schools differed in staff, they did not differ in supplies. The ESEA school had adequate levels of pencils, paper, art materials, and other supplies. The compensatory funds allowed the staff to scrap the state-supplied textbooks in favor of programmed learning texts. The middle-class school used the state-supplied texts along with workbooks bought through parent-supplied funds. Teachers in the middle-class school were more willing to ask children to bring arts and crafts supplies from home. The teachers themselves brought more materials to their classrooms, perhaps because they had been at the school longer and regarded their classrooms as more permanent.

Beyond these differences, there was little to choose between the two. The middle-class school was in a newer, more pleasant building. Classes in the ESEA school went on several trips a year, all funded by ESEA money. Classes in the middle-class school also went on several trips a year. Two of the trips were held jointly with an ESEA school and were paid for from ESEA funds. The other trips were paid for by student money brought from home. In the middle of the year, the district received a large supplementary ESEA grant for mathematics, and the ESEA school received two mathematics teaching machines in each classroom in grades 1–3. Because the middle-class school was an integration model school, it received one machine for every two classrooms. The machines in the middle-class school were used primarily by the children who were being bussed in, although some of the neighborhood children also used them.

Compared with both these schools, the school receiving only SB 28 money was in poor condition. SB 28 funds were restricted to hiring extra teachers, and the school did not have an active parents' organization. As a result the school was starved for supplies. Teachers were forced to rely on state-supplied textbooks (often inappropriate), though some teachers bought paperbacks out of their own salaries. Class sizes were as small as in the ESEA school, but practically no class had a teacher's aide. There was no librarian, and teachers ran the library themselves. The procedure was adequate for checking books in and out, but nobody had the funds or responsibility to get new books or magazines. Because the school had no connection with the ESEA program, it received no mathematics teaching machines under the supplementary grant. Any trips the children took (except for one bus trip to see a play at a neighboring school) were organized by individual teachers and were either walking trips or trips paid for by a combination of student and teacher funds. With one exception, no classroom went on many trips.

The author did not have a chance to observe a poor school with no compensatory funds. A good guess would be that those schools resembled the SB 28 school in its lack of supplies and resembled the middle-class school in its larger classes—the worst of both worlds.

The U-shaped Curve Again

The picture here reinforces the U-shaped relationship observed in the distribution of salary dollars in 1969/70. Schools in well-to-do neighborhoods get extra supplies through ad hoc parental supplementation. Schools in poor neighborhoods get extra supplies because they qualify for ESEA funds. But schools neither sufficiently rich nor sufficiently poor are tied directly to the district's financial situation and so do badly.

The existence of these U-shaped relationships in personnel and supplies again raises the question of aid restrictions. Both well-to-do schools and poor schools received above-average levels of resources. But the well-to-do schools received their extra resources through "neutral" administrative policies, while poor schools received theirs through restricted compensatory funds.

We saw that in 1969/70 well-to-do schools received a relatively high level of salary dollars per student. We explained this level by the district policy that allowed teachers with seniority to transfer within the system. While officially neutral, the policy had the effect of allowing experienced (and therefore high-salaried) teachers to move from poorer to richer schools. We saw also that well-to-do schools had a relatively high level of resources in the classroom, and this arose from a neutral policy: if parents wanted to make direct contributions to their children's schools, school officials would not stand in their way. Policies that were apparently neutral actually favored the richer, predominantly white schools.

In 1970/71, the new superintendent began to modify these "neutral" policies. He sharply reduced the number of approved transfers and he reduced student/teacher ratios in the poorest schools so that salary dollars per student of *district* personnel were equal among all schools. Both policy changes are important, and similar, moderate changes are possible in the future, but the superintendent has only limited freedom in this direction. In particular, he could never justify funding large compensatory programs from the tight district budget.

The 1969 ESEA guidelines required that each child enrolled in

an ESEA program receive $300 or more in services than he other-
wise would receive. This figure represents a 30 percent increase
over average district expenditure. Were the superintendent to attempt such a program for even a few schools, he would have to
explain why he was favoring such a program over all competing
demands: higher wages and salaries, increased supply and textbook allowances, full-time school nurses in all schools, and so on.
The poorest schools, like the richest schools, receive large amounts
of supplies and high salary dollars per student but only because
the funds for these extra resources are restricted to this purpose.
We shall return to this point in the next section when we discuss
the redesign of state educational aid.

PROSPECTS FOR THE FUTURE

We began this chapter by describing the financial problems faced
by the Oakland school district: the taxpayers' revolt, the increasing salary demands of employees, a possible recalculation of state
aid, heightened concern with the intradistrict distribution of
resources.

A school district is more, of course, than the value of its annual
budget. Over the year, it dispenses many nonfinancial resources:
teacher attitudes, the accessibility and attention of the administration, the use of school buildings for neighborhood groups. Some
of these resources are symbolic. Others may have direct impact
on the way in which children achieve. All of them influence outcomes because they affect the way in which the community re-
gards the schools.

In the years just ahead it appears that these nonfinancial resources will become increasingly important.[69] They will do so in
part by default because financial resources will be increasingly
hard to come by. We can emphasize this point by considering one
by one the potential sources of financial change.

69. There is some evidence that this kind of planning is beginning to
take hold. One of the new superintendent's concerns has been to redesign
the administration. He has reduced the staff at the central office and decentralized certain administrative functions to three assistant superintendents, each in charge of one part of the district. Through this kind of policy
and through numerous personal appearances, he hopes to increase the
district's accessibility. Ultimately, however, he hopes that these improved
community relations will lead to a successful tax election.

THE DISTRICT'S PARENTS

The district's parents have a limited kind of power. They want more resources for their children, but they do not have sufficient force in the electorate to pass a tax increase. They can get their children more resources by making larger direct contributions to their children's schools (if they can afford it) or by demanding a redistribution of the district's existing resources. The people most likely to want redistribution are the parents in the near-poor schools, the schools at the bottom of the U, too well-off for ESEA and too poor to make substantial direct contributions.

Under the new superintendent, some redistribution has already begun. His policy of smaller class sizes in the poorer schools (before compensatory personnel are counted) has roughly equalized salary dollars per child. His policy of sharply reducing approved transfers will, in the long run, equalize experience and education levels in all schools. But neither of these policies speaks to supplies, and supplies (or their absence) are one of the first things noticed by a visitor to a classroom.

In 1970/71, a district teacher in a poor school was paid about $12,000 per year. At this salary, staffing classes at thirty rather than twenty-eight results in a saving of about $840 per class, or $28 per child. If parents were asked to choose between the larger class with substantial supplies and the smaller class with few supplies, many would undoubtedly choose the former. To please these parents, the district might consider a policy of equal total dollars per child (rather than equal salary dollars per child) and equal class size. The near-poor schools would receive increased class sizes together with larger supply budgets.

It is, of course, easier to discuss such a policy than to implement it; the process of laying off teachers and transferring their salary savings into supply budgets has a number of pitfalls. Teachers may object to the trade-off (unless, perhaps, the staff reductions come through attrition). The money released from the salary budget will immediately become fair game for claims from other programs in the system. In addition, the ESEA regulations will force the program into a degree of inefficiency. Regulations require that before a district can receive compensatory funds, it must spread its own program evenly across all children. The regulations would force the district to provide extra supply monies not only to the near-poor schools, where they are needed, but also to the poorest schools, where large supply allotments are already provided by ESEA. Despite these difficulties, an equal expenditure (and equal class size) program would move toward satisfying parental demands.

THE TEACHERS

The district teachers, too, have a limited kind of power. They became important in our story only when the district received a large amount of unrestricted funds. If similar funds do not become available in the future (and we believe they will not), teachers will return to bargaining over marginal wage increments.

This conclusion is reenforced by both economic forces and district politics. In theory, teacher salary increases could arise from normal supply and demand factors. If teachers were in short supply and Oakland had a number of vacant positions, it would have to increase its salary schedule in order to lure teachers away from other districts. In fact, the Bay Area has a substantial oversupply of teachers. Even a relatively undesirable district like Oakland has enough applications to fill all vacancies at existing wages. Thus market pressures for wage increases no longer exist.

Alternatively, wage increases can arise from teachers' political power. In many cities the board of education is a stepping-stone to higher office, and board members must court political support. Since employee unions are often a crucial part of this support, board members must continue to pass sufficient wage increases to keep the unions satisfied. But again, Oakland does not fit the model. Here, board members rarely move to higher office, and in general they show a lack of political ambition and skill. Occasionally, these qualities can be a liability, as when the board was overwhelmed by teacher demands in 1969. Even a political board interested in teacher support could have obtained a more balanced settlement. But in periods of tight revenues, their lack of political ambition means that board members have little incentive to let wages increase faster than the cost of living.

THE STATE

The most likely change in Oakland's finances will come from the state: a new state-aid-to-education formula designed to comply with the *Serrano* decision. A new aid formula will affect the district both through the amount of money it provides and through any new regulations it imposes upon the money, but even in this case a large change is unlikely.

Serrano attacked the inequities of the current relationship between the school tax rate and educational expenditure. A property-rich district like Emeryville ($95,000/ADA) taxes itself at a low rate and still raises a large amount of revenue. A property-poor district like Hayward ($5,700/ADA) taxes itself at a high rate and raises a small amount of revenue.

Presumably an "equitable" relationship would reflect state averages. A district's tax rate would produce total revenue (local revenue plus state aid) as if the tax were being applied to the average tax base per child in the state. The state can move property taxes toward this relationship through a number of different plans.[70] Each plan contains an element of redistribution where higher taxes are collected from the property-rich districts and more aid goes to the property-poor districts. But under any of these plans, a district whose local tax base is close to the state average should remain relatively unaffected, for it already has an equitable relationship.

Oakland is such a district. In 1970, the average assessed valuation per child in all California school districts was $15,464. Oak-

70. The simplest plan is the statewide property tax. Under this plan the state chooses a per pupil allowance which is high enough to cover (or exceed) educational expenditures in most of the state's districts. They then calculate the property tax rate which, when applied to all taxable propery in the state, will raise enough funds to provide this allowance for every public school student. Presumably districts would be allowed to add local taxes to finance expenditures above the allowance. Under the plan everybody pays at the same tax *rate*. The plan is redistributive, since residents of high tax base districts pay more total revenue than do residents of low tax base districts even though all residents are receiving the same per pupil allowance in return. The per pupil allowance has to be large, since compliance with *Serrano* requires that districts have only a limited dependence on the local property tax for their educational expenditure. But the very fact that the expenditure level is large means that a number of districts may be receiving windfall increases in unrestricted revenues, whether or not their voters want increased educational spending. A more sophisticated (but harder to administer) plan which preserves local autonomy is described in: John Coons, et al., "Educational Opportunity: A Workable Constitutional Test for State Financial Structures," *University of California Law Review* 57, no. 2 (April 1969): 305–421.

land's assessed valuation per child was $15,755. Any plan which
equalized the relationship between tax rates and expenditures
across districts would leave Oakland unaffected.

Redistribution may not be based on the property tax alone.
The state may find more political support for a plan which raises
increased revenues from state income taxes and sales taxes. The
new money would still be concentrated in the property-poor districts, but as a sweetener the state might give slightly increased
aid to all districts. If a sweetener were provided, even average
tax base districts like Oakland might benefit to a limited extent.
Oakland would also benefit if the state modified uniform cost allowances and adopted an "urban factor," a slightly increased aid
figure for districts which have heavy concentrations of low-income
children, but neither of these alternatives promises much. The
limited impact of these plans highlights the paradox of *Serrano;*
low-income people don't always live in low tax base districts.
School tax base comes from expensive houses but also from industrial and business structures, valuable properties which don't add
children to the school system. In rural areas, low-income families
and low tax base often go hand in hand. In central cities low-
income families (and their low-value housing) are offset by commercial property. Under *Serrano,* poorer rural districts and lower-
income, residential suburbs stand to gain. But central cities like
Oakland will do well to break even.

Even if Oakland does not gain much money from a new state
aid formula, it may be affected by the restrictions which the
formula carries. One potential restriction involves a shift of power
from the local boards to the state. Several state legislators have
suggested that if a *Serrano* remedy requires substantially increased
state aid, the state should also increase its control over how the
money is spent. The state would assume this control through
mandating a statewide teacher salary schedule, tighter limits on
minimum and maximum class sizes for all grades, and other
spending regulations.

The legislators' concern is understandable in light of the experience reported in the previous section—Oakland's disposition
of the windfall in property tax revenues. Nonetheless, their solution to the problem raises new problems. Designing a statewide
salary schedule—especially one which accurately reflects market

conditions in different parts of the state—will be enormously difficult. Other problems may be raised by transforming salary negotiations from their current decentralized form to a single negotia-
tion between teachers' organizations and the state legislature and
the governor.

The objections take on greater weight because alternative solutions exist. Consider a property-poor district like Hayward. Compared with state averages, Hayward taxes itself too heavily for
what it spends, but this fact leads to two possible solutions. The
state can argue that Hayward should maintain its tax rate but
should have more money to spend. Or the state can argue that
Hayward should maintain its spending and levy lower taxes. Under either judgment, Hayward receives more state aid, but in the
first case, the extra aid would be given to the school district to
spend as it chooses, thus raising the problems of unrestricted
funds. In the second case, the state requires the district to pass
the extra aid on to the voters in the form of reduced property
taxes. In the first case the district can spend more on education
whether or not the voters approve. In the second, the district can
increase educational spending only if it can convince voters of
the need to increase taxes from their lower, post-aid level. By
placing the emphasis on lowered taxes, rather than increased
spending, the *Serrano* mandate can be satisfied without recourse
to new regulations and without undermining the existing balance
of power between the state, the local boards, and the voters.

We advocate this solution not because we believe the existing
balance of power is the only natural one. To the contrary, some
of the Oakland district's problems arise from the asymmetrical
treatment of school taxes and other municipal expenditures: the
city council can set its own tax rate while the board of education
cannot. It makes far more sense to put school expenditures and
other municipal expenditures on an equal footing, either by con-
solidating school expenditures with the rest of the city budget
and placing it under the city council or by giving the board of
education the power to set its own tax rate. In either situation,
the voter's control over school expenditures would diminish because he could only vote for candidates and could not vote on
taxes directly. But this shift of power is a far cry from removing
major school expenditure decisions to the state level.

A final change affecting Oakland may occur if the state wants to extend the redesign of state aid to include reassessment of current special-purpose programs and override taxes. The reassessment would be in the spirit of recent "special revenue sharing" proposals, motivated by the idea that local administrators know local problems best. Their logic suggests that existing special-purpose programs should be collapsed into general-purpose grants and given to local districts for their own priorities.

We have presented material to show that some consolidation is needed. The seventh and eighth grade override tax gives expenditures for these grades a de facto priority which has no logical basis. The system by which wages and salaries come from general monies, and fringe benefits come from an override tax, puts an unnecessary bias in employee settlements. Yet we cannot extend this logic too far. The two examples both affect broad groups of people. All students are in the seventh and eighth grades at one time or another. All teachers collect fringe benefits. The size of these groups guarantees that their interests will be safeguarded even without aid restrictions.

Other restricted programs affect much smaller groups. Compensatory education programs, dropout-prevention schools, and similar items represent large amounts of money spent on a relatively small number of children. The district allocates money in this fashion because it is forced to; the district either spends ESEA money on poor children or it doesn't get it. The situation is a kind of paradox. Restricted funds are "unrestricted" because they are not subject to all the competing claims placed upon the district's general money.[71] Were the programs to be reformulated into bloc grants, the relatively small number of beneficiaries could not apply sufficient pressure to regain the funds. Outcomes would change substantially.

Again, we do not argue wholly for the status quo. Compensatory education programs are far from a total success. A dropout-prevention program may have its own problems. But if the state decides that these, and similar programs with small numbers of beneficiaries, are worth undertaking, the state will have to continue financing them through restricted grants.

Having described these new restrictions, we should emphasize

71. We are indebted to Victor Goldberg for this point.

that all of them are at best problematic. The most likely result of *Serrano* is a new state aid formula which simply increases the funds available to the poorest districts and leaves Oakland relatively untouched.

CONCLUSION

We who study Oakland would be the first to say it does not encompass all of urban reality.[72] Yet the situation we have described—a budget that is tight now and that will continue to be tight—can be found in a number of other cities. Oakland's tight budget is due to a particular set of circumstances: a predominantly black and Chicano student body, a predominantly white electorate, and a fiscally independent school district which allows the electorate to hold down the tax rate. The demographic pattern is typical of many other cities. The fiscally independent district is less typical, but where a board of education has more control over spending, it becomes a better political stepping-stone. In such communities, board members must put greater emphasis on salary increases to cultivate political support. Where Oakland faces tight revenues, these communities face greater pressure on costs.

Oakland's tax base per child, a tax base near the state average, is also typical of many cities. We suggested that this tax base was deceptive in part: a low proportion of children in a low-to-moderate-income population which is already burdened by high property taxes for other municipal services. But this too is typical of central cities. Unless state aid formulas become sophisticated in their indices of district wealth, Oakland and cities like it will be in a poor position to benefit from *Serrano* and similar court decisions.

We could go on, but the point is clear. If Oakland and other central-city school systems are not in the midst of a true crisis, neither are they particularly comfortable nor will they become comfortable in the near future. What one makes of this depends upon how one feels about the schools. It may well be that other programs—a guaranteed income, direct employment programs for

72. See, for example: Jeffrey L. Pressman, "Preconditions of Mayoral Leadership," *American Political Science Review* 66, no. 2 (June 1972): 511–528.

the poor, catastrophic health insurance—simply have higher priority on tax funds. But we should not turn away from the schools, particularly the near-poor schools, with the feeling of a job well done.[73]

73. People familiar wih the Bay Area will recognize the new superintendent, referred to in this chapter, as Dr. Marcus Foster. As this book was being completed, Dr. Foster was murdered under circumstances which would have been ridiculous were they not so tragic. Both the Oakland Public Schools and Oakland itself were better for Foster's having worked there. They will be poorer for his absence.

2

Streets

We walk on them. We ride on them. We use and abuse them. Living in the modern city, we have always had streets; but most of us do not know how or through whom our streets came to be there. In no small part, streets contribute to the quality of urban life. Yet most of us take them for granted. As long as streets are clean, accessible, and without too many potholes, citizens are not terribly concerned. When we buy gasoline for that beneficiary of the streets, the automobile, most of us probably do not know that we are paying taxes to build streets and freeways. Despite their importance, streets remain an invisible public good—built and maintained by professional engineers, used and paid for by an indifferent public.

Just because the public is not aware does not mean that the allocation of street resources is trivial. On the contrary, how and why money is spent on streets is important both to the citizens who live in cities and for those of us who study them. The politics of streets involves who gets streets, whose streets are repaired, and where streets are built. It means having sidewalks to walk on and curbs, gutters, and storm drains to keep one's house from flooding. It involves our very safety not only when we drive our cars but also when our children go to school and the railroad crossings are suitably protected. In short, everyone has something to lose by not paying attention to street outcomes and their explanation; thus this study focuses on Oakland's Street and Engineering Department and two of its major activities—street construction and street resurfacing.

We will start with a brief explanation of the department's environment. The actors in its environment are mostly professionals with similar preferences. They make themselves felt by operating the revenue lever. By restricting the use of revenue, they affect what happens.

Having pointed out the importance of revenue restrictions, we go on to examine decision rules behind street construction projects and resurfacing of old streets. Despite some infrequent external intrusions, engineers eventually get their way. Being patient, able to manipulate their schedules, and having values that are compatible with their revenue sources, the engineers emphasize circulation of traffic by allocating resources to Oakland's major streets.

After discussing prior conditions, the environment and decision rules, we then turn our attention to outcomes. First comes the complex question of who benefits. In Oakland, those citizens with freeways and major streets in their neighborhoods may be the losers. Mostly, they are residents of the poor Oakland flatlands. The sure winners, in any event, are users of these major streets. Second, it is likely that the allocation of street resources is inefficient because cost considerations usually are ignored in decision-making—an outcome which may not surprise economists. Our third outcome will please planners who will be happy to learn that engineers make plans and use them; there is a stability of goals which comes from over fifty years of planning. And it is this stability, this concentration on allocating scarce resources to major streets which we question.

THE ENVIRONMENT: ACTORS

A street department is usually conceived of as operating within a closed, stable, and highly professional environment. One pictures engineers making decisions on the basis of technical considerations, free from disturbing influences and unpredictable interventions from city politicians or others in the outside world. After all, the general feeling is that engineers alone know how to solve street problems and that most people are not too excited about the subject. Educators, housing planners, and the like must be ready to adjust to a turbulent and emotional environment in which everyone has a different opinion about how to go about doing things, but no real knowledge. But in the technical world of engineers, one expects decision-making to proceed smoothly and efficiently, clad in rationality and objectivity, and founded upon the principle of long-range planning.

In some respects, decision-making in the Oakland Street and Engineering Department fits this idyllic description. Decision-making is by the few; long-range planning sometimes occurs; and decisions are usually, but not always, made on the basis of technical considerations. For the most part, allocation of resources under the street construction program is left to the judgment of the engineers. The city council and city manager hold to the principle that street planning is best left to experts. The manager limits himself to cutting from project requests only those amounts which will not be expended within the budget year. He is more concerned about limiting the department's total appropriation than about its internal allocations. The council generally learns of a planned street project only when requests for funds first appear in the budget, although it does have some advance knowledge of projects included in long-range plans. The council usually gives its approval for projects after a brief, formalized review.

Although the advice of the department is heavily taken into account, outsiders sometimes do make decisions. On occasion, the council (and sometimes the manager) will intervene by indicating to the department certain project priorities which they want to see observed. The council—as principal link between the public and the street department—occasionally will veto a project or legislate one of its own into existence.

Other city departments (particularly those whose functions are closely related to street activities) also intervene. Relations among the Police, City Planning, Traffic Engineering, and Street and Engineering departments have been formalized through a Traffic Committee in which each is represented at weekly meetings. By exchanging information on traffic problems, the other city departments get their viewpoint across to the street engineers.

More potentially disruptive relations exist between engineers and such outsiders as Oakland's Redevelopment Agency, which do not share goals. Cooperation among technicians, however, is the norm. After all, decisions made by other outside organizations can affect the makeup of the Street and Engineering Department's construction program. Most often such organizations are in the street business themselves—for example, the State Division of Highways, Alameda County, Port of Oakland, utilities companies, and railroads.

THE ENVIRONMENT: RESTRICTED REVENUES

One reason for cooperation is money; the street department cooperates with state, county, and city officials because they are the money-givers. These officials restrict the use of street money and reenforce the big street inclinations of Oakland's engineers. In short, revenue does influence the allocation of street resources. It is the central link between the department and its environment. With the exception of a charge for sewer service, restricted or earmarked revenues come from sources outside of the city. And outside sources bring with them outside influences—both from the state and from Alameda County.

Often the availability of outside funds for street activities becomes a rationale for the city manager and council to limit substantially the amount of general funds to be allocated to the department. A steady source of outside income thus does not guarantee that the department will escape the tight budgetary bind imposed throughout the city. Indeed, juggling between general fund and earmarked revenues is perhaps the department's central preoccupation. In the 1970/71 budget earmarked revenues accounted for about 67 percent of total budget appropriations (see table 2-1). We turn now to the earmarkers and fund manipulators —to the state, county, and city outsiders—who get what they want by controlling revenues.

STATE STREETS

Most outside street money comes from state gas taxes. The state collects gas taxes at the rate of seven cents per gallon of gasoline; it retains four cents and distributes the remainder to cities and counties. The state legislature gets what it wants by setting the

TABLE 2-1: Most of Oakland's Street Money Is Earmarked

Financing Source for 1970/71 Budget	Amount (in millions of dollars)	(in percent)
Earmarked:		
Alameda County Street Aid Fund	1.0	
Sewer Service Charge Fund	2.1	
Special Gas Tax Street Maintenance Fund	1.7	
Special Gas Tax Street Construction Fund	2.9	
Total Earmarked	7.7	67
General Fund:	3.8	33
Total	11.5	100

SOURCE: City of Oakland, *Preliminary Budget Fiscal Year 1971/72*, pp. B104–105.

apportionment rules for these gas taxes and by specifying the way money should be spent. By law these revenues must be kept in special funds separate from the city's general fund. Once the revenues are received by local governments, they may be spent on projects which meet the legal qualifications for gas tax funds. Once a year a state auditor checks to see that the revenues have been spent within these legal limits. In the past, local officials had to seek state approval for every proposed gas tax expenditure before projects could be undertaken.

Receiving state gas taxes means spending on state streets. It means following the state Streets and Highways Code (sections 2106 and 2107), and cooperating with the State Division of Highways in mapping out which streets will be built.[1] It means spending more on the construction of major streets and spending less on maintenance and on the construction of minor, neighborhood streets. Despite some recent lifting of restrictions by the state, much of Oakland's gas tax continues to be spent on major streets or what is called the "select system" of streets. In order to qualify as "select," a street must be a major arterial—that is, one that serves through traffic and not just motorists traveling within a city.

Oakland also is hurt by the state's apportionment formula. The

1. For a convenient summary of the state restrictions placed on the gas tax, see League of California Cities, *Limited Expenditure Funds* (Berkeley: League of California Cities, 1971), pp. 6–10.

apportionment of gas tax revenues among cities and counties in California is based essentially on population: the larger the population, the more the city is eligible for gas tax funds. This puts the faster growing, sprawling communities in the most favorable position, especially for receiving yearly increases. Older, denser, and more static cities with old streets, such as Oakland, are at a disadvantage; as Oakland loses population, so it loses gas tax revenues.

THE GENEROUS COUNTY?

Because Alameda County has the money while the cities have the problems, the county board of supervisors, perhaps feeling guilty, adopted the "Mayors' Formula" in 1956.[2] The county has not been entirely generous in using this formula; for example, out of a total $7,650,000, Alameda County distributed $2,455,848 of its gas tax revenue to its cities in 1970/71. We say not entirely generous because 80 percent of the streets in the county are maintained by the cities. For its 29 percent of those streets, Oakland receives only about $1 million a year.[3] Although officials of the Alameda County Road Division complain that they need more money for county road improvements, the board of supervisors still gives away one-third of its gas tax revenues.

Yet generosity can have its price. Indeed, county supervisors, just like state officials, influence city gas tax budgeting. In the fall of 1969, when the Mayors' Formula came up for its five-year term renewal, some interesting points of controversy arose between county supervisors and the cities of Alameda County, all revolving around the issue of how much control supervisors should exert over funds allocated under the Mayors' Formula.

The supervisors were in a fighting mood when the Mayors' Formula came up for renewal because they were experiencing a

2. Information regarding the "Mayors' Formula" was gathered through personal interviews with two Alameda County supervisors, Emmanuel Razeto and James Murphy, in November 1969.

3. These percentages refer to the miles of streets *maintained* by Alameda County and the cities and exclude those streets maintained by local property owners. Figures were provided by Mr. Ralph Lloyd, maintenance engineer, Alameda County Road Division, who obtained them from the State Division of Highways.

threatened incursion on their gas tax funds with no cooperation from the cities in staving it off. The East Bay Regional Park District had a bill pending in the state legislature at the time Mayors' Formula discussions were taking place, which would have allocated a $500,000 slice of the county share of gasoline tax revenues for building park district roads. The supervisors were angry when the cities (instead of backing them up in their efforts to defend against this raid) took the position—assuming that park streets should be considered county streets—that the park district should incorporate with the county and be given county revenues. The supervisors reacted by threatening to reduce each city's share of the proposed $500,000 figure on a prorated basis unless they helped the county oppose the bill. The mayors eventually agreed to offer their support.

The supervisors, making sure that the cities would appreciate where the money was coming from, voted to reduce the Mayors' Formula from a five-year to a three-year term. The mayors unanimously opposed this measure, because a five-year term gives them more stability in revenue forecasting and street planning. The supervisors were adamant. Frequent resource allocation would maintain the county's interest. One supervisor argued that reviewing the formula every three years instead of five would guarantee all future county supervisors (who serve four-year terms) the opportunity to express themselves regarding the formula.

Another point of controversy was over how much influence supervisors should have in determining project selection. Mayors' Formula gas tax revenues must be spent for constructing streets of "more than local importance" (a term open to various interpretations but apparently somewhat less restrictive than the state "select street system" requirement); under the formula each city must seek approval of the county supervisor in whose district the city is located for projects proposed to be funded with county revenues. Getting approval has never been much of a problem in city street planning. In the first place, there is some question whether individual supervisors actually can veto construction projects. Second, most supervisors have not wanted to try, feeling that city officials are closest to and better able to determine street needs of their own people. Although they take a fairly close interest in city proposals, supervisors generally do not object to city plans.

One supervisor, nevertheless, was unhappy with the approval mechanism because he felt that it gave the supervisors less than adequate control over the distribution of revenues in a city which contained several supervisorial districts. Such a city is Oakland, where this particular supervisor represents one of three districts. He complained that gas tax formula money was not being spent on street projects in his district in Oakland and that the needs of the citizens he represented were therefore not being met. Of course, needs do shift and political officials can take advantage of this. Consider the story of Fifty-first Street.

Several years ago the Street and Engineering Department planned to widen Fifty-first Street to four lanes, mainly to tie a major northwest arterial to the new Grove-Shafter Freeway and to improve traffic access from North Oakland to the central business district. The department built one unit of the project, and then was stopped by organized opposition from residents of the street between Telegraph Avenue and Broadway. Homeowners' groups and taxpayers' associations pleaded their case before the council, and the project was stopped.

By 1969, however, as engineers had predicted, traffic volume had increased substantially on Fifty-first Street, the street was congested, and some of the original remaining residents wanted to get the street project under way again and directed their demands to the supervisor, discussed above, who represents the district in which Fifty-first Street is located. At the same time, engineers themselves had decided to reinstate the much-needed widening project. The supervisor, nevertheless, saw a political opportunity. As champion of the people, he threatened to impose monetary sanctions on the street department if it did not undertake the Fifty-first Street project, thus making the engineers appear to be insensitive to residents' demands. He proposed to the board of supervisors that any city such as Oakland, which includes more than one county supervisorial district, be required to rotate its Mayors' Formula funds among those districts, alternating each year. The supervisors did not pass this proposal, partly because most of the other supervisors believed city councils knew best where the money should be spent. They were impressed also

by the argument of the city engineers that street needs do not in-
herently fall into one supervisorial district or another.

Next that same supervisor threatened to refuse to approve the
allocation of Alameda funds to any street project in his district
other than Fifty-first Street. Considering the uncertainty of the
supervisor's veto power, it is not known if his threat could have
been made real. But the city did commit all its county aid in
1970/71 to Fifty-first Street, and scheduled the project for immediate planning and construction. Oakland's engineers say they
would have undertaken the project anyway and believe that the
supervisor actually helped the department by convincing residents
who were still holding out against the project that it was a good
thing. Fifty-first Street illustrates that there is no such thing as a
block grant; whether for personal ambition or civic responsibility,
free funds soon acquire strings.

ENEMIES FROM WITHIN: CITY OFFICIALS

Administering and spending gas tax and other outside revenues
used to be left to Street and Engineering Department control.
Street department funds were its own business. Such a situation
was not tolerable to city officials who wanted to stabilize the
property tax rate (central revenue source for the general fund)
by protecting the general fund. If Oakland's officials spent less
from the general fund, they would not have to raise property
taxes. Thus, in the 1960s, the city manager began to protect the
general fund (1) by diverting flexible funds to other departments,
(2) by allocating gas tax funds to cover Street and Engineering
operating expenses, and (3) by exerting some influence over the
amounts expended on individual street projects.

Diversion of funds means giving less to the street department.
Reflect on the fate of the traffic safety fund. Established by state
law for collected motor vehicle fines and forfeitures, the fund was
traditionally regarded as the almost exclusive property of the
Street and Engineering Department until the mid-1960s and was
used for street construction and maintenance. In the 1961/62
budget all but $23,443 (about 2 percent of the traffic safety fund)
was expended for street department activities. In looking for
ways to get more money into the general fund, the city manager
soon discovered that traffic safety fund money could be spent for

many purposes other than street construction.[4] Faced with a choice between raising the tax rate and decreasing the money available for street projects, officials decided to divert traffic safety funds to the support of general fund activities.

The first transfer of traffic safety funds appeared in the 1962/63 budget when $228,047 was allocated to Traffic Engineering Department support and to the Police Department for the salaries of school crossing guards. By 1966/67, the Street and Engineering Department was receiving only 57 percent of the $1,390,000 fund, the remainder was diverted to other departments to pay for items previously financed by general fund revenues. In the 1967/68 budget the numerous invasions of the traffic safety fund continued. Out of a total of $1,608,000 in traffic safety money, only $611,000 was left for street construction projects. In 1969, there was none.

Another way to protect the general fund is to shift the department's operating expenses to its gas tax funds. The traditional city budgeting policy was to allow the department to use subventions for construction and the city's general fund for maintenance. Tax-minded officials, however, switched rules and diverted gas tax revenue from construction to maintenance. Until 1964, the state earmarking requirements attached to gas tax funds (Section 2107) stipulated that 60 percent of the money received by cities had to be spent on street construction, and the remainder could go to maintain major and secondary city streets. The state law was reversed in 1964 so that 60 percent of the funds could be spent for maintenance and 40 percent for construction. Until the 1964/65 budget the money had been used entirely for construction except a $20,000 sum for "sundry services and expenses." In 1969, officials established a special Gas Tax Street Maintenance Fund which not only met legal requirements but also formalized the 60 percent rule.

The maintenance tactic was also extended to other operating expenses. The 1966/67 budget laid down a new policy by which the cost of administering the gas taxes was shifted from the gen-

4. This includes the purchase and maintenance of traffic control devices, equipment and supplies for traffic law enforcement and accident prevention, and school crossing guards, in addition to the construction and maintenance of streets. Section 770, Vehicle Code of California.

eral fund to gas tax funds. By this means about $40,000 previously included in the Street and Engineering Department appropriation was removed.

Thus far we have discussed two tactics for protecting the general fund: the transfer of monies previously used for street activities to other departments, and control over allocation of funds among budget categories. More recently, the budget and finance office has been going a step further by exerting some control over expenditures for individual street projects. The allocation of gas tax funds among particular projects has historically been left almost exclusively to the judgment of engineers. One gas tax construction project was as good as another, so budget analysts usually ignored the distribution of funds among projects. In the 1970/71 budget, procedures changed—the amount of gas tax funds requested for three select street projects was cut, for a total decrease of $429,000.

The finance office's dissatisfaction with the way in which the street department kept its ledgers was the principal reason for the change. The accounting system for street project expenditures was loose and flexible. In past practice, money allocated to particular projects was not necessarily spent the way it was budgeted. Rather, funds were juggled from one project to another when money ran short—a case of robbing Peter to pay Paul. Juggling was relatively easy, since funds were usually accumulated for large projects over a number of years; although shown in the budget, the funds would not be expended until such time as actual work was begun on a project. With their own piggy bank, engineers could complete projects without worrying about cost overruns.

Fund juggling was ended by the finance director. Money allocated to a project must now be spent on it. Costs for the different phases of each project must now be shown: initial design work cost, property acquisition costs, and construction costs. Funds still can be accumulated for projects, but not for many years in advance, as they were previously. As far as possible, the finance director would like to see all expenditures shown in the budget actually spent in that year. Therefore, in 1970/71 some of the funds for the three projects were cut. These cuts were confined to appropriations for construction phases of the projects, which were not expected to begin for two or three years. The amounts requested for the planning and design work and property acquisition phases (scheduled to commence in 1970/71) were left intact.

In summary, having somebody else's money, the state gas tax, does not give complete discretion to Oakland's street engineers. There is always someone around who wants to restrict the engineers' discretion. Spend the gas tax on county streets; spend the gas tax on the streets in my district; better yet, spend the gas tax to protect the general fund and stabilize the propery tax. Earmarking, to be sure, helps explain the engineers' influence. Yet it is only a partial explanation; for the full story we must turn to Oakland's engineers and their decision rules. We will see that earmarking for select streets is consistent with their values and standards.

DECISION RULES: CAPITAL PROJECTS

Most street capital improvements in Oakland are reconstruction projects, in which old streets are substantially improved, rather than construction projects, in which new streets are built. Street improvement planning is a highly complex, technical, and time-consuming business. Seven or eight years usually elapse between the time when it is decided a project should be undertaken and the date of completion of construction. In that time, a myriad of decisions must be made regarding such factors as cost, design, route selection, materials, financing, and scheduling.

There are basically five steps from inception to completion of a street improvement project. First, the engineers decide that a project will be undertaken. When this decision is made, only two things are definitely determined: (1) gross cost estimates have been made, and (2) the route is fairly well established. Next, the selected project is placed on a timetable for budgeting and construction. Some projects lie around for years before a construction date is set and the department gets around to finding the money. Others may be decided upon suddenly and budgeted without delay. The process of budgeting and scheduling is important here because it involves setting priorities among projects.

The final three steps necessary to complete a street improvement project will not be relevant to our discussion of project se-

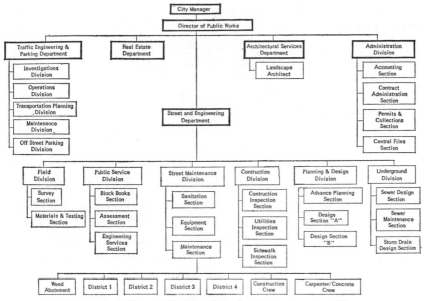

Figure 4. Office of Public Works Organization Chart

lection. These are (1) acquisition of right-of-way, (2) detailed planning and designing of a project, and (3) actual construction. Decisions made for these steps are mostly technical in nature—what type of pavement material should be used, what the landscaping scheme should be like, what contractor should receive the bid, and what price would be fair to pay for the property acquired. In other circumstances or other cities, these decisions might be the major issues.

Unforeseeable conditions such as storms and floods can damage streets, raise the level of complaints, and shift engineering priorities. Other agencies also can bother the engineers. In order to exert control over its environment, the department establishes close, cooperative, and informal relations with relevant outside agencies and city departments. Since unpredictability cannot be completely eliminated, the department builds into its selection of capital improvement projects an ability to adjust to new situations as they arise.

The work program generally proceeds on the basis of a "Five-Year Street Capital Improvement Plan," in which projects to be undertaken in that period are scheduled and budgeted. Deviations from the plan are common. If it is necessary or advanta-geous to undertake new projects or revise priorities, the depart-ment will do so. Longer range, comprehensive street plans have been formulated on occasion (twice in the past twenty-three years). Decisions to undertake projects are usually direct re-sponses to problems as they arise. The project selection process is incremental, informal, and confined for the most part to a closed fraternity within the top echelons of the department.

Four actors in the street department make decisions as to what projects will be undertaken; they establish the department's pri-orities. The city engineer and director of public works, and the assistant city engineer (also head of the street department) are by far the most influential (see organization chart, figure 4).[5] The character of the street construction program reflects their deci-sions and their influence, which is exercised at all stages of street planning. They approve proposals for projects, often initiate proj-ect selections, and are consulted whenever any important prob-lem in the administration or operations of the program arises.

The city engineer's most significant role is as a linking pin be-tween the top city policy-makers, other city departments, and the street department.[6] All political interventions in street planning are directed toward him, and he defends the street department when disputes arise. Most of his relations are not based on dis-agreement; he coordinates, or cooperates, rather than defends. He is well liked and highly respected in Oakland's city government, and his opinions carry heavy weight.

His assistant is more closely in touch with day-to-day street planning problems than the city engineer and spends consider-able time in the field to oversee personally what is happening.

5. Street and Engineering used to be a separate department. In 1968 it and the Traffic Engineering Department were consolidated under a newly created Office of Public Works. The consolidation and reorganization move brought few changes in practices, because the key decision-makers remained the same. The city engineer, who previously headed the street department, became director of the Office of Public Works. The assistant city engineer moved up to head the street department.

6. See Rensis Likert, *The Human Organization: Its Management and Value* (New York: McGraw-Hill, 1967), pp. 50, 164–165, 179–180; and *New Patterns of Management* (New York: McGraw-Hill, 1961), pp. 113–115.

Little occurs in the department without the assistant city engineer's being informed. Both of them have extensive contacts with their professional counterparts in such agencies as the State Division of Highways, the Bay Area Rapid Transit District (BARTD), and the county street department. Most negotiations between the department and private establishments interested in the street business (such as real estate developers) are handled by the assistant engineer.

The other two members of the decision-making team are the head of the planning and design division of the Street and Engineering Department, and his second-in-command, head of the advance planning section. They do not make final major decisions but rather participate as providers of information. The main task of the head of the advance planning section is to design the five-year program, matching projects with yearly revenues. The head of the design division is responsible for scheduling projects and design work. The two are consulted almost invariably before any major decisions on new projects or revised priorities.

The four men cooperate closely, communicate frequently, and make decisions informally as problems arise. There is little need to establish formal channels of communication or invoke strict hierarchical controls, since the actors are bound by a highly shared identification with their profession and with the goals of the department. Cooperation is further enhanced because they have worked together in the department for years.

Having briefly discussed the department's decision-makers, we can now focus upon their decision rules which govern the allocation of resources. Since decision-making is left primarily to engineers, the rules which they apply in project selection have the largest effect on total allocation outcomes. For the most part, engineers base their decisions upon professional and technical criteria of relative need. When the department must respond to the actions of outside agencies or the city council, however, professional criteria do not serve as the exclusive bases of decision-making; rather, projects occasionally will be undertaken because it is expedient to do so. Engineering values are never completely abandoned, but projects will be selected to which the department might not normally have assigned high priority on technical grounds.

PROFESSIONAL CRITERIA: FAST, SAFE, AND EFFICIENT

The principal objective of the Oakland street engineers is one common to their profession: to provide for a fast, safe, and efficient traffic circulation system. The best means to realize this objective (according to the profession) is to concentrate on improving streets that have the most traffic and to construct ones capable of carrying motorists long distances relatively quickly. High traffic volume is important in judging a street eligible for improvement. What Oakland needs is a fast, safe, and efficient street system.

In concrete terms, however, "fast, safe, and efficient" means to improve and construct only select streets. The select system is composed of arterials, or major thoroughfares, and selected collector streets whose function is to channel local traffic onto arterials.[7] One would expect that resources would be concentrated on select streets because of the restriction on the use of gas tax revenues. But two principal decision-makers both stated that, because they carry the most traffic, select streets would be chosen for improvement almost exclusively even if the state requirement did not exist.

The engineers have no argument with the earmarking requirements, and in fact view them as a form of protection for their professional goals. The assistant city engineer expressed fear that

7. According to the dictates of traffic engineering, a traffic circulation system should consist of a hierarchy of several different types of streets, each type designed to perform a certain function. *Freeways* and *expressways* are designed to handle extremely large volumes of through traffic for long distances. Expressways are built on a slightly smaller scale than freeways, and have some limited cross traffic while freeways allow no cross traffic at all. Coordinated with freeways and expressways are the *arterial streets*, which carry relatively large volumes of traffic through a city. Arterials thus serve as the principal network for through traffic flow within a city and connect areas of major traffic generation. They also provide for the distribution and collection of through traffic to and from collector and local streets. *Collector streets* serve to link residential neighborhoods and other areas of homogeneous land use with arterial streets. They also serve through traffic within a local area, although they are designed so as not to attract such volumes of traffic as to disrupt the area. Only the most important collector streets are assigned to the select system. At the bottom of the hierarchy are local streets, which provide access to abutting property and should not carry any through traffic.

if the gas tax requirement were lifted, intracity squabbling could develop over the location of street improvements; thus project selections might be made on the basis of politics and public opinion rather than according to engineering principles. Department administrators are convinced that they are the best judges of what is good for the public at large. They argue that politicians and pressure groups should not be allowed to influence street allocations, since the results might be detrimental for the larger community.

A corollary of engineering ideology says: Do not waste time, effort, or money improving local streets. There are 760 miles of streets in Oakland: 167 miles of arterials, 93 miles of collectors, and 500 miles—the vast preponderance—of local streets.[8] Yet resources available for street improvements are not concentrated on those local streets. There are obvious financial and legal imperatives for neglecting local streets. State and city policy makes local property owners pay for local street improvements, either by means of a special assessment or through hiring their own contractors. Nevertheless, certain local street improvements have been financed by the city. On the few occasions when the manager or council made such allocations, it was over the objections of the Street and Engineering Department.

The engineering rationale for not improving local streets is that "by the very nature of the function they perform, most local streets are not likely to be plagued by the problems of excess traffic volume, high accident rate and the like."[9] The force of this rationale is shown in table 2-2. Of street capital improvement projects budgeted between 1960 and 1971, 94 percent of the dollars spent went to select street improvements and only 6 percent to nonselect improvements.

In addition to the primary decision of constructing select streets, other engineering criteria influence resource allocation. Oakland's engineers reflect the transportation emphasis of our age. They will usually choose for construction streets that will provide access to freeways or will serve as crosstown arterials. They want to complete important linkages in the total traffic circulation system, so

8. *Oakland Preliminary Circulation Plan, 1966–1985*, City of Oakland, 701 Program, Advance Transportation Planning Team, 1966, p. 11.
9. Ibid.

TABLE 2-2: Resources Are Concentrated upon the Select Street System
1960–1971

	Number of Projects	Percent of Projects	Approximate Cost of Projects (millions of dollars)	Percent of Total Cost
Select streets	73	87	51.8	94
Local and minor collector streets (nonselect)	11	13	3.5	6
Total	84	100	55.3	100

SOURCE: Oakland, *Budgets, 1960/61–1970/71*. Oakland, *Capital Improvement Program, 1961/66* and *1965/70*. Oakland, *Oakland Preliminary Circulation Plan, 1966–1985*, 701 Program, Advance Transportation Study Team, p. 66, table 10.

that the majority of motorists can travel quickly and efficiently in and out of Oakland. As the city engineer put it: "Oakland's basic street system was structured in the early 1900's by the street rail-road system which essentially radiated from the central core. Many of the improvements that have been made are the cross-town connections that are necessary to join these 'spokes' based on this old radial system and, in effect, are additions to the system to provide circulation based on newer transportation concepts." [10]

The department aspires to an ideal street system mapped out in a document known as the "Bartholomew Report," regarded as the "bible" of street improvement planning by the Oakland engineers. It was drawn up in 1947 by the consultant firm Harland Bartholomew and Associates of St. Louis, who were commissioned by the city to devise a comprehensive plan for Oakland's streets. The plan *in toto,* adopted officially as the circulation element of Oakland's master plan in 1949, governs current planning and resource allocation. Much of it is yet to be completed.

Building major crosstown arterials and providing access to freeways is the department's number one priority. It was set in the Bartholomew Report, which provides access across town from north to south and east to west and ties the city street system into the freeway network. Of the projects we studied, 21 percent were undertaken to provide access to freeways, and 17 percent could

10. Letter to the authors from the city engineer, November 12, 1971.

be classified as crosstown arterials.[11] North-south arterials are constructed to connect the two important east-west freeways, (the MacArthur and the Nimitz which, incidentally, were planned by the Bartholomew firm). Oakland lacks sufficient north-south arterials, according to traffic engineering standards which prescribe that there be an arterial at every two-mile interval in both directions in a city. Furthermore, the areas north and south of Oakland are the largest generators of travel to and from Oakland.

Thirty-fifth Avenue and Redwood Road is an example of a north-south crosstown arterial project that has been assigned a top priority by the Oakland engineers. The two connecting streets will be widened to handle a higher volume of traffic from the Nimitz Freeway in the south of Oakland to the Warren Freeway in the northern Oakland hills. The project was first sketchily planned in the Bartholomew Report, and became seriously considered as an important project in the mid-1960s, when traffic volume increased on these roadways. The need for the project grew in importance when plans to build a new junior college at the top of Redwood Road were disclosed.

In addition to worrying about arterials, the engineers want to improve select streets which are no longer performing their assigned roles in the system. A street is deficient if it is congested or structurally unsound for carrying loads to which it is subject. Congestion is the more important of the two criteria.

If the engineers must choose between correcting deficiencies in a congested street and constructing either a freeway access or crosstown arterial, they will invariably select the latter. Crosstown arterials and freeway connections inevitably generate more traffic than the congested street; thus their construction is supposedly more beneficial to the community at large. Such is the rationale of the Oakland engineers.

A deficient street, in any case, turns out to be a state of mind. Officials do collect ample statistical information from which to determine where deficiencies in the system are located. A thor-

11. One of the ways used to determine what rules govern decision-making was to study the history behind a variety of street projects. All projects included in the Five-Year Street Improvement Program for 1970–1975 were studied, and others were selected at random as discussion of them arose in interviews with key decision-makers. Twenty-nine project histories were studied in all, covering the period from 1961–1975.

ough survey of the condition of Oakland's streets is conducted every four years, when a "Street Deficiency Report" is compiled in compliance with state requirements. Virtually every street in the Oakland system is examined, and statistics indicating their performance are compiled. But such statistics are often ignored because engineers, like many of us, tend to respond to problems as they arise. It is possible to isolate a few projects that were undertaken in the past ten years principally to correct inadequacies brought about by the normal increasing traffic exerted on streets. The reason these particular streets came to be improved, however, was not because engineers consulted their statistics in the Street Deficiency Report and selected for reconstruction roads with low service ratings. Rather, the need for these street improvements was made visible to the street department through other means.

An example is the reconstruction of Adeline Street overpass. This terribly dilapidated structure, which serves as an access to the West Oakland defense area, was built by the U.S. Navy and was supposed to be maintained by the navy under an agreement with the city. The navy recently passed title to the overpass to the General Services Administration, which in its turn unloaded it on the city. The navy had failed to live up to its maintenance responsibilities, and the overpass was transferred to the city in such an unsafe condition that the load limit for trucks had to be lowered immediately. The city had anticipated this move and engineers had worked on plans in advance to reconstruct the grade separation on Adeline. The overpass is particularly important because it carries a heavy volume of rush hour traffic. Because of monumental traffic problems here the need to improve the streets was quite visible to the department even without deficiency reports.

When land use or traffic patterns are expected to change, another professional justification for improving a street arises. Projects of this kind are *occasionally* undertaken in anticipation of future traffic volume or structural problems. One way in which the street department responds to anticipated future needs is to make special studies of an area at which an important facility will be built. A study was made of the streets surrounding the proposed site of a new junior college near Skyline Boulevard and

Redwood Road. Another example is the planned construction of a large postal receiving center in downtown Oakland which prompted engineers to study likely effects on the neighboring streets.

The largest study of future traffic needs was made in conjunction with the 701 Plan for 1985.[12] About sixty select streets were measured as to present and future (1985) traffic volumes. Future volumes were predicted on the basis of studies concerning future distribution of population, housing, businesses, and jobs. This study of long-range needs is an exception to the department's usual informal routine.

Even in the 701 effort the influence of future traffic needs, as compared with other criteria, was discounted. Future traffic appears not to have been an important consideration mainly because most projects included had been planned years before. Moreover, engineers tend to delay improving streets that are not deficient at present, unless the street is to be a crosstown arterial which will draw traffic to itself, or deficiencies are expected to develop in a few years with the advent of a new facility.

One might expect future land use to be an important engineering criterion for undertaking projects, but the usual approach of the engineers is not to anticipate change but rather to adjust to it as circumstances arise. The main exceptions to this rule are if an opportunity exists to share costs with the builder of a proposed land use development, or if political actors direct the department to undertake an improvement.

We can now summarize the engineers' notions of need in the form of decision rules for project selection. (1) Improve or construct select streets only; (2) of these, improve and construct first those which provide access to freeways or will serve as crosstown arterials; (3) next, improve select streets that have heavy traffic, choosing (a) those which are congested and (b) those which are structurally unsound; (4) improve other select streets that are deficient in traffic-carrying capacity; (5) deal with emer-

12. Funded by the federal government, the 701 activity was a city-wide planning effort involving surveys, economic analyses, and the production of a Comprehensive Development Plan for Oakland. The city became eligible for the 701 grant when it was designated a depressed area by the Area Redevelopment Administration of the U.S. Department of Commerce in 1964.

gency situations as they arise; (6) improve select streets in anticipation of future deficiencies (rarely used).

PROFESSIONAL CRITERIA: COST-SHARING

Oakland's engineers have one decision rule for project selection which has little to do with need: undertake capital improvements when costs can be shared with other agencies. Projects selected under this rule may receive priority over others which normally would be considered more important. Because the department cannot expect much from the general fund, cost-sharing is its only readily available means to expand upon the base of gas tax revenues. Between 1970 and 1975, the department expects to be reimbursed by outside agencies in at least the amount of $934,417.[13]

The biggest opportunity for cost-sharing in the last ten years has been the Bay Area Rapid Transit District's (BARTD) construction. BARTD was required by law to return to their original condition all streets torn up in subway construction. The department took this opportunity to widen several streets. BARTD paid for restoration to original condition while the city paid only for the extra lanes and got widened streets for about one-third the original cost. Some streets, such as Grove Street and East Eighth Street, would probably not have been so extensively widened if engineers had followed the usual criteria of congestion. However, by taking advantage of these cost-sharing opportunities as they arose engineers had avoided the possibility of having to widen streets in the future at their own expense.

The street department often shares costs with the railroad also, particularly in connection with grade separation projects and signal devices. Opportunities for sharing costs are also available in cooperation with private development. Private developers are supposed to be financially responsible for any street improvements which become necessary as a result of their development. When new subdivisions are built in the hills, for example, developers must pay for the widening of city streets that is necessary to handle the amount of new traffic they will generate. This policy is enforced by the Planning Commission, which will prevent construction if developers refuse to cooperate.

The widening of Keller Avenue and Fontaine Avenue to four-

13. Oakland, *Tentative Street Capital Improvement Program, 1970–75.*

lane roads are two projects which can be attributed primarily to cost-sharing with developers. Neither street carried much traffic, being in one of the least developed hill areas in Oakland. Two or three subdivisions were built in the area between Skyline Boulevard and the MacArthur Freeway; developers wanted these streets widened to provide good access from the freeway, since this was a selling point for their subdivisions. The projects were justified as "crosstown arterials." Developers agreed to contribute their share—the two extra lanes beyond the normal width of streets in undeveloped areas—either in the form of contributing right-of-way, grading a portion of the street, or as actual construction. The city took responsibility for further widening of the street beyond that needed for development. As with projects shared with BARTD, the city got arterial-width streets at a low cost.

Occasionally the department simply is given no choice by an outside agency; it must cooperate. Here the factor of *timing*, not just costs, is dominant. Consider the planned reconstruction of Fruitvale Avenue on both sides of the Fruitvale Avenue bridge. The Army Corps of Engineers owns the bridge and plans to reconstruct it completely at a cost of about $5 million. The city will have to put up $70,000 to $100,000 to reconstruct the city street access. Only recently informed by the army of its plans, the department must scurry around to find the money and must put off other street improvements to create the planning and designing man-hours necessary for this project. Parenthetically, engineers are not too unhappy about this, since a $5 million improvement is always welcomed.

POLITICAL CRITERIA: STREETS AS ECONOMIC DEVELOPMENT

Some observers outside the department believe that most street projects are undertaken for political reasons. In the broad sense of "political" they are right, because all allocation decisions are political. But in the narrow sense of the word, in which some kind of outside intrusion interferes with engineering criteria, they are wrong. Most street projects are not the pets of the manager, mayor, or city councilmen. Indeed, it was found that, of the twenty-nine projects whose histories we studied, only seven were undertaken principally because of nonengineering, political support. There are other projects in which politicians displayed an interest and perhaps influenced outcomes. But for our immediate purposes, we define a political project as one for which the city council makes the decision to undertake or to schedule. Sometimes the city manager influences such decisions; engineers, however, do not. They might favor the project, but they would not have undertaken it themselves at the time chosen.

There are two kinds of intrusions by top city policy-makers into project decision-making. The first is for a project which the manager and council believe necessary to fulfill their own city policies. The second is seen when the council acts as a sounding board for public opinion, bringing the influence of citizen groups into street planning. Here the council may either initiate or scrap projects. Of course, the council has the last word, and unless engineers can convince the councilmen to change their minds, political projects usually get top priority.

Our first concern will be with projects initiated by the city council as Oakland policy makers. One goal of the council, in addition to saving money, is to bring economic development to the city; therefore, the council usually supports street projects that are tied to such growth.

Building the Oakland Coliseum complex is a good example. It had a tremendous effect on street planning in the Street and Engineering Department. The coliseum was a highly political undertaking, backed by Oakland's public officials and business community as a means to focus the national spotlight on Oakland and bring quite a bit of money into the city. It would also add a large volume of cars and traffic; the Street and Engineering Department had to drop almost everything else and turn to this problem.

One project affected by the coliseum was the Hegenberger Expressway, or the East Oakland Crosstown Arterial. Plans to turn this two-lane road into a major six-lane crosstown expressway had been made years before, and construction had begun before the coliseum was under way. In the late 1940s a state freeway was planned to follow about the same route Hegenberger now follows. Nevertheless, the city decided to build an expressway with its own gas tax funds instead, for two reasons. First, a major arterial was needed in that section of town very quickly, because Hegenberger was the only road leading to the rapidly expanding

Oakland Airport. The state was not expected to build the freeway for several years, but the improvement was needed immediately. Second, the mayor at that time decided the city had about enough freeways. The three freeways constructed since 1950 had taken enough land off the Oakland tax rolls. The crosstown expressway, therefore, would wipe out any need for the state to build the freeway planned for East Oakland. In 1959, Hegenberger was included in the Oakland General Plan; in 1962, revised plans for the project were approved by the council. In the early 1960s the section of Hegenberger between the airport and the Nimitz Freeway was constructed. As time went on, it was decided that Hegenberger should logically extend all the way to the newly planned Warren Freeway in the Oakland hills.

Because of the coliseum, however, Hegenberger received higher priority than it had been assigned before, and the project became substantially more expensive. Hegenberger would serve as the major route to bring traffic from the other side of Oakland to the coliseum. It was decided to widen the section near the coliseum (between East fourteenth Street and San Leandro Avenue) to eight lanes instead of six. Total cost of the project rose to $9–10 million, the largest street project ever undertaken by the city, and all of this was accumulated and planned to be spent between 1962 and 1972, only ten years. Very rarely is this much money accumulated so quickly for a project. The Street and Engineering Department had to transfer funds from several other committed projects to pay for Hegenberger. Approval was given by Alameda County to transfer Alameda County Street Aid funds from their projects to Hegenberger; in fact, almost all the Alameda County money Oakland received for a few years went to this project.

Hegenberger is thus an example of a project already initiated by the department, with some political elements involved, which by legislative and administrative fiat suddenly becomes top priority. The street department's work program had to be entirely rescheduled to accommodate the project, and many other projects were driven out of the money for several years.

A favorite project of the mayor was the coliseum access road. Originally only one access road was planned for the coliseum, which was constructed by the Coliseum Corporation. Later on, however, it was decided that a second south access road was nec-

essary. The Coliseum Corporation contributed $200,000 toward
the $690,000 price tag, but the city had to provide the rest, and
quickly. Money again was transferred from fund to fund, the
urgency being necessary because $285,000 was needed to acquire
right-of-way. Being short of enough city money, Oakland's officials applied for and received a federal grant from the Economic
Development Administration to cover the city's share of this road.
The grant was justified by the EDA and the mayor on grounds
that the coliseum would provide employment for minority groups,
since the road would directly serve and connect East Oakland
poverty areas with the job-producing complex. Most observers
feel that this was just a convenient rationale. Rather, the road
gave the city something for helping EDA in other areas and
served to bring outsiders more quickly through a poverty area.

Here is another example of a political project motivated by
economic development. In 1969, the chief engineer, after discussions with the city manager, asked his assistant to find money to
acquire right-of-way for the airport access road, a project never
included on the five-year program. The road will be a one-way
street connecting two streets which join at a very bad intersection
on the approach to the airport. At a cost to the city of $804,000,
the new road is supposed to relieve considerable traffic congestion
at the intersection of Hegenberger Road and Doolittle Drive, increase the traffic-carrying capacity of airport roads, and improve
access to some of the hotels, restaurants, and other businesses in
the area.

The engineers had been disturbed about congestion at the intersection before, but had not contemplated doing anything for
quite a while. Action came at last when the Federal Aviation
Agency recently took a look at Oakland's airport and informed
the city that if air traffic and ground traffic capacity at the airport
did not increase substantially, it would lose out to San Jose Airport. Naturally, airport expansion is a top concern of Oakland's
officials, for airports generate economic development. The city
engineer therefore received the order to acquire land for the new
road as quickly as possible. A federal grant, designed to assist
cities in making streets safer, was awarded to Oakland for the
project.

Redevelopment is another area in which politics sets the engineer's priorities. The politics of streets in redevelopment areas is particularly interesting because it involves the city manager, the council, local citizens, and the independent Redevelopment Agency. Engineers have not been too happy with the situation. Three large redevelopment projects are in the process of being planned or constructed. Two—the Acorn and Oak Center projects —are housing projects in the West Oakland target area. The other is a large, city-center, hotel-convention-office complex. By decision of the city manager, mayor, and council, the city has committed itself to reconstructing, improving, or resurfacing almost every street in the Acorn and the Oak Center projects. Some of the work is being paid for by federal redevelopment funds. But the majority of the work, much of it on local street improvements, is being paid for by the city out of gas tax and general funds, to the extent of almost $2 million.

The city manager and council were willing to do this for two reasons, the more important being the incentive of federal dollars. Street improvements serve as a noncash contribution to the city's one-third share of redevelopment costs. For every one dollar of funds it spends (either gas tax or general fund), it receives three dollars from the federal government. What better place to spend two million dollars of gas tax funds?

The growing awareness of the community is the other reason why the city was willing to spend two million dollars for local street improvements. West Oakland residents, through their citizens planning council, wanted street improvements as a major priority for redevelopment. These residents had lived for years with bad streets, whose condition contributed greatly to general deterioration in the area.[14] The first problem was that many of the streets had no curbs. Temporary redwood curbs had originally been constructed by the area's private developers, but these had deteriorated because the city will maintain only concrete curbs. Without curbs, storm waters cause street problems, the city's street-cleaning equipment will not work, and trees cannot be planted. Local property owners could not afford to improve the

14. "How to Make a Slum," *Montclarion*, February 12, 1969, reprinted from the *Wall Street Journal*, January 30, 1969.

streets and, worse, could not obtain loans from the bank for this purpose—a vicious circle contributing to the gradual deterioration of the area.

The subject of redevelopment allows us to examine another aspect of the politics of streets—namely, bureaucratic infighting. The Redevelopment Agency and the Street and Engineering Department have had several bitter disagreements regarding street planning, in which each has played for the support of the manager and the council.

Planners and engineers do not appreciate one another. Planners regard engineers as overtechnical, unaware of larger value considerations, and highly unimaginative. Engineers believe that planners are dreamers, unrealistic and dreadfully impractical. Although planners and engineers get along fairly well in Oakland, there are occasional problems. As one engineer remarked, the agency planners tend to "plan and plan and plan!" More than once, a street redevelopment project has been completely designed and ready to be put out to bid when the planners have come up with a new concept for design.

Conflict over goals is often the source of bureaucratic disagreements. The Street and Engineering Department is interested most in traffic circulation, while the Redevelopment Agency sees the accumulation of land for profitable development as all-important. One example of this obvious difference in land usage policy involved a project proposed by the Redevelopment Agency for Seventh and Eighth streets in Oak Center. Each is a four-lane, one way street, quite sufficient in traffic-carrying capacity. The Redevelopment Agency wanted to widen Seventh Street, making it two-directional and divided, and to reclassify Eighth Street as a local street. As Redevelopment saw it, the area was slated for residential housing (in contrast to originally planned industrial use), and busy streets on each side of the houses were considered undesirable. More important, the reclassification of Eighth Street created the opportunity for additional land to become available in the future, at almost no cost, for more housing and development.

The engineers were quite upset with this plan. For one thing, there was absolutely nothing wrong with either street, and so gas tax funds could not justifiably be used. Secondly, the scheme was detrimental to traffic circulation in the area—not to a dangerous point, but enough to be bothersome. The city engineer commented that if traffic disruption had threatened to be worse he would have done everything in his power to stop the project. As it happened, the Redevelopment Agency managed to find not only federal money for the project, but also the support of the city manager.

The two agencies have also been fighting over a recently planned multimillion-dollar city-center redevelopment project. Politically, city center is a desirable project because the city council hopes it will bring business to Oakland and revitalize the town core. The project was planned by the original (but no longer present) developer, Dillingham Corporation, to include a huge 5,000-car underground parking garage. A traffic consultant firm, Gruen and Associates, made the studies for Dillingham and estimated that such a garage was necessary. Dillingham made its commitment to develop the area contingent upon the city's willingness to build the garage according to the consultant's specification. The council agreed—without commissioning any other studies regarding the desirability or profitability of the $20 million garage and without much public discussion. (All money spent on the garage is counted as a noncash contribution for future federal dollars, and this fact probably encouraged the council to make a quick decision.)

Once the Redevelopment Agency got its garage plan (which it pushed hard), it began fiddling with the engineers' state-approved plans for access roads from the planned Grove-Shafter Freeway to downtown Oakland. The section of the freeway in question, part of which has already been built, cuts between downtown Oakland and the West Oakland redevelopment areas. The Street and Engineering Department had planned to improve four streets to form two one-way couples over the depressed freeway—Seventeenth and Eighteenth streets, and Eleventh and Twelfth streets.[15] Gruen and Associates and the Redevelopment Agency did not think either would provide sufficient access to the city center project. So the Redevelopment Agency came up with a plan to build

15. A one-way couple consists of two parallel streets, usually separated by only one block, each of which carries traffic in the opposite direction from the other.

elaborate flying ramps, running from the freeway directly into the garage. The justification was that only such an arrangement would bring enough cars and people to the city center to generate profits (and therefore city revenues). When the planners met angry resistance from the engineers, they modified their scheme to include only one ramp, on Eleventh Street. Fourteenth Street would be made one-way and Twelfth Street would be completely closed off; the land thus made available could be used for future development.

The street department objected to this plan on several counts. First, in keeping with their cost-sharing notions they wanted to keep the original plan because it was possible that the state could build this portion of the freeway in the very near future. Second, they were angry because the plans for freeway connections had already been changed several times, more than once at the insistence of the redevelopment planners. The State Division of Highways was unhappy as well—they wanted no more changes made on the access plan. Third, and most salient, the ramp idea was quite undesirable from an engineering point of view. Downtown street circulation would be significantly affected. It would be difficult to make Fourteenth Street one-directional; there would be the problem of getting traffic from a high-speed freeway into a crowded garage within a few short blocks; the Police and Fire departments were worried that with Twelfth Street closed off their response time in emergencies would be lengthened dangerously. The Redevelopment Agency did, in the end, compromise with the engineers on a more suitable plan.

POLITICAL CRITERIA: CITIZEN DEMANDS

Citizen demands influence street project decision-making through the city council. Citizen groups generally find the Street and Engineering Department rather insensitive to their opinions, and so take their grievances to the council, which, for its part, tries to avoid conflict with Oakland's officials and citizens but nevertheless does become a somewhat reluctant mediator.

The council will hold hearings on projects planned by the street department when citizens, on occasion, demand it, and will stop a project when considerable public opposition exists. Usually the council is not required to hold special public hearings on street capital improvement projects. It gives these projects only a cursory review when they are presented in the department's budget requests; annual budget hearings are considered sufficient for presentation of opinions about projects.

Before describing individual cases of council mediation on behalf of citizen groups, let us briefly examine the attitude of the street department toward public demands. The engineers are rather paternalistic. They believe they have the best overall view of how properly to distribute benefits, because they are aware of the total effect of projects on the city. Although the widening of a street may be detrimental to the immediate residents, it might benefit many other people by reducing traffic on surrounding streets. From his experience, the city engineer believes that once engineering reasons for undertaking or not undertaking a project are explained to inquiring citizens, they usually will accept the explanation and cease complaining.

Opposition to a project generally appears after the project has been budgeted, but before design or construction is begun. Usually residents of an area first discover that their street is being widened or reconstructed when the city begins to survey the land and acquire property. Residents of a street on which improvements are planned are not interviewed, consulted, or otherwise notified in advance of a project. If opposition arises, the complaints are handled directly by the city engineer and his assistant. The city engineer usually meets personally with groups of complaining residents (often homeowners' associations and the like) and gives the department's reasons for undertaking a project. His approach seems to be that of explaining his point of view rather than listening to grievances.

If opposition is intense, engineers may go so far as to study alternative routes or designs. Consider the property owner who did not want his house torn down to make way for the planned widening of Thirty-fifth Avenue. He collected the signatures of 150 neighbors on a petition to the city and received publicity of his plight in a local newspaper. So the department took the petition seriously enough to study alternative alignment proposals for the street, and has postponed construction.

On the other hand, if the city engineer feels that complying with citizen demands would be detrimental for traffic or impossible according to engineering considerations, he will not comply with public opinion. Noncompliance is the typical situation. The residents of Fourteenth Street in the redevelopment area of West Oakland, for example, oppose the department's plans to widen the street considerably. They do not want a street with heavy traffic, nor such a large slice of their land covered by concrete. The engineers (and also the Redevelopment Agency, incidentally) have not allowed themselves to be swayed, contending that traffic projections indicate that the wider street will be essential.

Although most citizen groups do not find the department especially responsive to their complaints, there is one sector of the public to which the engineers are quite sensitive—namely, churches, schools, and hospitals. In order to avoid unfavorable publicity, the department is careful to avoid confrontation with these groups. Street alignments and routes are carefully planned to circumvent them. Tearing down a school to put in a street is a sure way to waste tax dollars and gain enemies.

The widening of Harrison Street—a project planned for years to relieve a bad traffic bottleneck at an intersection—is an example of the department's sensitivity. Unfortunately, the only side of the street topographically appropriate for widening happens to have a church located on it, part of whose land and trees would have to be sacrificed. The chairman of the church board was an avid environmentalist, who determined to fight the engineers in order to preserve his trees. He had the support of a quite influential congregation, including some Piedmont residents and Kaiser Corporation executives. Here, the street department, rather than fight the congregation and let the case be brought before the council, decided to wait out the storm and put off the project indefinitely. Eventually, the engineers got their way. The church became short of money and sold the controversial right-of-way.

In other instances the fight has gone to the council, where projects have been stopped because of public opposition. A project to widen Moraga Avenue, in the hills near Piedmont, was scrapped after a group of resident environmentalists campaigned to protect the trees. Once the council stopped a minor $39,300 pavement, curb, gutter, and sidewalk job in East Oakland because private property owners fronting the street did not want the improvements.[16] The street was fronted by large industrial acreage—big property owners. The city would have paid for all but $8,550 of the job, since it owned most of the property. The feeling of the council was Why do something only the city wants? The chief engineer could not persuade them that the improvements were necessary.

In one interesting case, known as the "high-crown streets" project, citizens managed to get the council to allocate $750,000 of general fund monies for local street reconstruction. In an old residential-industrial, mixed area of East Oakland, some of the streets had been built (at far below city standards) before 1920, when the area was under county jurisdiction. The drainage system was quite bad, so the streets were built with high crowns down the center. Now the streets are in terribly bad structural condition, very inconvenient for residents of the abutting property.

When a federally funded poverty agency located there, residents of the area formed an organized group, and demanded from the department that these streets be reconstructed with city money. They felt it was a city responsibility, since the streets never had been built to city standards. Residents themselves could not afford street improvements. The city engineer told them that his department did not have the money to improve the streets, since they could not be financed with gas tax funds. No doubt the department could have managed it somehow, but did not feel the project was as important as others needing money.

The residents then went to the council, which approved the $750,000 necessary for complete reconstruction of the streets. The engineers admit the streets are perhaps the worst in Oakland and should be repaired. They just would not have made the decision themselves, as they will not consider allocating resources to anything but major streets. Between $75,000 to $100,000 is being spent on the high-crown streets each year, to stretch over a ten-year period.

The only other situations in which the city has agreed to reconstruct or improve local streets have been in the redevelopment areas discussed above, and occasionally in small areas in the Oakland hills. Hill residents have received help only in emergency

16. "Street Job Vetoed by Council," *Oakland Tribune,* July 9, 1969.

situations, after storms and slides destroyed streets, and only after screaming long and loudly to the council for help.

The Uptown Merchants Association and the Central Business Association, among other business groups having suffered from BARTD construction in downtown Oakland, decided it would be some compensation if Broadway (the main downtown street) were glamorized after the BARTD system was completed. They felt that such additions as attractive street lighting, street benches, trees, fancy sidewalks, and poured-concrete striped crosswalks might bring more shoppers back to the center. The merchants hired an architect, who drew up plans which were presented to the city manager and council. The merchants agreed to assess themselves for the improvement at a very high rate.

Unfortunately, the lowest bid for the project was $1,451,000—almost 28 percent higher than original estimates. The city manager and the city council allowed themselves to be convinced by the merchants that the city should chip in $1 million (of gas tax funds), or two-thirds of the necessary amount. After all, as the manager said, "[Broadway is] our core and provides a great deal of the taxes necessary to run this city." [17]

The Street and Engineering Department was not particularly pleased with this decision. It was forced to reschedule projects, to shift funds from more important projects, and to devote four months of design man-hour time to the Broadway beautification project. Engineers believed the project was not entirely necessary, being mostly frills and trim, and would have been willing to deny the merchants assistance. But the council thought otherwise: what is good for business must be good for Oakland.

One learns this old lesson from the examples above: Do not waste time on the engineers; they will not help much. Citizens who want to improve streets or stop engineering improvements have to bring a well-supported and organized case to the city council. The council is visible, wants to be liked, and can be persuaded by economic arguments. A project can be stopped because it will save the city money, and a project can be started because it will bring the city money.

Thus far we have examined three sets of criteria for understanding the selection of street capital improvement projects, which we will summarize briefly.

17. "Broadway Gets Attention," *Montclarion*, March 18, 1970.

Engineering Criteria

In accord with the basic dictum of "fast, safe, and efficient," there are three purely "engineering" criteria for undertaking street projects: (1) to complete the overall circulation system, which means to construct freeway access facilities and crosstown arterials, (2) to correct deficiencies on the existing system (without changing the prevailing function of a street), and (3) to improve streets not as yet deficient in anticipation of near-future needs.

Cost-sharing and Coordination Criteria

The street department will undertake a project with another agency or private developer if costs can be shared, for the purpose of expanding its total financial resources. Engineers also will time a street improvement project to coordinate with another agency when they are given no other choice.

Political Criteria

The city council and sometimes the city manager determine that a project should be undertaken or should be scrapped. The council bases its decisions upon two objectives: (1) to promote economic development in Oakland, and (2) to avoid conflict with vocal segments of the public. Political projects are designed, then, to serve the purpose either of fulfilling the circulation element of city-wide development plans or of satisfying the demands of organized citizen claimants.

Although it may appear from our discussion that most street projects in Oakland are political projects, this is not so. Most projects are street department projects. As table 2-3 shows, engineers get their way. Of the twenty-nine projects we studied, covering a period from 1961 to 1975, 24 percent were undertaken primarily for political reasons and 17 percent in order to share costs and coordinate with another agency, while over 58 percent were undertaken for engineering purposes alone.[18]

Recall that it is usually select streets which are chosen for construction. Moreover, almost every project undertaken in Oakland

18. Alan A. Altshuler also found that highway engineers got their way. In a freeway case in Minnesota, he found the engineers' influence was due to their "clarity of standards and strength of conviction"; see his *The City Planning Process: A Political Analysis* (Ithaca: Cornell University Press, 1965), pp. 77–83.

TABLE 2-3: Engineers Get Their Way: Distribution of Projects
According to Reasons They Were Undertaken

| | Projects | |
Reasons	Number	Percent
STREET DEPARTMENT PROJECTS:		
ENGINEERS' TECHNICAL CRITERIA		
Links in Circulation System		
Freeway access	6	21
Crosstown arterials	5	17
Arterial improvements	4	14
Deficient Streets		
Congested streets	1	3
Structurally unsound streets	1	3
Subtotal	17	58
STREET DEPARTMENT PROJECTS:		
COORDINATION WITH AN OUTSIDE AGENCY		
Cost-sharing	4	14
Without Cost-sharing	1	3
Subtotal	5	17
POLITICAL PROJECTS		
City Development	5	17
Community Demands	2	7
Subtotal	7	24
Total Projects	29	99

complies with some engineering criteria which indicates a need
for improvement. The main effect of political criteria is to shift
priority schedules. When political projects arise suddenly, they
drive out all others. Cost-sharing opportunities and emergency
projects also will be seized upon, even if others must be postponed. In other words, although projects springing from political and coordinational circumstances will be given high priority
when they arise, these circumstances rarely occur in street planning. Decisions as to which projects to undertake are left for the
most part to the engineers, who base their decisions upon technical, engineering judgments.

DECISION RULES: RESURFACING

The street construction program is relatively better off than other
public works programs in Oakland, since there is every reason to

spend gas tax revenues. But programs which rely on the city's general fund, with its competition from other users, are more likely to run into trouble. Street resurfacing, administered by the street maintenance division of the department, is one such program. Although the maintenance division receives gas tax revenues, more than half of its money comes from the general fund. Resurfacing is the most important and expensive ($575,000 in 1970/71) of the division's various maintenance programs, which include street cleaning, minor street construction, and weed abatement.

BUDGETING: THE COMPROMISED "STANDARD"

Appropriations for street resurfacing have been declining steadily since the early 1960s, when Oakland's financial situation began seriously to deteriorate. The city's maintenance engineer believes the present level of financing for the program is not enough for an adequate level of service. After all, the maintenance division's minimum standard is that a street should be resurfaced every ten years. This is a shorter life expectancy than was assumed for streets in the past, but pavement deteriorates more rapidly nowadays because of heavier traffic and heavier truck loads. According to the ten-year standard, at least seventy or eighty miles should be resurfaced each year. This would require budget appropriations of approximately $1 million per year, as resurfacing one mile of a street costs about $13,500.

Once upon a time, the ten-year standard was a real decision rule.[19] In the late 1950s the division was getting up to $1 million per year and could resurface as many as a hundred miles of streets annually. The program began to be cut in the early 1960s, so that the division has been able to resurface only twenty to twenty-five miles in most years. The division's budget never meets the standard's expectations. Given more miles of streets to be resurfaced than the funds to finance them, the division's budget barely keeps up with price increases. Moreover, the program's

19. The city engineer does not believe the ten-year standard was ever a real decision rule. Yet he reflects the same ambivalence over its use as his maintenance engineers. In his comments to us, he said, "True, the assumed hoped-for 10-year cycle for resurfacing seems unreachable and is an arbitrary figure used for scheduling purposes only." Letter to the authors from the city engineer, November 12, 1971.

troubles are not over yet. The city manager has recommended that part of the decrease in gas tax revenues suffered since Oakland has lost population be dealt with by cutting gas tax allocations to the resurfacing program.

Cutting the resurfacing program and ignoring the division's standard can be attributed to a number of factors. Generally, maintenance activities have suffered because of the city manager's "hold the line" policy. The manager's instructions inevitably warn departments that maintenance must remain at its present level of service. Another contributing factor is that the city engineer does not attach much importance to resurfacing if it threatens to compete with the street construction program. (Indeed, in 1970/71 it was the manager who increased the department's maintenance request.)

Some part of the resurfacing program's difficulties are due to the attitude of the maintenance division's administrators when requesting budgetary appropriations. Compiling the maintenance division's budgetary requests is the responsibility of the assistant maintenance engineer. He is an idealist and feels strongly that he should request what is objectively needed and should justify requests in a straightforward way. For this reason, he bases his requests partly on the much abused ten-year standard, instead of adjusting his sights to revenue expectations. It is no surprise then that his requests are drastically cut. In 1967/68, for example, he asked $750,000 for the program; this was cut to $400,000 by the city engineer and further to $330,000 by the manager's budget officer. After making his requests, the assistant maintenance engineer does not try to get them approved. He does not slant his justifications for requests to agree with his supervisor's wishes. When asked what counts in getting money for a particular program, he said, "You just put it in the budget. If management thinks it is a worthwhile program, they will consider it." To him, justifications are straightforward; once objective information is given, decisions can be made. He does not see that his information is not being communicated and that no budget sells itself. And so cuts are made.

Within the framework of line-item budgeting, the assistant maintenance engineer uses simple rules-of-thumb to estimate his budget requests. He does not worry about particular street projects. Instead, for his resurfacing program he decides how many

miles of streets he would like to see resurfaced; next, using percentages based on past experience, he divides his program into
three types of resurfacing processes. For each type he then roughly
estimates the required line-item cash for materials, man-hours,
and equipment.

Although different budgeting procedures might lessen threats
to the resurfacing program, the program cannot overcome one
handicap it has in competition with others—lack of outside support. The street construction program, in comparison, has a great
deal of outside support. The resurfacing program can be compared also with the street sanitation program, for which budget
requests have met with much more success. The head of the sanitation section has a more strategic approach to budgeting—he
requests increases in incremental amounts, waits for the opportunity to increase the level of service, and slants his justifications.
However, the relative success of the sanitation program is mostly
due to support from three sources: a citizens group, the downtown
merchants, and most important, the city manager. The manager
attaches more importance to the appearance of streets than did
his predecessor, and the division was granted its request for some
new equipment and personnel, which had previously been rejected. The Downtown Retail Merchants Association has almost
a proprietary interest in clean streets in the business district and
pays a great deal of attention to the section's activities. Also, the
Oakland Pride Committee, which promotes city beautification,
has supported some of the sanitation section's requests. The resurfacing program, on the other hand, has few supporters. Citizen
interest in the program comes mostly in the form of complaints
which are received by the maintenance division. Complaints
about potholes, for example, are made by unrelated individuals
who do not come to the support of the resurfacing program when
the division requests money. Without support, what good is a
standard? Sometimes standards can influence allocations; here,
resurfacing a street every ten years is a potential decision rule
to which only a few pay attention.

WHICH STREET LOOKS THE WORST?
—ALLOCATION IN BUDGET EXECUTION

The determination of which streets should be resurfaced is separated from the budget process and is made *after* the yearly ap-

propriation is known. The maintenance engineer, his assistant, and four street maintenance district superintendents are the principal architects of the yearly resurfacing programs. Oakland is divided into four districts which serve as centers of operation for all maintenance programs. District superintendents are responsible for surveying streets in their territories and submitting to their superiors lists of those in need of improvement. Then the maintenance engineer and his assistant review the lists and determine which streets should be included in the yearly program. Both men spend a great deal of time in the field. For many years they have been "riding the streets" to evaluate surface conditions, and for many years their superiors in the street department left the allocation decisions to them.

Responsibility for surveying street surface conditions to discover which are in need of resurfacing belongs to the four district maintenance superintendents and their foremen. Streets are surveyed more or less continuously, but exactly how often, how thoroughly, and how accurately depends entirely upon the personality and standards of each superintendent. Visual examination is used to evaluate street surface conditions. Either riding in a car or walking the streets, the superintendents rely on their eyeballs and their experience to determine, subjectively, if resurfacing is needed. Conceivably, what one man labels a deficient street another might not. Little scientific testing of the street surface is undertaken until the decision is made as to what type of resurfacing is required. This takes place after the list of projects to be undertaken has been finalized.

The principal reason the division has never used a sophisticated method of testing street conditions is that until recently the only scientific techniques available were too expensive to be of practical use. In order to test precisely how well a street surface is holding up under its traffic load, the deflexion, or "give," of the pavement must be measured. The only method available to test deflexion was to measure with elaborate equipment how well a street withstood the weight of a loaded truck. This was simply too complex and time-consuming a process to use often. To determine the exact condition of the pavement and soil beneath the surface, the street had to be opened below the pavement to its base. This destructive and expensive method was feasible only when deciding what type and depth of resurfacing was required on streets already designated as needing improvement. The one sensible way of determining which streets needed resurfacing, then, was to rely on the experienced judgment of the superintendents, who knew which streets looked the worst.

Now, however, the street department is experimenting with a recently developed machine which tests both deflexion and base conditions easily and nondestructively. Known as the "road rater," the device is attached to the front of a truck and tests the deflexion of the pavement by sending vibrations into the street. The device can both measure pavement condition accurately and allow an operator to determine what kind of repaving is required, in a simple, inexpensive operation that takes only about one minute. The device suppiles accurate data with which to compare the serviceability of one street over another, although it could never completely replace professional experience. In the future, a machine will partly replace the eyeball in decision-making. Technology has come to Oakland.

HOW TO CHOOSE A DEFICIENT STREET WITHOUT A MACHINE

The superintendents submit to the assistant maintenance engineer lists of all the streets in their districts which need resurfacing. Usually they indicate which streets are most in need of repair, and give rough cost estimates based on unit costs. The maintenance engineer and his assistant, in reviewing the lists, use five criteria to determine which streets will be repaired.

The degree of deterioration of the street surface is the first criterion. Those streets in the worst condition should receive priority. To determine which these are and to compare conditions in the various districts, the maintenance engineer and his assistant go out to see for themselves.

The second criterion is how heavily the street is used. Streets which have a high traffic volume should receive priority over those which are little used. This conforms to a general departmental belief that you benefit the most people by providing the best service on those streets which the most motorists use.

The third criterion is citizen complaints. Streets about which complaints have been made and which are found to be in need of resurfacing receive priority. The volume of complaints is not too high; three complaints a week is the average. Complaints are handed over to the district superintendents, who investigate the streets in question and report their findings and recommendations to the assistant maintenance engineer. Though the streets are scrutinized carefully, they will be fixed only if need can be established.

Usually the Street and Engineering Department knows that a street should be resurfaced before they get citizen complaints. When many complaints about a particular street are made, however, the department may choose one which otherwise it might not have fixed. An example of this is Golf Links Road between the MacArthur Freeway and Ninety-eighth Avenue. The street department knew that this section of the street needed resurfacing badly but had put it off because Golf Links Road was slated for complete reconstruction. Many complaints were received about the condition of the street. In 1970, when the reconstruction project was postponed for a few years, the decision was made, partly because of complaints received, to go ahead and resurface the section of the street in question.

Another example concerns Stanley Avenue, an unimproved street located near the MacArthur Freeway. The street was used as a truck route, which resulted in serious deterioration. The street department was aware of the condition of the street, and had received complaints about it. Usually when an unimproved street (i.e., a street without curbs or gutters) is to be resurfaced or otherwise improved, it requires financial participation of local property owners. The city engineer, here, refused to approve resurfacing until property owners would agree to share the costs, yet the residents refused, asserting that they were unable to afford the cost. Eventually the residents won; the street department resurfaced Stanley Avenue with city money.

The purpose of the three criteria—deterioration, traffic, and complaints—is simply to weed out the most insignificant projects proposed by the superintendents, but not to cut down their lists drastically. Furthermore, the maintenance engineer and his assistant do not attempt to establish exact priorities among the projects; rather, they indicate, after a mental weighing of need, which projects are most important. At this point, cost is not a consideration, and evaluation is not more careful, because no final decisions can be made until the utilities are consulted.

The fourth criterion—the engineer's principal decision rule, which guided street repair until recently—was to let someone else decide. The utilities must be informed of the city's resurfacing plans since they are prohibited by the Street and Engineering Department from making a cut in a street (in order to make underground repairs) for five years after it has been repaved. In the past the maintenance division tried to coordinate with the utilities companies by sending them a long list of all proposed resurfacing projects and allowing them to scratch off the list any streets on which they might expect to do underground work. Thus the utilities significantly influenced the decisions as to what would be included in yearly resurfacing programs.

This procedure made the engineer's original criteria nonoperational. For the most part the same criteria guided the utilities' maintenance work. Older streets with the most deficient surfaces generally also have the most deteriorated underground facilities; so, the utilities as well gave them high priority. Similarly, major streets with heavy traffic are a priority for both the utilities and the maintenance division. They carry a great proportion of Oakland's underground facilities and consequently require a good deal of the utilities' maintenance attention. Thus streets considered the most deficient by the maintenance division were oftentimes subjected to attrition by the utilities, and resurfacing had to be deferred. The list of proposed street projects was reduced by about 50 percent after the utilities were through with it.

The final criterion, to determine which remaining projects on the list will be undertaken, is geography. When resurfacing work is let out for contract, each contractor generally is given a number of streets to resurface, usually all those which call for the same resurfacing process. It saves money for the city if the contractor resurfaces all deficient streets in one small area at the same time. Consequently, the maintenance engineer and his assistant attempt to line up groups of the most deficient streets. Occasionally some streets not on the yearly project list or with a low priority are repaved because they are located in an area in which resurfacing projects are concentrated. Grouping, however, is not regarded as essential; seriously deficient or heavily trafficked substandard streets will be resurfaced even if no surrounding streets can be found for which repairs could be justified. Because of grouping, one area of Oakland may get a very large number of projects in a year. This is countered by concentrating resurfacing in different areas each year.

Criteria do not always make a decision rule. Sometimes criteria are used to justify arbitrary decisions; sometimes they conflict with one another. In resurfacing, only one criterion came close to a decision rule: "Let the utilities people decide." Priorities set by engineers—worst deterioration, heavy use, and even citizen complaints—were by and large unusable. With no objective standards by which to compare even the degree of deterioration of various streets, and with no simple way of making decisions, engineers have quite understandably found it easier to shift the decision to the utilities.[20]

The deficiencies in administering the resurfacing program were recognized by a team of leading Oakland businessmen whom the city manager commissioned in 1967 to study the organization and efficiency of city public works agencies. "Emphasis should be placed on preventive maintenance," the team stated in their report, "rather than on reacting to complaints, which now characterizes much of the city's street, sewer and electrical activity." [21] In late 1969 the maintenance division was put under the authority of the assistant city engineer. He takes considerable interest in the resurfacing program and has ordered some policy changes. His most important innovation has been to institute a program of long-range planning for resurfacing. Among other things, this helps solve the problem with the utilities companies. A five-year plan is being formulated which will indicate the year in which each project is to be undertaken by the division. This will be circulated among the utilities, who will be required to plan their

20. The city engineer does not agree with our interpretation. His comment speaks for itself: "I feel the implication that the City yielded to utilities on decisions on street resurfacing is in error—true, compromises have been necessary but we try to consider the taxpayer/ratepayer (who is one and the same) as the prime beneficiary." Letter to the authors from the city engineer, November 12, 1971.

21. "Oakland Urged to Modify Municipal Works Activities," *Oakland Tribune*, April 7, 1968.

maintenance activities around the division's schedule. The utilities will have to adjust to the city's plans, rather than vice versa.

OUTCOMES

Identifying decision rules gives only a partial view of the allocation of street resources. To complete the view, we turn our attention to the consequences of these rules, to outcomes. Who benefits is one obvious question for an analysis of outcomes, but we will find that it is difficult to answer with precision. Another outcome of some importance is the efficiency of the department's allocations. It is unlikely that Oakland's engineers are using their resources wisely, because they avoid cost information. Finally, stability of goals is also an outcome. The engineers put their goals in their plans and then have the patience to realize them; schedules may shift, but past plans do influence present allocations.

WHO BENEFITS?

No doubt the automobile is the prime beneficiary of Oakland's street politics. Who benefits, then, would depend on who has a car and uses the streets. In 1960, 26.5 percent of Oakland's households had no car.[22] Of those who own cars, we do not know exactly which segment makes heaviest use of any particular improved street. We do know, however, that Oakland's street system is used by its residents and commuters. A recent transportation study reported the following traffic flow for 1965: (1) through traffic on freeways only, 106,000 vehicle trips per day; (2) traffic in and out of Oakland, 403,000 vehicle trips per day; (3) traffic strictly within Oakland, 586,000 vehicle trips per day.[23] The street system is certainly serving Oaklanders, but which Oaklanders?

While it is true that more people from the (poorer) flatlands than from the hills use public transportation and walk, it is incor-

22. According to 1960 Census data, there are fewer cars per household in Oakland than in the rest of Alameda County; see Donald L. Foley and John Redwood III, *Auto Nonavailability as a Component of Transportation Disadvantage* (Berkeley: Institute of Urban and Regional Development, University of California, 1972), p. 7.

23. Oakland City Planning Department, *Options for Oakland*, Oakland 701 Project, 1969, pp. 108–110, from Bay Area Transportation Study Commission Report, Berkeley, 1969.

TABLE 2-4: All Oakland Citizens Use Their Streets (1965)

	Hill Areas			Flatland Areas		
	A	B	C	A	B	C
Population	15,142	23,245	9,777	16,430	22,714	8,280
Number of vehicle trips per day, for all purposes	24,811	19,770	14,629	19,765	23,879	11,250
Number of trips per person	1.6	.85	1.5	1.2	1.1	1.4

SOURCES: Bay Area Transportation Study Commission, "BATSC 1965 HISF Linked Weekday Vehicle Trip Tables," Berkeley, 1968; and BATSC *"Controlled Trends" Zonal Forecasts, 1965–1980–1990*, Berkeley, 1969.

rect to say that they do not drive on Oakland's streets. Using trip studies made in 1965,[24] we compared traffic volume and flow from three hill and three flatland aggregated census tract areas. Table 2-4 shows that flatland residents have driving patterns similar to those of hill people. We found also that both groups do most of their driving within Oakland.

Knowing that city streets benefit Oaklanders in general, we can gain some further insights about beneficiaries by examining a geographical distribution of street projects. The department generally pays only slight attention to geographical distribution. In resurfacing, projects may be grouped by area to save costs. In construction, projects will not be confined to one area and will be spread out as a hedge against unanticipated effects on the circulation system. Conceptually, equality in the geographical distribution of street improvements should mean that the residents of every area should have decent (or equally indecent) streets and should have easy motoring access to any other area of Oakland. This does not mean, however, that improvement projects will be distributed equally among all areas. Rather, areas with traffic problems—which are in most need of improved streets—should be receiving the most benefits in order to bring them up to par with the circulation system in other areas. The engineers believe this but do not always act on it.

By dividing Oakland into ten areas (see figure 5) fairly equal

24. Bay Area Transportation Study Commission, "BATSC 1965 HISF Linked Weekday Vehicle Trip Tables," Berkeley, 1968.

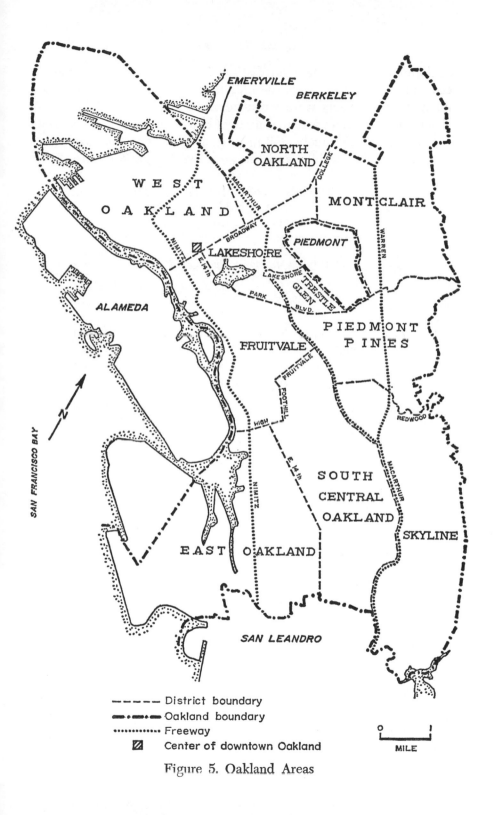

EMERYVILLE

BERKELEY

NORTH OAKLAND

WEST OAKLAND

MONTCLAIR

PIEDMONT

LAKESHORE

TRESTLE GLEN

ALAMEDA

PIEDMONT PINES

FRUITVALE

SOUTH CENTRAL OAKLAND

SKYLINE

EAST OAKLAND

SAN FRANCISCO BAY

SAN LEANDRO

N

MACARTHUR

BROADWAY

NIMITZ

E. 14th

COLLEGE

WARREN

LAKESHORE

PARK BLVD.

FRUITVALE

FOOTHILL

HIGH

REDWOOD

MACARTHUR

------- District boundary
--·--·-- Oakland boundary
············· Freeway
▨ Center of downtown Oakland

0   1
MILE

Figure 5. Oakland Areas

in population and somewhat distinct from one another in socio-economic class and residential character, we can determine how many street projects were constructed in each area.[25] The location of projects in a particular area, of course, does not necessarily mean that its residents benefit most from them. For the most part, the rich live in the hills and the poor live in the flatlands; each

TABLE 2-5: The Flatlands Receive More Projects Than the Hills: Distribution of Street Capital Improvement Projects in Oakland, 1960–1971

Area	Description of Area	Number of Projects			Percentage of projects		
		Select	Local	Total	Select	Local	Total
OAKLAND HILLS							
Piedmont Pines	Residential. Wealthy white	6½	0	6½	9	0	8
Skyline	Residential. Wealthy, white. Low population density	11	2	13	15	18	15
Montclair	Residential. Middle to upper-middle class. Liberal politically	1	2	3	1	18	4
Trestle Glen	Residential. Upper middle class. Integrated, including black professionals	0	0	0	0	0	0
Subtotal		18½	4	22½	25	36	27

25. The ten areas delineated here for studying the distribution of benefits represent a modification of the historical divisions of Oakland. Although none is completely homogeneous in regard to socioeconomic characteristics, each is dominated by the characteristics we have assigned to it. There is a bias in that the areas do differ in geographical size, and naturally there is a higher probability of larger areas having more street work (since they have more miles of streets) than smaller areas. It was more important to distinguish between socioeconomic groups than to worry about equal size. All street construction projects undertaken between 1960 and 1970, or at least budgeted in those years for future construction, were included in the analysis. If projects were budgeted and constructed in units (i.e., divided into sections), each unit was counted as a separate project in the tally. In analyzing the resurfacing program, only those streets resurfaced between 1968 and 1970 were included, since there is a lack of sufficient data for earlier years.

Area	Description of Area	Number of Projects			Percentage of projects		
		Select	Local	Total	Select	Local	Total
FLATLANDS							
Lakeshore, Adams Point	Middle and upper-middle class. Many retired people. Very conservative politically. Includes part of downtown area	7	0	7	10	0	8
South Central Oakland	Working class, blue collar. Primarily white. Conservative politically	11½	1	12½	16	9	15
North Oakland *	Working and lower-middle class mostly. Includes black areas, poor	5	0	5	7	0	6
Fruitvale *	Poor. Primarily minority groups: blacks and Mexican-Americans. Wealthy whites live near Lake Merritt	9	1	10	12	9	12
East Oakland *	Industrial-residential mix. Primarily black. Poor	11	3	14	15	27	17
West Oakland *	Primarily black, mostly poor. Includes part of downtown area. Scene of rede-velopment projects	11	2	13	15	18	15
Subtotal		54½	7	61½	75	63	73
Grand Total		73	11	84	100	99	100

* Officially designated poverty target areas.

Sources: Oakland, *Budgets*, 1960/61–1970/71. Oakland, *Capital Improvements Program*, 1961/66 and 1965/70. *Oakland Preliminary Circulation Plan, 1966–1985*, 701 Program, Advance Transportation Study Team, 1966, table 10.

group thinks the other group gets what the city has to give. Without committing an ecological fallacy, we can see from tables 2-5 and 2-6 that the flatlands, for both select and local street improvements, get more projects and more money than the hills; 73 per-

TABLE 2-6: More Money Is Spent on Streets in the Flatlands,
Distribution of Street Capital Improvement Project Resources
in Oakland, 1960–1971

Area	Approximate Cost (in millions of $)			Percentage of Cost		
	Select Streets	Local Streets	Total	Select Streets	Local Streets	Total
OAKLAND HILLS						
Piedmont Pines	2.50	0.00	2.50	4.8	0.0	4.5
Skyline	9.16	0.14	9.30	17.7	4.0	16.8
Montclair	0.04	0.07	0.11	0.1	2.0	0.2
Trestle Glen	0.00	0.00	0.00	0.0	0.0	0.0
Subtotal	11.70	0.21	11.91	22.6	6.0	21.5
FLATLANDS						
Lakeshore, Adams Point	2.60	0.00	2.60	5.0	0.0	4.7
South Central Oakland	12.85	0.35	13.20	24.8	10.2	23.9
North Oakland *	4.50	0.00	4.50	8.7	0.0	8.1
Fruitvale *	1.66	0.04	1.70	3.2	1.2	3.1
East Oakland *	14.10	0.90	15.00	27.2	26.0	27.1
West Oakland *	4.44	1.96	6.40	8.5	56.6	11.6
Subtotal	40.15	3.25	43.40	77.4	94.0	78.5
Grand Total	51.85	3.46	55.31	100.0	100.0	100.0

* Officially designated poverty target areas.

SOURCES: City of Oakland, *Budgets*, 1960/61–1970/71; *Capital Improvements Program*, 1961–66 and 1965–70; *Oakland Preliminary Circulation Plan, 1966–1985*, 701 Program, Advance Transportation Planning Team, 1966, table 10.

cent of the streets improved were in the flatlands, while only 27 percent were in the hills. Three of the five areas with the most projects happen to be the poorest sections—West Oakland, East Oakland, and Fruitvale. South Central Oakland, a working-class area, did equally well. The fifth one, Skyline, is one of the wealthier hill sections; another hill area, Trestle Glen, received no projects at all.

It would be foolish to conclude prematurely that the poor are primary beneficiaries of Oakland's street construction program. The street in your neighborhood may not be built for you. Closer examination shows that the top three areas receiving of projects were those with the highest concentration of public and private development. East Oakland contains the airport and the coliseum complex; West Oakland has been the scene of considerable urban renewal activity, and Skyline is undergoing more private residential development, particularly of subdivisions, than any other area of Oakland. Moreover, South Central Oakland and Fruitvale were the scenes of improvements related to freeways. Street work in these areas can be attributed to their central location in Oakland, crisscrossed by important arterials and flanked on both sides by major freeways. Most of the street work there consisted of freeway connections and arterial reconstruction.

Did the residents of an area benefit from these development and freeway projects? For the Skyline area projects, yes. Those certainly were constructed to benefit residents of the hills almost exclusively. This least developed area of Oakland is almost completely residential. Six of the eight streets improved (winding two-lane roads) were widened and realigned as major arterials to carry traffic to growing subdivisions. Five connect with the MacArthur Freeway and continue south to the flatlands and from there as crosstown arterials; their purpose was to provide access for the residents of the areas to freeways, that is, of Oakland, and to downtown Oakland. Although part of a crosstown system, the improvements are of slight value to the rest of Oakland because the hills are a "dead end." Although there is a park and a new college at the top of the hills, to which some Oakland residents drive, the Skyline projects chiefly benefit hill residents.

But to get some idea of how much more hill people use flatland streets than flatland residents use those in the hills, table 2-7 com-

TABLE 2-7: The Flatlands Get the Traffic

	Percentage of Vehicle Trips					
	From hill areas			*From flatland areas*		
	A	B	C	A	B	C
To all hills areas	47	28	45	1	13	4
To all flatlands areas	53	72	55	99	87	96
	100	100	100	100	100	100

SOURCE: Bay Area Transportation Study Commission, "BATSC 1965 HISF Linked Week-day Vehicle Trip Tables," Berkeley, 1968.

pares hill- and flatland-bound traffic from six areas. Area C in the table corresponds quite closely to the Skyline area boundaries we drew (see figure 3). Most of Oakland's traffic goes to the flatlands.

East Oakland flatland residents, on the other hand, were not the chief beneficiaries of most of the projects constructed in their areas. Most of the street work was built in conjunction with the Oakland coliseum and airport. The two large crosstown arterials routed through East Oakland were built to connect the Nimitz and MacArthur freeways, serving primarily commuters from the north and south of Oakland, as well as sports fans and air travelers from all over the East Bay. This is not to say these streets will not improve travel conditions for East Oakland residents; but they can only be a minority of the users. Probably they will incur more costs than benefits from the improvements, since more traffic is being brought into their area.

West Oakland is a mixed bag in terms of who benefits. The most expensive projects were built in conjunction with redevelopment, for the almost exclusive benefit of residents of the area. Local street improvements were substantial. The residents do undoubtedly bear costs, however, from a freeway which is being built between the renewal area and downtown and for which several other street projects in the area were built. The freeway is depressed, and the connections do give access from West Oakland to downtown, so the area's inhabitants are being harmed as little as possible by the freeway. Nevertheless, it is not an aesthetic addition to their neighborhood.

It may seem surprising that downtown Oakland (in the Lakeshore area) received so few projects. Actually, this is in the

Central District Plan, whose principal objective is to minimize through traffic and maximize pedestrian and public transit. The main project in the downtown core was Broadway Beautification, designed to attract pedestrians.

The only kind of improvement that benefits residents exclusively is local street improvement. Residential streets are reconstructed now and then in wealthy hill areas, usually in emergency situations when landslides and cracks occur in the area. East Oakland, where there are badly deficient high-crown streets, and West Oakland, where local streets are being repaired in conjunction with redevelopment, are the only other areas improved. All of these situations led to help by the city only after considerable citizen agitation.

Resurfacing is a different matter from construction; engineers do pour asphalt on minor streets. When reviewing the lists of streets resurfaced in the last three years, one notices how very few major arterial or fairly important cross streets were repaved. Most of those repaved were located downtown. Collector streets and local streets got by far the most attention. Obviously, the criterion of "heavy traffic volume" did not guide project selection. In a sense, then, the resurfacing program counterbalances the construction program's concentration on select streets.

Since repaving applies primarily to minor streets, it is easier to determine who benefits from resource allocation. Minor streets are likely to be used only by residents of the immediate area, and surely no one is disadvantaged by having an unimportant street in his area repaved.

In comparing table 2-8 with table 2-5, one of the first things to note is how the distribution of projects between the hills and the flatlands differs. Whereas the hills received 23 percent of street construction projects, they received 42 percent of the resurfacing projects. It is true that the hills constitute almost one-half of the area of Oakland, and so it might seem that this proportion of benefits is perfectly justifiable. According to the maintenance division's criteria, however, it is not. In the first place, many of the streets repaved in the hills—small residential and cul-de-sac streets—are very little used, some with the lightest traffic in Oakland. Second, the most deteriorated streets are located primarily in the oldest sections of the city—in the flatlands, not in the hills.

TABLE 2-8: The Hills Receive Some Attention: Distribution of Street Resurfacing Projects in Oakland, November 1968 to June 1970

| | Resurfaced Streets | | Resurfacing Costs | |
| | Number | Percent | Thousands of $ | Percent |
Area				
Oakland Hills				
Piedmont Pines	18	13	25	4
Skyline	15	11	48	9
Montclair	23	17	76	14
Trestle Glen	1	1	20	4
Subtotal	57	42	169	31
Flatlands				
Lakeshore, Adams Point	25	19	84	15
South Central	10½	8	59	11
North Oakland *	14½	11	64	12
Fruitvale *	12½	9	98	18
East Oakland *	4	3	12	2
West Oakland *	10½	8	59	11
Subtotal	77	58	376	69
Total	134	100	545	100

* Officially designated poverty target areas.

SOURCE: Oakland, Department of Streets and Engineering, *Street Resurfacing Program,* 1968–1970.

This is not to say that the hill area should not receive a fair share of benefits, nor that it does not contain streets badly in need of repair. In fact, the hill area streets often present the worst maintenance and emergency problems, because the hills are made up of fairly new geological formations, prone to crack and slide, and because the storm drainage system is not the best. Understandably, streets in the hills deteriorate more quickly than streets in other sections of Oakland. Problems do not occur so often, however, that so many streets should have to have been repaved there—particularly minor streets. For example, in one year (1969) 54 percent of the streets resurfaced in Oakland were located in a small, fairly isolated corner of the Montclair hill area, though there are countless deficient streets in all areas of Oakland.

The work that has been done in the Oakland hills embarrasses the resurfacing engineers, who admit that priorities were misplaced. The blame is placed on the utilities companies. The maintenance engineer claims that after the utilities companies got through slashing the most important projects from the division's lists, almost all remaining streets were in the hills. Although this is plausible, it also implies that the maintenance people included many hill projects on their list in the first place.

Another likely explanation is that hill residents complained more about their streets. We have no factual evidence to support this hypothesis, but until recently it was generally true that higher income groups were more likely than lower income groups to voice complaints about city services, particularly in regard to such often-experienced inconveniences as potholes and the need for stop signs. When one considers that the maintenance division pays more attention to written complaints than to those which are phoned in, the hypothesis becomes more plausible.

In terms of the total proportion of projects, poverty target areas in the flatlands fared better in the street construction program than in resurfacing. Whereas 50 percent of construction projects were in target areas, only about 30 percent of the streets resurfaced were located there. Residents of the core poverty areas did not necessarily receive whatever benefits were distributed. The core poverty areas are burdened with the oldest and the most deteriorated streets in Oakland, streets which for the most part were not repaired. Rather, streets in more commercial sections were resurfaced.

One explanation for this may be that the utilities may have had many underground maintenance problems on these streets. Another is that several streets were so deteriorated that repaving would have accomplished little, and complete reconstruction was called for. Finally, the street department has a policy not to maintain streets not originally built to their own standards. This policy applies to a block of streets in West and East Oakland.

These ills are soon to be corrected. In the first five-year plan for resurfacing, the division plans to include several of these deteriorated target area streets, partly out of their own recognition that the distribution of benefits has been somewhat unbalanced. For the most part, however, it is due to wholesale concentration on improving streets in redevelopment areas.

The south central, working-class area of Oakland received 8 percent of the total resurfacing projects. The streets in the area are fairly old, many built with high crowns and obviously not repaved in years. The area has the disadvantage of being in the center of the continuum of relative need—there is not as much traffic as there is in the rest of the flatlands, and it does not experience the severe physical problems which occur occasionally in the hills. Lakeshore received the greatest number of projects—about 19 percent of the total. Those repaired were fairly well traveled collector and residential streets in middle-class neighborhoods. The streets were as normally deficient as most of those in Oakland.

It is hard to answer the question of who benefits. Resurfacing, for the most part, seems to be spread evenly around the city, while construction is centered in the flatlands. In one situation, minor streets are repaired; in the other, traffic circulation improvements and development objectives dominate. Streets improved according to engineers' decision rules were primarily major thoroughfares and freeway connections. Unintentionally (since in their decisions the engineers did not consider likely differential outcomes on Oakland's citizens), residents of hill areas and motorists traveling to and from Oakland benefited, while poorer areas of the flatlands bore costs. No doubt residents of West Oakland, East Oakland, and Fruitvale did profit in terms of having better access to points outside and inside the city. Unlike hill dwellers and commuters, however, they had to suffer the discomforts of increased traffic volumes and more air pollution near their homes.

LIKELY INEFFICIENCY

Cost information is slighted in departmental decision-making. One might expect costs to be an important consideration. But costs dampen aspirations. In practice, therefore, the economic choice of projects, in terms of benefits received in relation to costs incurred, is never squarely faced in Oakland. Projects are undertaken according to the importance of the purpose they serve. If the project is considered essential, the effects on the total street program of allocating a great proportion of resources to one project are not carefully calculated. Take the Hegenberger Expressway, for which the city allocated an unprecedented $9 to $10 million. That money could pay for a number of other major streets and for improving many minor streets. But tradeoffs or other objectives are ignored. No one in the department thinks in cost-effectiveness terms.

The most telling indicator of inefficiency is that a firm estimate of cost is not calculated until *after* the decision has been made to undertake a project. There are three possible stages at which project costs are estimated. The first time is when a project is planned to be undertaken in the future (in conjunction with a long-range plan, for example). Using standard unit costs known from past experience, gross cost estimates are made. The engineers use unit cost analysis, where the cost of one foot of the street project is estimated and then unit cost is multiplied by length. Similarly, cost for each foot of sidewalk, curb, and gutter is computed. The amount is inflated appropriately if unusual construction problems are anticipated, such as could be expected with street building in the Oakland hills. The real estate division estimates the cost of property acquisition for a project, which is added to the total estimate. After unit construction costs and property prices are computed, 10 percent of this total is added on for engineering costs, and another 10 percent for contingency expenses.

Costs are estimated also when projects are selected for the five-year street capital improvement program. This is the basic working program for the street department. It tells how much money will be budgeted for which projects in what years and for what phases of construction work. Again, costs for each project are estimated only roughly, using the unit cost analysis method. The original cost estimate may be accepted for the five-year program or may be revised to account for rising costs or design changes. A breakdown of the total cost into the various phases each project will go through is shown: acquisition of right-of-way, preliminary planning and design, and construction and post-construction. The amount budgeted for each phase is computed by allocating a standard percentage of the total cost to each.

Detailed cost estimates finally are calculated when firm plans and designs for a project are drawn up. This generally takes place after acquisition of right-of-way has begun, and about a year before actual construction is budgeted to commence. Cost estimation here is more accurate and elaborate than the unit cost estimation used in earlier stages because the cost for all materials used, man-hour time, and all the various components of a project are figured.

Engineers try to be generous in making estimates. A sort of contingency fund is built into each project estimate to deal with surprises. Besides, rising prices and unanticipated changes in the design concept at a late date may raise the price of a project, so it is useful to have a cushion.

Underestimated costs rarely, if ever, result in a project's being scrapped. Other ways of getting around the problem include such tactics as these: (1) Other projects included in the five-year program may be postponed until later, so that the project in question can be undertaken according to its original timetable; (2) only one section of a street will be constructed instead of the entire part planned in the five-year program, the rest being postponed until later; or (3) the date for letting out the contract for bid may be postponed.

Determination of which streets should be chosen as the route of a crosstown arterial depends only partly on cost. Topography, for instance, is important; one must determine which side of a street or which of two routes is best suited topographically for street construction. Closely related to this consideration is safety. The street must be so aligned that it is safe for all motorists traveling at the designated speed limit. Another factor is the avoidance of public institutions, such as hospitals and schools. The engineers must also consider which of two routes will be most likely to generate and serve the desired volume of future traffic on an improved street. Finally, the problems of acquiring right-of-way on two alternate routes, or on either side of one street, are given a great deal of attention.

Cost is probably more important in choosing alternate routes and alignments than it is in determining the design and quality of constructing a street. Here standards rule. In order to determine what method of construction and types of materials are needed, the basic measurement taken is that of soil condition. The soil over which the street will run is tested to determine what kind of street surface is required. The depth and quantity of material is based on a comparison of the soil condition to the average daily traffic volume on a street. Streets that are heavily used naturally need a stronger surface.

Engineers consider their standards more important than costs. Although standards are issued by the state or city, sometimes they have to be made out of whole cloth. There are no explicit standards, for instance, to determine asphalt depth. The depth of resurfacing depends on the condition and volume of traffic on a street. The city engineers contract for as much asphalting as they believe necessary for an "acceptable job." What constitutes "acceptable" is determined subjectively. The maintenance division even disregards the state gas tax regulation that defines any more than 1¼ inches of asphalt as reconstruction rather than maintenance. Engineers have an implicit standard which considers maintenance to be whatever amount of asphalt is necessary to keep the street in reasonable condition for the next ten years.

The maintenance division, moreover, does not know how much it costs to maintain a street. Files are kept of resurfacing projects, but these consist only of records of contracts let out to bid on groups of streets. It is difficult and time-consuming (although not impossible) to ascertain exactly how much it costs to resurface each street. No data are available which show how often particular streets or types of streets have had to be resurfaced, how much is saved by resurfacing a street now rather than later, or how many man-hours are required for specific street jobs.

In short, cost is not a very important consideration in engineering decisions. The rule is that if it costs too much, look for more money—do not eliminate projects. When project costs overrun estimates, juggle project scheduling. As a consequence of the lack of economic calculus, one can hardly expect that resources are efficiently allocated.

PERMANENT PLANS AND TEMPORARY SCHEDULES

As political scientists, more often than not we expect planning efforts to be comprised by political events. As we have seen, however, engineers usually get their way. Their plans, despite difficulties such as determining street deficiencies, set their agenda. Political projects and the lure of cost-sharing will shift the schedule.[26]

26. The deferring of professional projects by politicians was also noted by W. H. Brown and C. E. Gilbert in *Planning Municipal Investment: A Case Study of Philadelphia* (Philadelphia: University of Pennsylvania Press, 1961), pp. 196–201. Although the initiative for projects in Philadelphia

TABLE 2-9: Plans Influence Budget Allocations of Engineers' Projects

	First Year Project/Unit Was Budgeted	First 5-Year Program on Which Project Appeared	Appeared in	
			701 Plan (1969)	Bartholomew Report (1949)
Freeway Access				
Beaumont Avenue	1961/62	1961/66	X	
18th Street	1967/68	1965/70	X	X
17th Street	1970/71	1970/75	X	
East 8th Street	1966/67	1961/66		X
11th and 12 Streets		1970/75	X	
Lincoln Ave. Extension	1967/68	1965/70	X	
Crosstown Arterials				
35th Ave. & Redwood Rd.	1964/65	1961/66	X	X
Hegenberger Blvd.	1961/62	1961/66	X	X
Golf Links Road	1961/62	1961/66	X	X
98th Avenue	1969/70	1961/66	X	X
High Street		1970/75	X	X
Major Arterials				
51st Street	1964/65	1961/66	X	
Embarcadero	1961/62	1961/66	X	X
Market Street	1963/64	1965/70	X	X
14th Street	1967/68	1965/70	X	X
Congested or Unsound				
Harrison Street	1961/62	1961/66	X	
Adeline St. Bridge		1970/75		

SOURCES: Oakland, *Budgets,* 1960/61–1970/71. Oakland, *Capital Improvement Program,* 1961/66 and 1965/70. *Oakland Preliminary Circulation Plan, 1966–1985,* 701 Program, Advance Transportation Study Team, 1966, table 10. "Freeways and Major Streets in Oakland, Calif.," *Oakland Master Plan,* City Planning Commission, prepared by Bartholomew and Associates, City Planners, St. Louis, Mo., 1949.

But what is a few years between friends, when ultimately the engineers' projects will be funded and constructed?

The influence of planning can be seen when we trace the origins of our twenty-nine projects (see table 2-3, p. 134). In table 2-9 we show how the seventeen strictly engineering projects came

generally came from the administrative decision-makers, the council would respond to political pressures by rescheduling project alternatives. "Such projects set off a series of scheduling changes, by both administration and Council, in which the changes made by the administration will frequently be altered by Council" (p. 197). The administration's projects were usually deferred and seldom scrapped.

to be. Clearly, the Bartholomew Report of 1949 influenced subsequent plans, and the five-year program set the agenda for budgeting projects or components (units) of a project. Another evidence of the influence of planning is that 75 percent of the projects included in the five-year program for 1971/1975 were taken from the 701 Plan. In any event, most projects undertaken by the engineers according to technical criteria were decided upon in conjunction with long-range planning. Most of the political projects and those undertaken by the engineers in order to share costs, however, were never included in long-range plans, but rather appeared first in an annual budget. In a budget year, the latter type of projects would temporarily drive out some of the planned, technical projects.

If planning influences budgeting, budgeting also influences planning. The first project engineers will include in a five-year program is the one previously budgeted but not completed. In long-range plans the same things occur; projects already budgeted and yet to be completed were first to be included in the 701 Plan. A budgeted project (either for design work or actual construction) creates a commitment.[27] Committed projects, as seen in table 2-10, then determine the contents of the plan, particularly in the earlier years.

Planning implies the ability to set priorities and ascertain deficiencies and needs. City officials do have standards of deficiency (such as travel-time delay rate, accident rate, and street surface

TABLE 2-10: Committed Projects Are Scheduled in the Early Phases of the 701 Plan

Phase of Plan	Number of Committed Projects	Number of Uncommitted Projects	Total Projects
I 1969/74	16	5	21
II 1975/79	5	10	15
III 1980/84	2	7	9
IV After 1984	2	11	13
Total:	25	33	58

27. Past commitments have a way of limiting future actions; for an interesting discussion of commitments see Philip Selznick, *T.V.A. and the Grass Roots: A Study in the Sociology of Formal Organization* (Berkeley: University of California Press, 1953), pp. 255–259.

TABLE 2-11: Committed Projects Are Scheduled Earlier Than
Their Priority Rating Would Justify

	Number of Committed Projects	*Number of Uncommitted Projects*
Scheduled earlier than their Priority Index Rating would advise	21	14
Scheduled later than their Priority Index Rating would advise	4	19

conditions) with which to rate future projects and assign priorities. For the 701 Plan, officials supposedly used a priority rating index based on a system developed by the League of California Cities.[28] The rating system assigns priorities according to certain prescribed standards of need and deficiency in order "to hold to a minimum political and community pressures in highway planning and construction" and "to minimize or eliminate the element of personal judgment in the expenditure of road funds."[29]

Yet when prior commitments, cost-sharing opportunities, timing problems, and political demands come into play, the rating system has to be shoved aside. There is practically no relationship between a project's priority index rating and its scheduling in the 701 Plan. Most committed projects, as we expected, were scheduled earlier than their priority rating would have warranted (see table 2-11).[30] Uncommitted projects also were not scheduled according to their ratings; more than half were scheduled later than indicated by the rating system. The committed drove out the uncommitted.

28. *Oakland Preliminary Circulation Plan, 1966–1985.*
29. Ibid.
30. Each project included in the 701 Plan was assigned a "priority index rating" by the engineers based upon measurements of deficiency such as surface condition, miles traveled per day, accident rate, and delay rates. To arrive at the information shown in table 2-11, we first listed projects in order of their priority index ratings, or relative deficiency. We then compared this with a listing of the projects in the order in which they were actually scheduled for construction in the 701 Plan. "Committed" projects are those which had already been decided upon and budgeted before the 701 Plan was formulated, but had to be included because they were scheduled for construction during some of the years covered by the plan.

The rating index itself is imperfect. It does not, for instance, include a measurement of the structural condition of streets at their base; only the street's surface condition is evaluated. Doing more than that would require costly spot destruction of the street surface. But what good is an index that cannot highlight hazardous conditions? The Adeline Street Bridge is an example of a project scheduled ahead of others with a higher priority index rating. The priority index rating did not reflect that the bridge is so structurally unsound it may soon fall into the railroad track beneath it.

Another factor which the priority index rating does not take into account is infrequent but serious deficiencies on a street. Coliseum Way, for instance, is usually an empty street, but on days when the sports arena is used it is congested. Since the "vehicle miles per day" component of the index measures only averages, Coliseum Way ended up with a low priority, which did not reflect the actual need for improvement. It was, therefore, moved up in scheduling.

Political popularity also serves to push low priority projects up in scheduling. Grass Valley Road moved up because it enjoyed outside support. The street will be widened to provide better access to a subdivision in the Oakland hills. Developers got their way.

The priority ranking system cannot cope with the imperatives of property acquisition. Sometimes it is advantageous to acquire property far in advance of the time when actual construction will begin. Consider Skyline Boulevard, which is to be widened as a scenic route along the top of the Oakland hills. Objectively, the project is not vital and has a low priority rating. It was included in an early phase of the plan, however, since the street department wants to acquire property at a reasonable rate before anticipated development along the route begins. Actually, property acquisition problems more often cause higher priority projects to be put off in scheduling than to be moved up. Difficulties in acquiring right-of-way are fairly common. Grand Avenue is one street that was seriously considered for the plan, since it needs to be widened, but it was omitted originally because the cost of acquiring necessary property was prohibitive. Then Kaiser Corporation came to the rescue and agreed to donate some of the right-of-way which it owns; so Grand Avenue was put back into the plan.

Postponing projects is a way of displacing conflict. In order to widen Third Street, property would have to be acquired from a railroad, which was reluctant to sell. Engineers wanted to avoid a confrontation with the railroad, so they put the project in the later phases of the plan. Another project, widening Twenty-second Avenue, was postponed because a number of houses in a "sensitive" area would have to be acquired. Racially mixed, the neighborhood is in a period of transition, and an attempt to buy houses there would make the street department very unpopular. The engineers believe it is easier to acquire property in middle-class areas, from which the homeowners can afford to move, than in poorer neighborhoods. In order to buy time, the department shifted that project into the no-conflict future.

Projects are put off to leave time for a better alternative to be considered. Both High Street and Seventy-third Avenue are included in the 701 Plan to be widened eventually as crosstown arterials. The department, at the same time, is considering the possibility of a freeway in the corridor between these streets. Most of the High Street construction is scheduled later than its index rating would advise, so that ample time will be available to gather information on the feasibility of a freeway.

Similarly, the department scheduled high-ranking projects late when traffic conditions surrounding a street are in a state of flux. Telegraph Avenue was to be reconstructed and widened because of severe congestion (it is used as a major Oakland arterial). The new Grove-Shafter Freeway lies in the same corridor, however, and the engineers waited to see how much traffic would be diverted to the freeway from Telegraph before widening the street.

Large dollar requirements of projects influence priorities. Some projects that were scheduled earlier than their priority rating called for large sums of money; therefore, other projects with a high priority rating had to be scheduled later. Because of the limitation of funding, it is hard to plan for many high cost projects during the same time period.

We have seen that in scheduling projects and establishing priorities, value judgments, uncontrollable circumstances (such as the need to coordinate with city projects), and political and economic imperatives are more influential than standards of need and deficiency. The Street and Engineering Department is so dependent on other agencies and city plans and on the need to find outside money that it must compromise its own values. The entire exercise of attempting to objectify and rationalize decision-making—to base choices on measurable standards—seems futile. Even if one could design a perfect index of deficiency, the index would never be capable of fixing a schedule. There seem to be more reasons why a project is shifted than there are projects. The city engineer agrees; he commented once that although the rating system might be a good guide, "you can't just plug in a formula and come out with the right decisions."

When a particular project will be undertaken is anybody's guess. Of course plans and priorities should be modified as conditions change. But a fascinating feature of Oakland's street planning is the stability of goals which it establishes. Planning provides the menu for street construction. Regardless of short term changing conditions, engineers keep putting resources into major streets—into filling in the spokes of the street system of the early 1900s. One wonders whether it is time now to reconsider these goals.

CONCLUSION

Public works elsewhere may be a pork barrel, but in honest Oakland street decisions are straight. Hardworking engineers—professionals who know their business—make the major decisions. Engineers are very protective of their own values. They plan improvements when and where necessary according to their own criteria, not according to citizens' requests. Engineers believe they are the best judges of how to benefit the public. The degree to which a project will better the public welfare is evaluated by its contribution to improve traffic circulation and motorist safety; the effect of street improvement on other aspects of people's lives is given much less consideration. Hence the automobile is the prime beneficiary of Oakland's street program.

Engineers modify their schedule when fitting plans to the constraints of their environment. By waiting, they do get their way.

What if the construction schedule slips? After all, there is an opportunity to share costs with other agencies. What if engineers
slight costs? They know what is good for the citizens of Oakland.
As responsive civil servants they answer citizen complaints and
accept council intervention; as professionals they dominate the
politics of streets.

Combining their goal of improving circulation of traffic with
the highway emphasis of the gas tax, the engineers have made the
city a convenient place for Oaklanders to drive across and for
other Californians to pass through. Neighborhood streets for the
most part are neglected, though occasionally a real estate entre-
preneur can lure the city council into spending money because
of the prospects of economic development, and poor areas of the
city once in a while get a sliver of the action because of federal
largesse. To see the distribution of street resources solely in terms
of rich or poor, hills or flatlands, however, is to miss the central
allocation decision. The winners in Oakland are those who use
the select system of streets.

Engineers are not the bad guys either; they have been trained
to worry about traffic, not necessarily about people. But even if
they wanted to repair nonexistent curbs in a rundown neighborhood, where would they get the money? The city does not have
enough money to keep up its streets, let alone build new ones.
The state, with its mushrooming automobile population, has to
provide the means for moving them from one place to the other.
The federal government is looking for low-cost innovative solutions to the "urban crisis," and street repair is usually not very
innovative. Policy makers at all levels are blinded by a transportation fixation. But while we agree that improved traffic circulation is desirable, we feel it desirable also to improve our neighborhoods and cities so that people will enjoy living in them more than
driving away from them during rush hours.

3

Libraries

There is safety in the past. It already happened. There is no way now it can happen differently. Explanation of past behavior can never be conclusive but neither can it be decisively refuted. Unless it suffers from internal logical contradictions, an explanation may be challenged, even derided, but it can hardly be proved wrong. For refutation requires a problematical element; life must be given a chance to do the unexpected. If only a single event is possible, nothing else could have occurred and there is no point in waiting around for the inevitable. Prediction is replaced by observation, contingency by reporting, planning by history.

How have things been? The chapters on education and streets tell us how the participants made outputs from their inputs and distributed them (or permitted them to be distributed) in certain ways. These outcomes are the outcomes that were. They are what they became. Maybe, we hope, they could have been other than they turned out to be. But we shall never know and neither will anyone else.

Changing the future depends on understanding the past. That we have tried to do. Controlling the future consequences of present actions (planning or policy analyses, as this effort to shape man's fate is called) requires a venture into the unknown. Unless the problem is trivial or mechanical, or both, there are bound to be substantial uncertainties connected with attempted solutions. Data that would be useful is frequently missing, distorted, or incomplete. Theories of human behavior, which must undergird efforts to predict events under varying conditions, are usually nonexistent, partial, or suspect. The people involved are interested in the outcome; rarely are they completely cooperative.

Everything was normal when we attempted to prescribe for the Oakland Branch Libraries. Existing data was insufficient. We would have liked to have known consumer preferences for different types of library services, for instance, but no survey exists (though we did impute preferences in various neighborhoods by sampling patterns of actual use). Nor were we certain whether the people in whom we were most interested—people who used the libraries least—would be able to predict accurately their future use (or lack thereof) on the basis of hypothetical questions we might put to them, if we had money and time for sample surveys. We had the time but the city had no money. Officials wanted fast and cheap advice. The reader may well conclude they got their money's worth.

If relevant data was not exactly superabundant, neither was theory. We could only guess whether people who stayed away in large numbers would be attracted by the untried measures we recommended. Theory on why people read or what makes them want to read was not available. So we recommended different ways of learning from experience. Perhaps, the more demanding will say, practitioners don't need analysts to learn from the school of hard knocks. The people doing the jobs did not always know why they did what they did and were not always willing to share their best hunches with us. And why should they? It was our task to prove ourselves to them and not vice versa. In the end, like the perspicacious consumers they are, city officials bought from us what they wanted (a hefty transfer of funds from personnel to books) and left us to peddle our other nostrums elsewhere, which we are doing.

Rather than duplicate the well-worn pattern of the previous two chapters, therefore, we have rearranged the same sort of data on the distribution of outputs and their relation to financial inputs, in a form better suited to policy analyses. Suddenly gaps in data, chasms in theory, become manifest before our eyes. To become more relevant, apparently, is to increase vulnerability. Analysis is a risky enterprise. But it is also fun. The reader, we hope, will appreciate both aspects of our presentation.

If we were content to describe the allocation of resources in branch libraries, there would be no need to raise the fundamental question of whether they should exist. They do exist; therefore they allocate resources. But there would be no point in recommending changes in branch libraries unless we believed it was right for them to exist. Since our clients would have thought we were crazy to have explicitly raised an issue "everyone knows" has been settled, we did not impose this arcane discussion on them. Instead we have saved it for you.

SHOULD THERE BE PUBLIC LIBRARIES?

Before giving an unthinking affirmative reply, it is worth stating the contrary argument as persuasively as possible. The vast majority of books and services provided through libraries are designed either to entertain, stimulate, or divert the populace. Why should tax dollars be used for those purposes in direct competition with rental libraries and booksellers?

The usual answer is that it is good for people to read, and the city has an interest in helping them. And, where the rich can pay, the poor cannot, so it is right for the city to meet the demand. Yet it seems meaningless to talk about what people "want" in the absence of some indication of what they would be willing to give up in order to get it. The fact that somebody comes in and asks for something does not suggest there is a demand; it becomes a demand only when people are willing to sacrifice something else in order to get it.

There is a reasonable case against government subsidy of reading. There may be, for instance, a large public purpose served by providing at no charge automobile repair manuals or brochures on how to pass civil service examinations. If governments wish to engage in vocational education and training, however, they should examine alternative institutional settings that may make more sense than a library. Civil service exams, for example, could be distributed by the city and state personnel system and linked directly to training programs designed to help people qualify for public employment.

In talking about streets, one deals, at least, with benefits that are more collective in nature, whereas in the case of libraries the benefits are almost entirely individual. Thus the city has no obligation to produce more book reading among poor people even if (perhaps especially if) it means less free book reading among rich people. The state has no business concerning itself with the private reading habits of its citizens, especially if what the citizens are interested in would not, if consumed, produce any benefits for other people. To go from the assumption that the poor ought to read more to the assumption that the library ought to seek out poor readers and somehow induce them to read more takes a lot of explaining.

This position, reflecting the literature on welfare economics and the definition of public goods, is not obviously wrong. Just because public libraries have "always" been provided by cities does not mean that this error should necessarily be perpetuated. Subsidizing the rich and belaboring the poor to read requires a more convincing rationale than it has received.

When it is said that allowing popular preferences to prevail in the economic marketplace is efficient, the assumption always is that the distribution of income is taken for granted. For if the prevailing distribution of income is believed to be wrong, then the "votes" or "bids" in the marketplace are weighted more heavily in favor of the rich than they ought to be. This consideration takes on special force in the case of libraries because the alternative is to satisfy reading desires through the private market in the form of lending libraries or bookstores. The rich can afford to do this much more than the poor. Yet the poor would have to be more highly motivated because the marginal value of a dollar means more to them. Such a market might test the virtue (but not necessarily the reading desires) of the poor.

Asking why libraries should be supported unfairly puts the burden on them. Indeed most local services in the past were supplied by the private sector. Today police, fire, and education can be (and sometimes are) private activities for which a fee is paid directly by the citizen or household. Yet few suggest that these ought to be entirely private activities. There is absolutely no reason to mandate that any municipality have a public library. But what is wrong with having one if its citizens so desire? These people might believe that the reading habits thus inculcated have socially desirable effects, or they may believe that it is worthwhile having libraries available even if relatively few people, including themselves, use them. Why question Ben Franklin and go behind these long-standing citizen preferences?

One objection is that the rich use the library but the poor pay for it. While such a statement is not entirely accurate, it does suggest that the poor pay more than their proportionate share. The solution to this problem, to the extent that there is one, is for library services to be distributed more in the direction of the poor, not to have them abolished.

Libraries may be undesirable because they provide a good that citizens could otherwise obtain in the market. A central economic rationale for a public library, then, would be market imperfections that do not permit citizens to collectively receive services they would otherwise prefer. But following this line of thought would lead to perverse actions on the part of city governments. Cities would run libraries only if they provided services no private party would supply in its own interest. Hence an anomaly we will point out—the Oakland Library specializing in arcane studies like the teaching of English in eighteenth century England— would be a candidate for city support precisely because no one in his right mind would contemplate spending his own money for it.

Political costs should be considered, especially since depriving people of a customary indulgence angers them more than refusal to begin a new one. Libraries exist. They represent a considerable financial investment. Citizens show no inclination to sell them off. They will protest to prevent closing of smaller branches. The interesting question then is how to amortize this investment by using the favorable feelings about libraries in the best way.

In a different era, the Oakland Library might have been considered a model of its kind. Its Main Library is an intellectual resource for the entire Bay Area; people come from far outside the city to use its specialized collections and the services of its professional reference librarians. Its California Room contains the best collection of early state history of any similar library; the sources kept there are indispensable for the historian. Its branches enable interested citizens to read quality material with professional librarians available for guidance. Indeed, it was good for its time, and those who built up the Oakland Library deserve ample credit.

If this study is critical, it is not because we fail to appreciate important contributions the library has made to Oakland or the inspired services of past librarians, but because it was not (when we made our study) taking advantage of current opportunities. New people moved to the city in the past thirty years but the library still served only its old clientele. Reading needs and patterns among its potential users changed markedly, but not the kinds of books the library normally ordered. As a result, the Oakland Library provided poor service at high cost for high-income whites and low-income blacks and Chicanos.

One concern we have is to make the library system more efficient; it is possible to achieve considerably higher circulation for the same budget. Our major concern, however, is to help make the library more effective; it should reach out and attract more people who need its services but who have previously stayed away. Attracting new clients can be done without reducing the quality of services to old ones. Accepting the official diagnosis that the city has little money, we will show that the Oakland library system could be made more efficient with only modest increases in costs.

We begin by looking at the major purposes libraries are designed to serve, purposes which Oakland does not achieve very well. The sources of these failures are found in the patterns of staff recruitment and resource allocation which characterize the library system; the librarians use norms that emphasize recruitment of professionals to an extent which overshadows the goal of expanding services to those not presently using them. The failure to reach out is documented in a detailed examination of the operation of the branch system. We end the chapter with a series of recommendations for improvement.

THE PUBLIC LIBRARY AS REPOSITORY, EDUCATIONAL INSTITUTION, AND RECREATIONAL FACILITY

Leigh, in 1950,[1] laid out the three objectives which guide librarians in their work. The first two are assembling, preserving, and administering books and related educational materials in organized collections, and serving the community as a general center

1. Robert Leigh, *The Public Library in the U.S.* (New York: Columbia University Press, 1950).

of reliable information. Munn, in 1954, stated that librarians' chief attention still is directed to "selecting, organizing . . . books, and having service available." [2] The California Library Association (CLA) in 1953 declared: "The public library's function is to assemble, preserve, and to make easily and freely available to all the printed and other materials. . . ." [3] Such statements clearly point to the notion of the library as a repository.

The third objective in the Leigh paper is "providing an opportunity for all people to educate themselves continuously." The CLA expands this brief statement by listing various things libraries should assist people in doing: continuing to learn, keeping pace with progress in all fields, becoming better political and social citizens, growing capable in daily occupations, developing creative and spiritual capacities, and contributing to the growth of knowledge. All these activities involve education.

This clearly educational purpose of the library was, until quite recently, predicated on the belief that the motivation to learn did exist in the community. The function of a good collection and well-trained staff of reference librarians presumably would activate those already motivated. McFadden (in a 1953 paper which anticipates the realization that motivation might have to be actively developed), says that "the popular faith in the self-education of the adult still persists." For this reason, he continues, librarians have stocked good books but failed to sell them to the public through promotional activities.[4]

We would like to suggest a new approach, which stresses the importance of getting people to the repository (or the repository to the people) in order to realize that educational role. Different kinds of people may require different kinds of education; the new outlook dictates an active program of reaching out to potential clients and guiding and stimulating them in their use of library facilities.

There are pessimists in the field. Since the new orientation lends itself to a concern for low-income persons who often lack much formal education, questions must arise as to whether the library

2. Ralph Munn, "The Librarian" in *Library Trends* (July 1954).
3. *Public Library Service Standards for California,* California Library Association, November 14, 1953.
4. Marion McFadden, "Objectives and Functions of Public Libraries" in *Library Trends* (April 1953).

can get to them, and whether it is the appropriate institution through which to reach them. Leigh addressed himself to precisely those questions and concluded that, aside from the population that now uses public libraries regularly, "the process of enlargement is slow, requiring intensive efforts and not producing numerically spectacular results." [5] He based this conclusion on the fact that the commercial media, who compete successfully for large numbers of consumers, use personalities, sensationalism, and distortion to overwhelm competitors (including libraries to the extent that they try to increase their own clientele). To the degree that libraries confine themselves to material the commercial mass media does not carry—older, standard, quality works—Leigh argues they will not be able to greatly enlarge their clientele.

It would be interesting to find out if the current social mobilization of the urban poor can defeat the pessimism of some commentators on libraries. This drive may create—in part already has created—a more insistent demand for educational materials and literature concerning current social issues than librarians and educators ever thought possible a few years ago.

Another goal of the public library is to provide community recreation. In discussions with librarians, Leigh discovered that recreation comprises a large part of the total library services. The recreation purpose dictates that the library stock books that people demand, regardless of "intrinsic worth." The problem of what kinds of materials the library will stock—relevant to recreation—in part reflects, in part dictates, the type of public the library will serve. This follows from the observation that various occupational and income groups have different reading tastes and needs. Traditionally, the three library goals—repository, education, and recreation—converged in a tendency for libraries to stock quality and standard works to be read for recreation by the upper classes and for education by the middle. Thus lower-income persons have not been attracted to libraries because their recreational reading centers on lighter, "temporary" works, to the extent that reading is pursued at all; librarians traditionally have felt that they should not stock such "nonquality" material.

5. Leigh, *Public Library in the U.S.*

THE OAKLAND PUBLIC LIBRARY

How well does Oakland meet the three great goals of a public library?

AS A REPOSITORY

A recent survey of thirteen large public libraries in California [6] showed that Oakland was fifth in bookstock per capita. For the last fifteen years, however, the library has been putting only about 6 to 8 percent of its annual budgetary appropriation into buying professional materials and upkeep of all sorts, including books, periodicals, records, films, pictures, and binding. (It ranked lowest of the thirteen in new books added per capita.) This low level of acquisition does not allow for sufficient turnover or enlargement of the book collection to keep it from becoming antiquated. As one looks through the collection, one is struck by the great age of most of the books, even in rapidly evolving fields. It is quite an experience to discover a 1915 science encyclopedia on the reference shelf!

AS AN EDUCATIONAL INSTITUTION

The kind of collection a library has affects the role it can perform as an educational facility. The Oakland library does not purchase much in the way of vocational materials. In a report sent by the library to the Budget and Finance Department, it was stated: "We daily must turn away an average of 203 people seeking circulating copies of civil service test booklets, because our book budget is not big enough to buy this type of material in quantity." [7] Similarly, the library has not obtained material in other media, such as film, which may be effective in adult education. That same report says that, according to American Library Association standards, a library the size of Oakland's should have at least a thousand film titles. Oakland has only fifty-seven, of which twenty-three were recently purchased with a federal grant. Lower-income groups, especially recently, have begun to ask for

6. *Newsnotes of California Libraries*, Statistical Issue (Winter 1966).
7. From notes sent to Department Heads and Regional Supervisors from the office of the Assistant Librarian, March 13, 1968.

materials on current events and social issues. But the library has not had a big enough book budget to buy books such as these with a short reader-lifetime. The library has been able to meet the demand for educational materials by higher-income persons who may find what they need among the classics, but even they are frustrated when trying to learn about areas where they must have access to up-to-date materials. Thus, apart from any question of enlarging its educational clientele among lower-income groups, the Oakland library is not even able to meet the current level of general demand.

AS A RECREATIONAL FACILITY

The library provides recreation for higher-income groups, especially with its large picture collection at the main library and the fine arts collection at one of the better branches in a moderately well-to-do neighborhood. Its book collection does contain traditional quality fiction, which might provide recreation for such groups, although the absence of recent works limits its role in recreation. It provides little recreative enjoyment for lower-income groups, for whom popular and temporary works are in higher demand. The one exception to the library's weakness is with respect to children's books: most branches have an adequate and well-used children's collection.

The Oakland library does not try to overcome its defects as an educational facility by allocating resources at the branch level in order to stimulate interest in reading. Although there are more branches in Oakland than in other comparable systems (which would seem to indicate an outreach to the community), most resources go into the main library. Only about 39 percent of the library budget goes to the branches, although they account for 75 percent of the total circulation in the system.[8]

The library staff goes out of its way to avoid any community involvement that might attract people to the library. Such involvement is clearly antithetical to what the staff feels is their proper role, as in the words of a typical branch librarian: "We aren't social workers; we are librarians. Our duty is to provide facilities and books for those who come to use them. . . . Librar-

8. Unpublished paper by David Lyon, under Michael Teitz, Department of City Planning, University of California, Berkeley, 1966.

ians don't go out and make sales pitches. . . . I'm not a sales-man." [9] The lack of concern for stimulating usage or attracting clients is reflected in the status of the Public Relations division of the library. It has been placed under Personnel, gets no budget, and does nothing.

When we asked a high library official about efforts to attract new clientele, he said that his restricted budget means that he can barely satisfy the demands of present users. He said that his low budget already has forced him to put many books on a reference basis (to be used at the library) rather than on a circu-lating basis, and that to court new clients would be only to in-crease demand to the intolerable point.

HOW DOES THE EFFICIENCY OF OAKLAND LIBRARIES COMPARE WITH OTHER SYSTEMS?

Comparing the effectiveness of Oakland libraries with other similar institutions is not simple because there are no acceptable performance criteria. (See Appendix B.) Moreover, there are no demand studies to reveal whether libraries are effective in creating and meeting demand for services. Data do exist, however, for the purpose of comparing Oakland with other libraries in the effi-ciency with which it circulates books. A comparatively high cost of circulation suggests, at least, that there is a lack of effectiveness in expanding demand. If more people were using the library, there would be a substantial reduction in the cost per book circulated. We shall compare Oakland with twelve large library systems, and with all libraries in California. No matter how one performs the comparison, Oakland comes out badly.

The Oakland library's aging collection and failure to attract new clients for either education or recreation results in very low circulation. In a survey of thirteen libraries in California cities with over 100,000 population (see fig. 6), Oakland was the lowest in circulation per capita. This combination of low circulation and high staff costs puts Oakland's highest by far of the thirteen Cal-ifornia libraries surveyed with regard to operating expenses per book circulated, and second highest in operating expenditure per capita.

9. Commission meeting of February 1968.

Oakland Has Second Highest Operating Cost per Capita Population

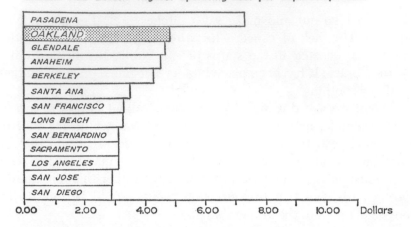

Oakland Is Lowest in Books Circulated per Capita

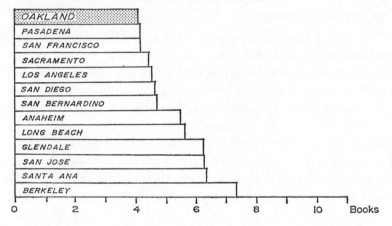

Oakland Is Third Highest in Staff per Ten Thousand Population

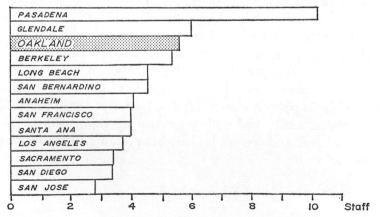

Figure 6. Summary Efficiency Measures for Thirteen California Library Systems, 1965/66, in Cities with over 100,000 Population

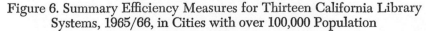

Oakland Has by Far the Highest Operating Cost per Book Circulated

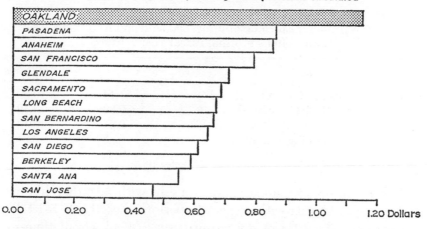

OAKLAND	
PASADENA	
ANAHEIM	
SAN FRANCISCO	
GLENDALE	
SACRAMENTO	
LONG BEACH	
SAN BERNARDINO	
LOS ANGELES	
SAN DIEGO	
BERKELEY	
SANTA ANA	
SAN JOSE	

0.00   0.20   0.40   0.60   0.80   1.00   1.20 Dollars

Oakland Has the Lowest Proportion of Books Circulated per Staff Member

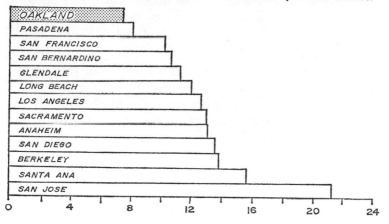

OAKLAND	
PASADENA	
SAN FRANCISCO	
SAN BERNARDINO	
GLENDALE	
LONG BEACH	
LOS ANGELES	
SACRAMENTO	
ANAHEIM	
SAN DIEGO	
BERKELEY	
SANTA ANA	
SAN JOSE	

0   4   8   12   16   20   24

Oakland Has the Highest Proportion of Professionals to Nonprofessionals

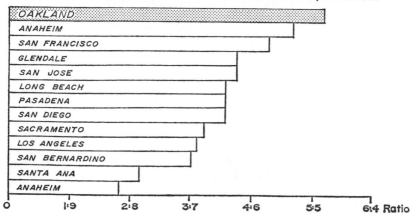

OAKLAND	
ANAHEIM	
SAN FRANCISCO	
GLENDALE	
SAN JOSE	
LONG BEACH	
PASADENA	
SAN DIEGO	
SACRAMENTO	
LOS ANGELES	
SAN BERNARDINO	
SANTA ANA	
ANAHEIM	

0   1:9   2:8   3:7   4:6   5:5   6:4 Ratio

TABLE 3-1: Oakland Libraries Spend More Money to Circulate
Fewer Books: Efficiency Ratios, Oakland and All Public
Libraries in California, Fiscal Year 1965/66

Ratios	Oakland	California
Operating Costs per Book Circulated	$1.14	$0.62
Salary Cost per Book Circulated	0.89	0.42
New Book Cost per Book Circulated	0.07	0.10
Books Circulated to Book Stock	2.48	3.65

SOURCE: *Newsnotes of Caifornia Libraries,* Winter 1966.

Oakland libraries compare unfavorably with all other library
systems in California with respect to performance. Table 3-1 tells
a sad story. The ratio of operating costs to book circulation—a
reasonable measure of efficiency in the absence of better ones—is
almost twice as high in Oakland as in the rest of the state, as is the
cost of salaries compared with books circulated. Where Oakland
should score high if it were keeping up with the times by buying
new books—the cost of new books as a proportion of those circulated—it scores only 70 percent of the rest of the state. Oakland
libraries also circulate fewer books compared with their total stock
than do other libraries. Only the city of Pasadena rivals Oakland
in the race for inefficiency.

WHY IS THE OAKLAND LIBRARY INEFFICIENT AND
PROBABLY INEFFECTIVE?

Library performance results from three factors: (1) the cultural
setting, which largely determines the significance of library services for the city; (2) the organizational context in which those allocations are made; and (3) objectives as reflected in resource
allocations.

Let us begin at the end by focusing on allocations of men and
money to different kinds of activity.

The Budget Game

The library calculates separately each of three budgeting categories—Personnel, Operations and Maintenance (O&M), and
Capital Outlay. Personnel requests consist, first, of the basic request for salary and salary increases to cover the current staff.

Second, requests include funds for additional personnel. For professional staff, the head librarian himself determines need with little or no staff consultation. For nonprofessional staff, he normally includes in his budget any requests from principal librarians.

The principal librarians select and purchase professional materials. The head librarian asks for a much larger professional materials allowance than he knows he can get, and then appeals the initial recommendation by the city manager or budget analyst prior to its going over to the city council for approval. We will discuss operation and maintenance later.

Capital outlay items, such as typewriters and shelves, are requested initially by principal librarians and usually are forwarded by the head librarian to the city. The Budget and Finance department and the city manager make substantial cuts in the requests and recommend appropriations to each of several categories.

Until 1968 the library, as an autonomous commission, could choose how to spend its total appropriation from the city. Although the city allocated money to specific categories of expenditure, these directions were not binding. Now, as a result of a charter reform, the library reports to the city manager, and he is introducing the usual controls exerted over all city departments.

Allocations: Causes, Procedure, Results

Professionalism is the key to understanding library allocations. The library is run by a staff of trained professionals as loyal to professional mores and practices as to the city and community they serve. Their standards of behavior stem from concepts fashionable years ago when they received their professional training; others derive from professional associations such as the American Library Association and California Library Association. In view of the advanced age of most of the principal librarians (over half are over fifty), as well as the highly centralized library organization under the former head librarian, it is not surprising that library standards of conduct appear to be those of another age.

The role of professionalism is enhanced by the city's acquiescence to expertise. Librarians determine their own needs for both staff and materials.

Experts Instead of Clerks

The 1940s were the years of growth for library personnel. In 1940 the main library and its branches were staffed by 170 full-time and 31 part-time employees. By 1948 the staff had grown to 234 full-time and 19 part-time persons. The basic full-time staff since 1958 has stayed at about 220 (219 being the benchmark established for full-time employees in 1962). In the thirteen-library survey in California. Oakland ranks third highest in staff per 10,000 population. Equally important is the fact that the *ratio* of professional to nonprofessional workers is very high. While most libraries the size of Oakland's have three nonprofessional employees to every two professional trained librarians, over half of Oakland's staff are professional librarians.

The large total staff and the emphasis on recruiting professionals has resulted in Oakland's high operating costs. Most large public libraries spent about 68 percent of their total budgets for salaries in 1965, but Oakland spent 85 percent.

Both staff level and the high ratio of professional to nonprofessional are rooted in the city's capitulation to the former head librarian. Though the city was unwilling to create a layoff crisis by cutting back on staff or to interfere with his decisions, it was faced with a severe revenue gap. The resulting fiscal squeeze meant that while staff was maintained, money was tight in other areas, especially for books, a category in which cuts do not create an immediate crisis. Not until 1950 did the city begin to hold back on funding new staff positions in general, and only in the 1960s did it seriously question the need for the large number of professionals.

Recruit and Promote the Congenial

The former head librarian (1943–1969) delegated no authority to members of his staff in selecting high-level professional librarians. Civil service tests—the only constraints within which he worked—produced candidates eligible for his final selection. The head librarian, in fact, had a voice in the scores applicants received on the tests, especially in the oral portion, and thus was usually able to decide whom he wanted to fill high positions on the staff. For this reason, his personality (values, needs, dispositions) became crucial in high-level personnel decisions.[10] Although personnel recruitment per se is not part of budgeting, the kind of people who are recruited largely determines where the rest of the budget (the 15 percent left over after salaries) will be spent.

To that former head librarian the two most important qualifications in choosing persons for high staff positions were, first, how closely they conformed to what he felt were the proper standards of a professional librarian, and second, how well he knew the person and how satisfactory their relationship was. Since he was an enormously energetic person who preferred to centralize much of the library work in his own office rather than delegate it, the people he got along with best were those who tended to agree with his administrative philosophy and who let him make most of the decisions. Wight and Merritt's 1955 study of the Oakland library's administrative organization illustrates this centralization, for example, by showing that eighteen persons reported directly to the head librarian.

The librarian in charge of hiring junior personnel takes into consideration what staff interviewers say about the applicant and his qualifications for the particular job, but relies even more on his personal impression of the person, the most important thing being for the applicant to be outgoing and without idiosyncrasies, that is, to be a "normal, average person." The former head librarian established this criterion for junior librarians. Sometimes he visited them personally and decided whether or not they could get along with people. If the applicant indicated that he had been unhappy with a previous job, it would rouse suspicion because he might well be unhappy in another, and no one likes unhappy people on the staff. A good candidate should be able to get along with other people; the bulk of a staff member's time was with other staff, so that harmony among staff members was most crucial when making selections. This same attitude makes the librarian reluctant to pull people off jobs after their probation periods. Failure to abide by efficiency reports for promotions within the system is explained by that emphasis on congeniality: the ability to get along counts in promotion.

The difference between the civil service and the library in

10. All statements about librarians are based on interviews with thirty-four librarians in Oakland.

choice of personnel is that civil service chooses qualified people and the library chooses nice people. Since the library has wielded more influence, nice people get to the top and qualified people who are not nice stay at the bottom. As people get closer to the top their promotions are more directly influenced by the library, and the head librarian takes an even more intense interest in who is promoted. The higher the level for hiring by the civil service, the more influential is the library in oral boards, and oral boards are the more influential in the total qualifying score of the candidate.

Leadership can maintain old values instead of introducing new ones. Because the head librarian saw the library ideally as a cultural storehouse of quality, standard works in the medium of the printed word, his staff members tended to perpetuate those values. And because of his great demand for personal loyalty on the part of those he promoted, he chose people who had stayed in the Oakland Library for some time and who would accommodate themselves to his centralized control. By this selection system, old-liners with the traditional values of the library profession of a previous generation inexorably rose to important positions.

Because the traditional professional mores of librarians dictate an attitude of aloofness, high-level staff members do not like to engage in what they call "salesmanship," that is, to reach out to potential clients and offer practical materials that might be useful when they go job hunting. They prefer to avoid community involvement, confining themselves to routine activities unless otherwise instructed by the head librarian. And because the professional ratio is so high, there is no budget money for necessary, nonprofessional work; thus professionals spend most of their time doing tasks that clerks and pages could handle. Much time is also spent trying to get supplies from the Finance Office (see below), as well as doing such actual maintenance as cleaning because the budget for that purpose is so small.

Professionals Without Professional Materials

The two major library departments which buy professional materials are Reference and Branch. The Reference Department consists of five divisions, each headed by a supervising librarian, who make the initial selections of books they hope to purchase, and send their requests to the principal librarian in charge of the Reference Department for weeding. A long and selective recruitment process has insured that both supervising and principal librarians will comply with traditional library standards in selection. They will stick with books and not try other media, and they will select standard works, with few popular and vocational books (unless there are available outside funds).

The Branch Department differs from Reference in that many book requests are initiated by librarians in charge of branches. Sifting such requests, a task perormed by the supervising librarians in charge of regions within the city, and by the department head, is thus far more extensive and selective, since these librarians have not yet passed their test of time in the system.

Because branch librarians are peculiarly exposed to community demands, as well as isolated from the scrutiny and sanctions of higher staff in the main library, they may deviate somewhat from book selection standards preferred by old-liners. But the weeding process soon brings out-of-line requests back in. Requests are homogenized as they go up the hierarchy.

The kinds of books chosen are severely limited by the small budgetary allocation for professional materials. High staff costs, a city-wide fiscal crisis, and the predominance of "uncuttable" items in the budget means that such "cuttables" as professional materials are slighted and get only residual and miniscule appropriations. Since 1954, as table 3-2 shows, the budget for professional materials has never exceeded 8.3 percent of the total budget. American Library Standards specify 20 percent as more appropriate, although the average large public library (population over 100,000) in 1960 was putting out only 14.2 percent of its budget for professional materials.[11]

While the average cost of all kinds of books (of the kind purchased by libraries) went up 49 percent from 1953/54 to 1961/62,[12] the Oakland Library increased its professional materials expenditures (of which books are the major category) by only 17

11. Helen Welch, "Costs of Library Material," *Library Trends* (April 1963).
12. Welch, ibid.

TABLE 3-2: Professional Materials (Mostly Books) Constitute Only
6 to 8 Percent of the Library Budget

Fiscal Year	Amount of Professional Material in Thousands of Dollars	Professional Material as a Percentage of Total Budget *
1953	94.0	8.9
1954	78.8	7.5
1955	90.2	8.1
1956	94.7	7.8
1957	104.7	7.9
1958	113.7	8.2
1959	126.4	8.3
1960	128.2	7.9
1961	113.3	6.8
1962	103.7	5.9
1963	106.6	7.2
1964	132.4	8.0
1965	131.7	6.3
1966	146.2	6.8

SOURCE: The Auditor-Controller's Annual Reports, unless otherwise stated.

* From Library records in Order Department.

percent. At the same time, the volume of books published has mushroomed, further increasing the costs of trying to keep up. The result is a deteriorating collection of old books.

In order to see how professional materials fit into the larger budget picture, consider its position in Operations and Maintenance. O&M consists of six categories: commodities, utilities, transportation, rent, insurance, and interest, communications, and sundry services taken together. Except for commodities all of these categories are relatively fixed in the sense that once a decision is made to establish basic facilities such as branches or reference divisions, the city is committed to spend certain amounts for utilities, transportation, rent, insurance, and communications. The two variables—commodities and sundry services—are, therefore, negotiable and cuttable. Commodities is by far the largest (normally well over half of O&M expenditure) and consists chiefly of office supplies and professional materials. Office supplies are automatically calculated on the basis of rising costs to meet standard office needs as defined by previous outlay experience. The budget officer of the library submits a request for supplies, and in recent years has simply added about $1,000 to each previous year's budget unless, for example, the opening of a new facility dictates a larger adjustment. The city does not severely cut supply requests.

But the professional materials budget is another story. This budget is controllable because it can be cut without creating a crisis. Accordingly, the head librarian submits a large request for this item, expecting a large cut. After the tentative recommendation from the city's Budget and Finance Department, he makes a pitch for an increase. Nevertheless, high salary costs along with the city's reluctance to expand revenues means that there is not enough money to meet his desires. This is true also for sundry services and expenses, including maintenance of grounds and buildings, another negotiable item. In 1964/65, for instance, the city cut the library's O&M request by $47,187. Of that figure, $29,085 came from commodities and all but less than $100 of the rest came from sundry services and expenses. In 1965/66, of the total O&M cut of $33,844, $28,706 came from commodities, most of the rest from sundry services and expenses. And in 1966/67, the total cut was $80,520, of which $63,965 came from commodities and all but $200 of the rest from sundry services and expenses. Though the budget does not specify just where cuts in these two categories are made, interviews led to the conclusion that the commodities cut was in professional materials, and the slash in sundry services came from maintenance. The high ratio of professional to nonprofessional, and the rigidity of the budget make painfully clear the implication of the professional as clerk and janitor.

The squeeze of salaries and O&M "automatics" on a relatively fixed total city appropriation to the library has led to a lopsided expenditure pattern for the library. Professional materials (see table 3-3) have slowly declined as a percentage of total expenditure from approximately 9 percent in 1953/54 to 6 percent in 1962/63, with a slight rise to nearly 7 percent in 1966/67.

Capital Outlay

Capital Outlay (usually a larger, one-time expenditure) is deferable; hence cuts are drastic. The average reduction in the Capital

Outlay request was 47.8 percent from 1960/61 to 1966/67. In 1965/66 and 1966/67 the cut was as high as 70 percent. Since 1950, Capital Outlay has represented more than 1 percent of the total expenditure for only four budget years, two of which (1965/66 and 1966/67) involved expenditures upgrading a single branch (Montclair). A similar fate has befallen Oakland's Capital Improvements program, which each year since 1963 has promised major investments in the future development of all city departments. The city council has yet to approve it.

Two things make for such meat-chopper cutting. For one thing, the head librarian normally forwards requests he gets from his principal librarians without doing any pruning himself. He only has his finance officer calculate cost estimates for requested items and establish some sort of ranking. The library really lets the city do all the cutting for Capital Outlay. For another, the head librarian does not make a strong pitch for Capital Outlay. This division of labor reflects his own attitude toward professionalism. He expects deference to his expertise in matters concerning librarianship, and reciprocates by letting financial people determine finances.

Summary: Books Are What Is Left Over

The central problem in the allocation of resources is residual budgeting. Oakland has had to live with large staff buildups inherited from the past. Substantial sums required to pay salaries have, therefore, largely squeezed out other expenditures. Books are a residual category. That is why Oakland spends less on library materials (see table 3-3) than twelve comparable cities. In fact, the next lowest city spends 60 percent more and the top three spend over 300 percent more than does Oakland.

To the extent that calculating across categories is attempted, it is on a bottleneck basis: an appropriate response is made only when the bad expenditure mix creates a crisis. Books have been purchased over the years, for instance, without a proportionate investment in shelf space. Thus many books have had to be stored or kept in places where rapid deterioration has occurred.

THE BRANCHES: WHERE THEY ARE, HOW THEY LOOK

Our purpose in analyzing the Oakland Library branch system is to determine whether its personnel, facilities, and services could

TABLE 3-3: Oakland Spends Less Than Comparable Cities
on Professional Materials
Operating Expenditures 1965/66

	Total	Per Capita	Salaries Expenditure (%)	Library Materials Expenditure (%)	Salary Expenditure Per Capita	Book Expenditure Per Capita
Anaheim	$ 695,956	$4.63	$ 446,818 (64)	$ 145,000 (21)	$2.96	$0.97
Berkeley	527,308	4.38	380,268 (72)	82,682 (16)	3.15	0.70
Glendale	646,056	4.76	434,289 (67)	69,547 (11)	3.19	0.52
Long Beach	1,418,330	3.81	1,117,380 (79)	144,095 (10)	3.01	0.38
Los Angeles	8,568,016	3.08	6,488,446 (76)	1,163,018 (14)	2.34	0.43
Oakland	1,864,186	4.83	1,465,160 (79)	118,721 (6)	3.81	0.29
Pasadena	912,607	7.30	725,551 (80)	92,241 (10)	5.84	0.73
Sacramento	801,707	3.11	557,899 (70)	98,192 (12)	2.18	0.37
San Bernardino	315,219	3.14	236,398 (75)	38,569 (12)	2.36	0.38
San Diego	1,937,535	2.89	1,281,467 (66)	252,549 (13)	1.91	0.38
San Francisco	2,994,693	4.03	2,014,274 (67)	599,734 (20)	2.70	0.81
San Jose	1,035,591	2.88	577,018 (56)	114,440 (11)	1.61	0.32
Santa Ana	473,915	3.49	314,403 (66)	88,252 (19)	2.30	0.66

SOURCE: *Newsnotes of California Libraries*, Winter 1967.

be put to better use. We first ask about how things work now, which is important if one wants to suggest doing things differently in the future. Thus we ask: Where are branches now located? Why? Where should they be? What kind of people do the branch libraries now serve? Why? Should the branches serve other types of people as well? What kind of books does the library buy for each branch? Why? Should it buy different books? Our basic assumption is that the library should be adapted to the people and not the other way around.

Historically the Oakland Library branch system developed through the initiative of local citizen groups. At various times these groups petitioned the Library Commission and the city council for branch facilities. In addition to the main library, at the time of this study, there were twenty-two branches, most of which were located along Oakland's two major north-south channels, MacArthur Boulevard and East Fourteenth Street. Of the branch buildings, the city owned thirteen and rented nine others. Each branch is intended to be a miniature main library and to service a geographically defined area.

The Oakland Library has also set up six regional service areas, each of which has one branch designated as the regional branch, with a larger staff and a more comprehensive collection. In theory they are scaled-down main libraries, bridging the gap between the main library and local branches. Their existence, however, does not seem to make any significant contribution to the branch system.

The location, size, and appearance of the branches are very important in determining library use. Although library services are provided free of charge, their consumption still involves a cost to the user in terms of travel, time, and inconvenience as well as actual transportation costs. The quality of the branches and their accessibility to the public can be viewed as directly determining this cost.

The present sites were not selected with effective library service in mind. A local benefactor donated some of the land or the building, or the city had a piece of vacant land available in the vicinity of the desired location, or a local school had a vacant site it could donate to the library. If all these possibilities failed, the library staff and the local citizens contacted realtors to find an inexpensive lot. While such practices may have appeared to save money at the time, they did not always contribute to long-run effectiveness. The John Swett branch, for example, was given free to the library, but it was six blocks from the nearest shopping area and eighteen blocks from the closest high school. Undoubtedly this unfavorable site contributed to the fact that this branch, with the third lowest circulation in the whole system in 1965/66, was abolished. The Gibson branch, also donated to the library (and with the next lowest circulation), is in a hilly area, which discourages pedestrian use, and lacks adequate parking facilities.

The physical appearance of the branches is nondescript or worse. There are no distinguishing characteristics to attract the passerby, no prominent signs or window displays (with Fruitvale a notable exception). Inside the branches are institutional and uninviting. Many have inadequate space. Improvements in atmosphere and physical setting would make the library a more pleasant place to be and might encourage use.

The sites of many branches could be improved. Dimond, for example, needs larger quarters. Elmhurst and Ina B. Coolbrith are set back too far off the street to attract passersby. Lockwood is so short of space that books are piled on tables and jammed into inadequate shelf space. Inadequate maintenance results in the deterioration of facilities. The burden of poor maintenance falls disproportionately on poverty-area branches where low demand for standard works is taken to indicate lesser need for allocations. The consequent deterioration further reduces the desire of residents to use the facilities; one has only to glance through a city report on maintenance of library facilities to understand this: table 3-4 shows defects ranging from cracked toilet seats to peeling walls. All branches have their troubles but some have more than their share. In this way, as in so many others, the city called Oakland looks different at the top of the hills than it does in the flatlands.

A Single City But Many Styles

The historical concept of a library service area as a circle of some radius around the library now has little value. The mobility and travel habits of library users effectively determine the size and shape of the service areas that develop today. User patterns

TABLE 3-4: Maintenance Condition of Main and Branch Library
Buildings in Oakland

Branch of Library by Income	Defects	
	Functional (Safety Hazards)	Aesthetic (Appearance)
Main	Walls, plaster cracked and falling; ceiling tile and moulding loose and hanging	Ceiling vents have rings of soot from exhaust; dirty walls, windows, ledges, blinds, radiators, skylight, etc.; walls and ceiling need painting; restrooms need cleaning—smell
$0 to $5,000 Jack London	Ceiling leaking; floor tile cracking; holes in walls; tile floor bleeding; toilet, ceiling plaster falling; toilet vent hanging	Walls and ceiling cracking; floor needs stripping and waxing; walls need painting
C. S. Green	*First Floor:* All floor tile is buckling; door warped, hard to open and close; toilets need new seats, flush tank covers, general cleaning; janitor room needs general repair. *Second Floor:* Radiators leak; linoleum cracking and buckling; staffroom window broken; utility room has a toilet floor rotting, walls half-painted, very bad wood floor, half of ceiling fallen, bad leaky radiators, general deplorable conditions; library stacks have glass floor with several broken squares	*First Floor:* Ceiling water-marked and paint chipping; wall needs painting, water-marks; auditorium has wax build-up on floor, stained floors, and lost finish on window facing, ledges, and baseboards; outside granite steps need cleaning. *Second Floor:* Staffroom has water-stained ceiling (extensive), walls very cracked and peeled, wax build-up; library stacks walls need painting, shelves to dust
West Oakland	Windows rotten; concrete floor in toilet cracked and patched; stacks of paper that appear to be fire hazard	Linoleum cracked; ceiling cracked; wax build-up; wood slat blinds in bad shape

Branch of Library by Income	Defects	
	Functional (Safety Hazards)	Aesthetic (Appearance)
$5,000 to $7,000 Melrose		Floor stained, wax build-up; basement linoleum worn out
Temescal	Wide cracks in linoleum; toilet seat needs changing (wood); weak floor in spots; one room in basement completely rotted floor	Wax build-up; basement walls peeling
Elmhurst	Sink top rotten; ceiling tile loose; door and window broken	Tables need refinishing; window needs painting; walls cracked
Lockwood		Blinds dusty; counter and tables refinish
Fruitvale (Latin-American)	Weak spot in floor; ceiling leaks; plaster water-soaked	Shades under skylight need replacing; wood floor needs refinishing; toilet floor needs painting; steps need painting; water-soaked window ledge; mezzanine floor refinish
Coolbrith	Toilets need new covers; basement toilet needs flush tank tops and toilet seat; a number of windows broken out	Pock-marked and patched floor tile; battleship linoleum old, cracked and patched; tables badly need refinishing; basement walls need painting; steps need refinishing
Golden Gate	South wall leaks, water-stained and peeling; wood floor in basement all rotted away	Walls in basement peeling
$7,000 and over Rockridge		Floor tile chipped and cracked; wax build-up; moulding cracked

TABLE 3-4: (*continued*)

Branch of Library by Income	Defects	
	Functional (Safety Hazards)	Aesthetic (Appearance)
Montclair	Crash bar on door front out of order; improper light fixtures—some tied with string	Corners dirty; slight wax build-up. Air vents dusty; desks and tables need refinishing
Piedmont		Wood slat blinds need changing; linoleum old and dry in spots; wax build-up
Brookfield	Ceiling leaks, needs painting; back door broken; weather strip on door falling apart	Wax build-up; window ledges need painting
Dimond	Flush tank top missing	Wax build-up; blinds dirty and broken
Glenview	Ceiling leaks	Wood blinds need destroying; picture window ledge needs painting; tables, refinishing; linoleum pockmarked, cracked, chipped; light fixtures dirty; windows dirty; wax build-up; floor vents dirty; brass rail unpolished
Laurel	Sink top tile rotten and loose; plate glass window loose, may fall; tile floor broken, chipped	Tile wall under window front broken; wax build-up; wall paint peeling; refinish tables
Eastmont	Need new toilet seats	Paint peeling on wall and ceiling; ceiling cracked; tile floor cracked and chipped; blinds paint chipping; wax build-up; tables need refinishing
Baymont	Hole in wall	Wax build-up; floor tile cracking; glass front dirty; ceiling paint peeling; corner cracked from floor to ceiling; blinds dirty

Branch of Library by Income	Defects	
	Functional (Safety Hazards)	*Aesthetic (Appearance)*
Lakeview	Hole in linoleum	Wax build-up; linoleum buckling; counter and tables need refinishing
Park Blvd.		Linoleum old, stained and cracked; wax build-up; plaster wall water-soaked

SOURCE: Caliph Johnson, "Report on Library Janitorial Transfer," City of Oakland, November 6, 1968.

vary in different parts of the city. The variety of the population in Oakland is reflected in different patterns of library use.

A quick glance at selected demographic data in table 3-5 indicates Oakland's diversity. We see three different neighborhoods, which vary in education, income, and racial composition. Not surprisingly, more education goes with higher income and a lower percentage of blacks.

Patrons of branches in areas of high per capita income and educational levels use their automobiles to travel to the library more frequently than do other groups. These people are also likely to combine trips to the library with shopping and, therefore, often do not frequent the branch nearest home. For them, proximity to a branch is not important in determining library use. The Baymont, Dimond, and Rockridge branches, which they use, display spread-out service areas, drawing some of their patrons from far beyond what would be considered their local service area: 75 to 80 percent of their users drive to the library.

People in areas of medium income and educational level exhibit slightly different user patterns. They are more evenly split be-

TABLE 3-5: Income, Education, and Race Vary According to Neighborhood in Oakland

Area	*Years of Median Education*	*Median Family Income*	*Percentage of Blacks*
Montclair	13.2	$10,000	0.8
Park Boulevard	11.1	5,851	17.1
West Oakland	8.8	3,500	80.4

tween the automobile and foot as a means of travel to the library. In these areas, too, branches in or near shopping centers tend to have larger circulations and a higher proportion of use by adults. The Lockwood and Elmhurst branches have slightly tighter user patterns than the previous group, but their service areas are still skewed in favor of traffic along major arterial highways.

Libraries in lower socioeconomic areas have smaller user areas. More of their patrons are juveniles and there are fewer adults than elsewhere. A large proportion of people using these branches walk, partly because of the large proportion of juvenile users, but also because in high-density population neighborhoods it makes more sense to walk than in suburban, low-density neighborhoods where destinations are normally greater distances from one another.

Library users in low-income areas do not combine library trips with shopping, nor do they commonly make use of other branches in the system, indicating a low level of interest in whatever libraries have (or are perceived to have) to offer.

The Oakland resident can choose from many branches; his choice depends largely on the distance to be traveled and his mobility, as well as the relative quality of the branch. If all branches were identical, the user would choose the closest. If they are not, however, as in Oakland, a user (with a car) might be willing to travel farther if he considered the branch to be of high enough quality to compensate for the extra distance.

In a further study of the distribution of Oakland's library users, Teitz and one of his students, James Gibbs, drew a random sample of borrowers' cards from the file in several branches and plotted their addresses on a map to find the distances traveled by these users. Except for those in Piedmont and Baymont, at least 80 percent of the users lived within a one-mile radius. Very few traveled more than 2.5 miles, which may give a rough idea of the maximum distance people are likely to go for library services.

Let us take two branches—Jack London and Piedmont—to illustrate spatial relationships. All users in the Jack London branch live within six-tenths of a mile of it. This suggests that most people walk because it is in a poor area where population mobility is low, where a high proportion of use is by children, and where the branch collection is not of sufficient quality to attract people from farther away. The Piedmont branch, on the other hand, has users from fairly great distances. This suggests that the people are mobile, that the area for which it is the closest branch is large, and that it has a good enough collection to attract people from as far as three miles away. All branches in the Oakland library clearly are not alike and should not be treated the same.

Centralized Books and Decentralized Preferences

The number and type of books ordered in the branches depends on (1) the standards of the librarians and (2) a formula for ordering based on previous circulation.

Branch librarians are uniquely exposed to the needs and desires of community residents. If they hope to move up to higher positions in the system, however, they must accommodate themselves instead to current "professional" standards. That is, they must maintain some degree of aloofness from the preferences of community residents, except for those who request "quality" works. Involvement in community affairs is disdained by the old-liners and those at the top. Those who do get involved tend to remain branch librarians for many years.

The *same kinds* of books are purchased for *all* branches, regardless of the characteristics, needs, and desires of the local population. Few vocational books and manuals, no temporary or popular fiction, and hardly any books on current issues are purchased in lower-income areas although they are in high demand. Because limited book budgets make tight priority purchasing mandatory, quality works are ordered only if prior circulation indicates future demand. Hence, most of the book money goes into quality books for branches in middle- and upper-income neighborhoods where circulation is already high. Treatment is uniform but unresponsive. There is equal treatment for different neighborhoods.

Because existing circulation is used as a basis for ordering books, a vicious circle is created in which inappropriate book stocks in lower-income areas reduces circulation; this in turn leads to fewer book purhases for such branches; fewer new book acquisitions lead to further declines in circulation. The fewer books you have, the fewer you get. It works in reverse, of course, for branches in wealthy areas where quality works are in use.[13]

13. See circulation figures in "Library Operations Preliminary Analysis," Thomas Huebner, Budget and Finance Department, Oakland, California, 1968.

In order to determine the pattern of demand for book acquisitions and circulation among branches, Michael Teitz and his students studied requests and borrowing by using the Dewey decimal system under which books are ordered in catalogs. They found, by and large, the same demands in all branches. Since Oakland's population manifests considerable variety and there are geographic concentrations of groups by race, income, and education, they concluded that the library attracted a certain type of user, who is found to some extent in all areas of the city. But there are more of these typical users in some neighborhoods. Circulation statistics show they are found disproportionately in areas with high income and educational levels. Circulation is high where they are concentrated and low where they are not. Library service evidently is appropriate only for a particular life style, and it is this life style that is crucial in determining use of library facilities.

Recognizing the possibility that the Dewey decimal categories conceal variations in supply and demand among branches, Teitz and his students decided to conduct a more sensitive study. They chose a high-income branch (Montclair) and a low-income branch (West Oakland) for a detailed comparison. They took several samples of data that gave actual book titles at each branch. One was a sample of book orders not filled (March 1966 to May 1967). To this was added a sample of books received by the branches but for which catalog cards had not arrived. The other sample was one of circulation for a two-week period (May 10 to May 31, 1967).[14]

Titles of the books for which cards were drawn were examined and assigned to categories following divisions of the Dewey decimal system. New decimal categories had already been assigned for the circulated books, but this was not true for ordered books. Here, classification was made by using titles as clues to subject matter; occasional errors in judgment, therefore, are entirely possible.[15]

14. The sample of books ordered, taken at random, represents 20 to 30 percent of all unfilled orders. The sampling of books circulated at Montclair was random (about 10 to 15 percent of total circulation). At the West Oakland branch every third and fifth card, respectively, was taken because the records there are kept by category rather than date due, as is done at Montclair.

15. The magnitudes of the proportions for West Oakland and Montclair

TABLE 3-6: West Oakland Readers Differ from Montclair's:
West Oakland Readers Like Sociology and Government
and Montclair Likes Fiction

Number of books in:	Assignment of Circulation Samples to Storage Categories (Actual Decimal Classification Known)												
	Gen 000	Philo 100	Relig 200	Soc *Gov* 300	Lang 400	Sci 500	Tech 600	Art 700	Lit 800	Hist 900	Trav 900	Biog	Fic
West Oakland Branch	6	0	4	21	2	8	9	11	8	0	8	4	19
Montclair Branch	0	5	1	8	0	4	12	11	7	7	8	3	35

West Oakland and Montclair (see table 3-6) exhibit general similarities in circulation for most of the Dewey decimal categories. Montclair readers, however, show a stronger preference for fiction, and a really strong differential appears which suggests that West Oakland branch users prefer books about sociology and government. When the titles in these categories are examined more closely, it can be seen that a large part of the demand in West Oakland is accounted for by the fact that books on jobs and careers are predominant in the 300-series circulation. Five of the eleven books that appeared in the circulation sample from West Oakland are job related. Another four are books on the civil rights movement and on current Negro affairs. The remaining two deal with the basic institutions of state and local government. The titles in the 300-series that appear in the circulation sample at the Montclair branch, on the other hand, deal with more general topics: international relations, economic history, the sociology of contemporary American life, and political studies.

A look at titles circulated in the 500-series (Science) shows that half of those circulated at the West Oakland branch were basic arithmetic texts. In the 700-series, books on the arts predominated

generally conform well to the previous tabulations on yearly circulation, which suggests that the smaller sample is indicative of the general pattern. But none of the variations in demand indicated by this more detailed breakdown are very great. These remarks should be thought of as marginal refinements of the conclusions based on the full-year statistics of circulation.

at Montclair, while books on sports, games, and entertainment were most in evidence at West Oakland. Significantly, perhaps, orders at Montclair often involved sports that require an investment in equipment, the availability of leisure time, and mobility, such as mountaineering and hiking. Noteworthy differences in book orders also appear in the 800-series on Literature and Fiction. At Montclair there was relative emphasis on the classics, which was not seen at West Oakland, where mysteries seem to be popular, both in circulation and in requests.

Although an overview of branch circulation suggests that more or less the same kind of people (with higher education and income) use branches, the more refined analysis above suggests that reader preferences do differ significantly from one area of the city to another. It should be possible to capitalize on these differences, therefore, by buying different books for branches whose clientele varies and would probably vary more if wider services were available. In order to effect such changes the pattern by which book orders are based on past circulation must be altered. If the branch that has gets, the branches that have not will continue to receive even less. Branch librarians should be encouraged to be more responsive than they are now to consumer preferences when ordering books. Central librarians should not be permitted to veto requests that reflect local preferences. In our final set of recommendations we will develop an alternative to present library organization that will meet these requirements. For the time being, we must look at the libraries' present efforts to stimulate demand for its services.

Promotional Programs: Is the Library Stimulating Demand?

Many people are unaware of the existence of the library, and many who already use the library are unaware of the variety of services offered. Though promotional programs exist to introduce people to the library and to encourage more intensive use by present users, they are now a subordinate function of the personnel department and no money is budgeted specifically for them. Instead, money is received from several categories, such as "miscellaneous" or "office supplies" so the exact amount being spent is hard to determine. It is safe to say, however, that it is small.

Promotional programs include (1) *Visits to organizations*. At the request of various groups the library will send out speakers to inform people about its services. This is a major program in terms of time and effort on the part of the staff. (2) *Calendar of events.* Perhaps the most ambitious program, this is a quarterly publication announcing the time, place, and nature of a number of special events presented by the library, which include films, lectures, and special classes. Three thousand are printed, half of which are sent to the "Friends of the Library" and to others who have requested them; the remainder are distributed to the library itself. This is relatively inexpensive and worthwhile. (3) *Book lists.* These are sometimes prepared to complement events such as garden and hobby shows. They are useful and inexpensive, but they do not reach very many people. (4) *Advertising.* The library purchases time on radio and television during National Library Week. Some librarians have indicated a distaste for this because they felt it was "too commercial."

The most serious weakness of the promotional programs is that they reach only a limited audience, most of whom already use the library. Such programs do not touch the large number of potential users who are unaware of or presently uninterested in library services. One librarian complained that she had wanted to put up a sign in front of her branch so that people might see the branch more readily, but that she had not been able to because approval had not been received from the head librarian's office.

When we asked a librarian about the role of the branch vis-à-vis its potential clientele, she began by denying that a library can really be successful in inducing people to use it. She said that book reading is like dope—you either get hooked, or you don't. We asked whether the library could hook people who weren't hooked yet, and she replied that "local cultural and social patterns leave no room for reading." According to her, low circulation is rooted in a situation which the library can never hope to change. The community is "semi-illiterate" with the exception of junior college students and professionals, who have access to better libraries. She feels, therefore, that the library can play only a passive role in the community.

Another librarian said that she spends most of her time keeping up with all the recent book reviews. She justified her passive attitude toward low circulation by pointing out that her branch was unnecessary, inconveniently located, and in a "deteriorating neighborhood." Her low book budget, she said, and not her own passivity, was the cause of poor circulation. The people in her service area now want how-to books, occupational books, mysteries, and temporary (undesirable) literature. She has responded by ordering more occupational and repair manuals, but she doesn't want to order literature with little educational value or a short user-life. Her major interest, not surprisingly, is in getting out of her branch. She made several passing remarks about the "bad neighborhood" and "bad reading habits" of people in her area, though the neighborhood still is a much higher income area than that of the majority of the branches.

Is the Branch System Fair?

We can summarize our previous discussion by saying that while the educational and recreational needs of persons in middle- and upper-income areas are being met (qualitatively, if not quantitatively), those of lower-income persons are not. The combination of poor and often irrelevant collections, a small total branch budget, the vicious circulation-allocation cycle, and the consequent deterioration of poverty-area buildings means that the branch system provides little education or recreation for those city residents who need it most.

The notion of equity in public services has to do with who gets the benefits with respect to who pays. In Oakland the library is financed indirectly through property taxes and we know that everyone is not paying the same amount; given this method of financing, two ways of distributing the benefits could be considered equitable. One is that everyone receives the same amount of benefit; another is that everyone receives a share of the total benefits equal to his share of the total cost. Neither rule is "better." Which to adopt reflects the values of the institution or person choosing.

Everyone Should Get the Same Amount of Benefit

The equity rule here would be for everyone to receive the same amount of benefit regardless of the amount that they pay. If we assume that the marginal benefit of another unit of library service is the same for everyone in Oakland, then we can say that if everyone receives the same amount of input, everyone receives the same amount of benefit. (Inputs, like expenditures, are not measures of outputs, like books read, but we have no choice.) If we use expenditures at a branch as the input, then the distribution of benefits is equitable if the expenditures per resident of the service areas are equal. Table 3-7 shows that the situation in Oakland, except for the Golden Gate branch, is inequitable by this criterion.

Taking six branches with 20,000 to 26,000 residents in their service areas, the expenditure per resident varies from $2.53 at Greene to $.65 at Lockwood. Greene might be expected to have higher expenditures because of its storage function for periodicals, but the combined Glenview and Dimond branches have an expenditure of $1.96 per resident, which is significantly larger than the $.65 spent at Lockwood and the $.75 at Temescal. If we assume that everyone should receive the same amount of benefit, the distribution of library benefits in Oakland is not equitable.

TABLE 3-7: Distribution of Library Benefits Is Not Equitable: Total Cost per Resident in Branch Service Area

Branch	Cost per Resident	Income Group *	Branch	Cost per Resident	Income Group *
			West		
Golden Gate	$3.62	Poor	Oakland	$1.83	Poor
Montclair	2.80	Comfortable	Laurel	1.51	Comfortable
Gibson/					
Eastmont	2.56	Average	Melrose	1.41	Average
			Fruitvale/Ina		
Greene	2.53	Poor	Coolbrith	1.22	Poor
			Park Blvd./		
Piedmont	2.46	Average	Lakeview	1.05	Comfortable
Rockridge	2.14	Comfortable	Baymont	1.00	Average
Glenview/					
Dimond	1.96	Comfortable	Temescal	.80	Average
Swett	1.95	Comfortable	Elmhurst	.79	Poor
			Lockwood	.65	Poor
			J. London	.50	Poor

* Income group determined by response of librarians on Branch Questionnaire.

The Share of Benefits a Person Receives Should Be Equal
to the Share of the Costs He Pays

To evaluate the branch system, to determine whether people get what they pay for, we would have to know which ones actually contribute to Oakland's revenues. It has not been possible to assess the specific proportion of taxes stemming from different income groups in Oakland, but property tax studies include independently compiled estimates that are quite consistent from region to region in the United States. Table 3-8, column (1), shows the average median income for service area residents taken from 1960 U.S. Census data. Column (2) shows the percentage of total property tax receipts paid by three income groups; the percentages are from Netzer's 1966 study of the *Economics of the Property Tax* for the Brookings Institution.[16] His data are presented for these income groups; comparisons thus are based on an aggregation of the branches into the three income categories.

Whether the output is measured by expenditures or by circulation, table 3-8 shows that low-income areas of Oakland are receiving a smaller share of the benefits from the library branch system than their share of contributions to total tax revenues. Our conclusion is that, if the goal of equity is to be achieved, a general shift of expenditures must be made from high- and middle- to low-income area branches.

There is one Oakland branch library—the Latin American Library—to which many of the criticisms made in this evaluation do not apply. This library, established in 1965, is located in the Fruitvale neighborhood, which has a large Mexican-American population. It is unique in respect to the other Oakland libraries in that it was purposely established as a compensatory institution tailored to meet the needs of the particular group of people who use it. It offers classes in Spanish and English, in citizenship and consumer education, Latin American cultural programs and art exhibits, community meeting space, and a bilingual collection of 20,000 books. The capacity of this library to reach the community

16. These percentages allow us to make some crude comparisons although the distribution of property tax may differ for Oakland and there are considerable nonproperty-tax supports of the library (e.g. sales tax and utilities tax).

TABLE 3-8: Low-Income Groups Receive Fewer Benefits from Library
Branches Than Their Total Tax Contribution: Comparison of
Proportionate Taxes Paid with Total Library Expenditures,
and Total Circulation, by Income Group

(1) Average Median Income by Branches (families) [a]	(2) Distribution of [b] Tax Payments (percent)	(3) Distribution of Library Expenditures (percent)	(4) Col. 3 — Col. 2	(5) Distribution of Circulation (percent)	(6) Col. 5 — Col. 2
$7,000 and over	45.8	52.9 [$264,607]	+7.1	70.1 [$818,319]	+24.3
Lockridge Montclair Piedmont Swett Dimond/ Glenview Laurel Gibson/ Eastmont Baymont Park/ Lakeview					
$5,000 to $7,000	22.3	30.3 [$151,537]	+8.0	26.2 [$305,174]	+3.9
Melrose Temescal Elmhurst Lockwood Fruitvale/ Coolbrith Golden Gate					
$0 to $5,000	31.9	16.8 [$83,977]	−15.1	3.7 [$42,703]	−28.2
Jack London Greene West Oakland					

[a] 1960 U.S. Census Data, Average for Tracts in Branch Service Area.
[b] SOURCE: Table 3-9, Estimated Property Taxes on Nonfarm Housing, 1959–60, by Income Class, in D. Netzer, *Economics of the Property Tax* (Washington, D.C.: The Brookings Institution, 1966), p. 54.

is enhanced by its operation of a Bookmobile, which circulates throughout the community a representative selection of the library's resources. All twelve of the staff members who work with the public are bilingual, and eight of these twelve are Mexican American.

The funding for the library has been primarily federal. Under the Library Services and Construction Act of 1965, the library has received approximately $90,000 in federal funds each year from 1966 through 1972. Over this period, the federal government paid $338,293 and the city paid $69,993 for salaries for the library staff. Throughout the twenty-eight months from December, 1969, to April, 1972, circulation has fluctuated from a monthly low of 2,978 volumes to a high of 5,715 volumes. During the thirty-six months of 1966–1969, each volume cost approximately $2.04 to circulate, though many activities not directly related to circulation were carried out. The language element makes it difficult to compare circulation in the Fruitvale branch with the others in Oakland.

1968: The Bubble Bursts

"It is obvious to anyone concerned that the Oakland library system is in a state of crisis. Costs are increasing and circulation is declining. Changes *must* be made if our library system is to survive as a viable public institution meeting the needs of our citizens." So said a budget analyst in the City of Oakland. As the inadequacy of the library has been cumulative over the last twenty years, it is not surprising that a city management devoted to increasing efficiency should eventually blow the whistle.

Until 1968 the past ruled the present: past commitments (in staff and basic facilities) were maintained, and the library retained substantial autonomy by allocating increases to staff rather than operating or capital outlay expenses. Then the city cracked down. The budget analyst recommended that the proportion of professional staff be reduced, and that branches with very low circulation be eliminated. The city manager instructed civil service to fill no open positions in the library until he was satisfied that future changes in staffing would be effected. Compared with staff, the book budget was increased in the 1970 budget. "I've been riding the Library harder than any other department," City Manager

Keithley declared at the city council budget hearings. Councilman Binns complained, "Why, I walked into the Jack London square branch once and found the employees outnumbered the patrons. They invited me to sit down and play bridge with them." As the *Oakland Tribune* reported on June 17, 1970, "There were murmurs of a 10 percent slash in the library's proposed $2.3 million budget for 1970–71 and threats to close some of the branches." Since then one branch has been closed and others have been threatened, only to be saved by last minute political protest.

RECOMMENDATIONS FOR THE OAKLAND LIBRARY SYSTEM

The city government is interested in efficiency and economy. It wants to see its money go into inputs that produce the greatest output (here, circulation) and it would like, as well, to reduce inputs of tax money wherever possible, regardless of potential output. Unfortunately, the coupling of efficiency with economy in determining library inputs could have adverse effects on effectiveness. The problem is that, in addition to the gross inefficiencies of the library (its low circulation and usage counts relative to the resources it gets), there is little serious attempt to improve library performance by attracting new clients, or recombining the same resources to produce better results. Rather, inefficient units (chiefly branches) are given fewer resources or are even eliminated. We recommend trying to combine efficiency (producing the most output for a specified input) with effectiveness (reaching the people who ought to benefit from library services). City outputs would be more efficient, and outcomes for citizens would be more desirable.

Is there unfulfilled demand for the services libraries in Oakland might offer? Fragmentary evidence suggests so. Branch libraries have difficulty in purchasing a sufficient number of civil service exams and in meeting requests for popular literature. Preferences for books do vary significantly among the branches, yet some branch librarians have had difficulty in honoring these requests or have not even tried. Librarians at various levels are disinclined to meet the existing demand or to cultivate new ones. Here we are on firmer ground. The library system does not try very hard to reach low-income people. If it did make serious and strenuous efforts without improving effective demand, we might then ask whether the people wanted library services. Since the library has not moved in this direction, however, it cannot say that its best efforts have failed. The library must bear the onus for failure until (like Avis) it tries harder. Recommendations of this study are designed to further that effort.

Since our objective is to help make the branch system of the Oakland Library more efficient and more effective, we begin with recommendations designed (given the present level of expenditures) to increase use of library services, and conclude with recommendations to increase effectiveness by reaching people the library does not now serve and by giving present users better service. The library system has an opportunity to serve more people

TABLE 3-9: The Cost of Circulating a Book in the Branches
Varies Greatly (1965/66)

Branch	Circulation	Cost per Book Circulated
Montclair	96,182	.349
Piedmont	63,575	.319
Gibson	30,544	.577
Eastmont	60,665	.333
Rockridge	54,024	.368
Laurel	87,071	.346
Park Blvd.	44,304	.422
Lakeview	132,475	.275
Golden Gate	26,386	.805
J. Swett [since closed]	27,856	.620
Melrose	61,593	.529
Glenview	66,200	.327
Dimond	79,533	.292
Baymont	55,972	.431
Fruitvale	32,590	.603
I. Coolbrith	40,764	.477
Elmhurst	55,056	.460
Temescal	53,875	.483
W. Oakland	14,800	1.130
Lockwood	34,910	.552
Greene	25,098	1.428
J. London	2,805	2.669

in better ways with only modest increases in costs. Everything depends on willingness to adjust library activities to the substantial change in population and reading preferences of the past decade.

USE OF RESOURCES

Inefficient use of resources results in high average cost in the library as a whole and in some branches in particular (see table 3-1, p. 178, and table 3-9). Leaving aside for a moment the question of who should be encouraged to use the library, the ideal allocation of resources is the one that results in the highest circulation (or other usage) for a given budget. Hence, we recommend that:

TABLE 3-10: In Many Branches Not Enough Books per Employee
Are Handled (1965–1966)

Wages and Salary Cost	Branch	Books per Employee *
$14,000–17,000	I. Coolbrith	22,275
	Gibson	16,161
	Eastmont	29,738
	Fruitvale	16,377
	Piedmont	31,164
	Park Blvd.	18,083
	Lockwood	18,277
	J. Swett	14,817
	W. Oakland	7,668
	Rockridge	26,353
$17,000–20,000	Baymont	23,034
	Elmhurst	24,254
	Glenview	29,163
	Temescal	20,801
$23,000–26,000	Dimond	35,421
	Greene	8,228
	Laurel	27,997
	Melrose	21,461
$27,000–30,000	Montclair	28,797
	Lakeview	34,862

* Includes librarians, pages, and clerk-typists, weighted by salary.

Wages and Salaries (dollars)

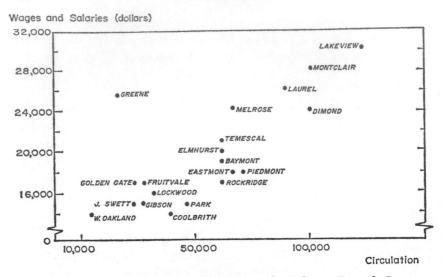

Figure 7. An Excess Capacity of Labor in the Library Branch System,
1965/66

The Library Should Spend Less on Labor

The branch system is overstaffed. Many branches could handle increased book circulation without increased labor costs.

Figure 7 shows that branches spending $14,000–$17,000 a year on labor (two employees) can circulate up to 66,000 books a year. Further evidence of overcapacity can be found in table 3-10, which shows the number of books circulated per employee. It appears that although it is possible to handle as many as 35,000 books per employee, some branches achieve less than 10,000 per employee. These tables indicate the increase in circulation which could be handled with the current staff.

An attempt to reduce the high labor cost could include either reducing the size of the staff or maintaining current staff and increasing circulation. Another way to reduce labor costs is to hire people with less expensive formal qualifications who can do the job. The present policy is to staff each branch with at least two professionals—one senior and one junior librarian. In branches such as Golden Gate and Lakeview, the demand is much less than two professional staff persons would normally handle. While it is arguable whether even one professional is needed at every branch, other personnel in smaller branches could and should be nonprofessionals. As the current professional staff moves and retires (many are elderly) they should be replaced until a proper balance is achieved.

The Library Should Spend More Money on Books

Though library policy discourages weeding branch stocks of old and unused titles, current stock needs a heavy pruning that might reduce its size as much as 10 to 15 percent. A policy based on book-stock figures which overstates the number of books that still have active use has tended to understate the need for new book expenditures. Since book prices have increased at a faster rate in the past ten years than the amount allocated for books, the undersupply is getting worse rather than better. Buying more books must, of course, go hand in hand with reduction of personnel costs as stated in the first recommendation.

The Library Should Allocate More Book Funds to Branches of Currently Low Circulation

Low-circulation branches receive the smallest allocations for new books. When a neighborhood is not making full use of the library, this does not imply that fewer books should be bought for that branch than for one that is more heavily used. In economic terms, if there is an untapped market, the marginal productivity of a dollar spent in this new market is likely to be higher than one in an established market.

Since the branch system is overloaded with personnel (see fig. 5 and table 3-11), new expenditures for other needed inputs would be more effective in increasing library use. More labor inputs can be characterized as having decreasing returns to circulation. The incremental value of more books is likely to be high, since they are an underutilized input.

The Library Should Spend More Money on Rent

A major factor influencing use of a library is the building itself. A number of improvements might be made that would encourage library use and not involve major capital expenditure. The image of the library as being dull and institutional discourages use; this could be changed by renovating existing buildings or by moving to different rented sites. Changes in lighting to make the library

TABLE 3-11: The Library Is Not Reaching Everyone

Branch	Type of Area	1965 Population	Books Circulated per Resident (1965/66)
Montclair	Comfortable	10,250	9.30
Piedmont	Average	7,890	8.05
Gibson Eastmont	Average	14,113	6.46
Rockridge	Comfortable	8,900	6.07
Laurel	Comfortable	16,913	5.15
Park Blvd. Lakeview	Comfortable	46,155	3.80
Golden Gate	Poor	7,150	3.68
J. Swett	Comfortable	8,073	3.45
Melrose	Average	18,500	3.30
Glenview Dimond	Comfortable	25,020	2.64
Baymont	Average	22,070	2.53
Fruitvale I. Coolbrith	Poor	31,840	2.30
Elmhurst	Poor	29,090	2.11
Temescal	Average	30,030	1.79
W. Oakland	Poor	9,670	1.53
Lockwood	Poor	24,490	1.42
Greene	Poor	22,210	1.13
Jack London	Poor	20,580	Closed

a more pleasant place, for example, would undoubtedly pay off in greater use of library facilities. Unfortunately, it is impossible to determine in advance what increase in circulation would result from given improvements in the buildings. Learning by doing must be the motto.

The library could do better with what it already has. By altering proportions of funds spent on books, rent, and labor, higher circulation levels are possible at the same budget level. While specific allocation problems have been stressed, it has not been possible to determine whether $100 spent on books will result in the same addition to circulation figures as $100 spent on rent. Neither have we suggested that circulation is the only comparative measure of benefits. One could hardly argue, however, that low circulation is positive benefit. Nor is there evidence to suggest that other activities in the branches make up for this deficit. A look at the total cost of the three inputs does suggest a measure of slack in the system; book and rent inputs could be used to pick up this slack. The lowest average price of a librarian, for example, is $6,363. Changing the policy of having three employees at each branch by eliminating just one staff member would make available one and a half times as much money as is currently spent on books at the system's busiest location (which happens to be $4,000). Of the now available $6,363, books expenditures could be increased to $4,000, say, and the additional $2,000 used for rent.

CONSUMPTION OF LIBRARY SERVICES

Our evidence of low consumption of library services is the small per capita circulation rate. Oakland circulates 4.2 books per capita annually against a state average of 5.3. While this comparison alone should not be taken too seriously, it does support our suspicions that the full potential for use has not be exploited.

Consumption of library services (see table 3-11) is low in some parts of the city. There are a number of ways that use could be increased. Basically these involve improving the services offered and making more people aware that the library exists and has much to offer.

Existing programs are directed primarily at people already using the library; this points out the most serious deficiency. Nonusers present a much greater potential for increased use of library services than do present users. Another serious deficiency is that promotional programs are only a subordinate function of the Personnel Department. The format of promotional programs must depend on the particular client. Variations in user groups must be taken into account. More extensive use of facilities by people already using the library can probably be accomplished by relatively simple in-library displays, book lists, and so on, but more substantial programs are needed to attract nonusers. A change in services may be necessary.

Promotional Programs Should be Designed and Carried Out
Largely at the Branch Level by Local People

If the branch professional staffs were reduced, funds would be available to hire part-time local personnel to go out into the community and encourage people to use the library, and also to inform the library of neighborhood needs. It is to be hoped that these would be reflected in the book selections. Such a program would develop the library in a much more community-oriented direction. At present, each branch tries to be a miniature Main Library, but because of population differences this is not appropriate. An effective promotional program, designed and directed at the local branch level, we believe, is crucial to success of the library as a community service.

Expenditure Policy Should Emphasize Low-income, Low-circulation Areas

Present library policy is to allocate additional books and staff to libraries with high circulation rates. While there is real need for more books at these branches, the implication of the present policy is bad for the library system as a whole because it strengthens already strong branches at the expense of the weak ones. One reason that some branches have low circulation rates may be that their book stock, appearance, and other facilities are poor. A larger expenditure for these branches might well result in an increase in circulation. A shift away from the existing policy would result in more balanced growth of the system as a whole, enabling the library to provide a larger number of people with good library service. On grounds of equity, we have previously shown (see table 3-8) that poor people get fewer benefits from libraries than is justified by the taxes they contribute.

As Funds Permit, Some Locations Should Be Changed

Another way to reach more people is to change the locations of some of the branches so that they are in areas potential clients normally frequent. Many locations were decided on because the site or building was a gift, or the rent or cost of land was low. Such criteria result in no real savings over time.

THE MAIN LIBRARY

A Study Should Be Made of the Main Library, with a View Toward Diverting Some of Its Resources to Branches in Low-income Areas

Clearly the financial facts of the situation—approximately three-quarters of the circulation is at the branches, but three-fifths of the funds go to the main library—cry out for analysis. Oakland can be justly proud of the California Room, with its fine collection concerning California history dating from the 1850s. Members of the Oakland Project themselves have benefited from using documents and books there. Nevertheless, one might ask if it would not be more appropriate for the University of California, possibly the Bancroft Library, to take over the historical collection. Since the collection really serves the state rather than the city, perhaps there should be state sharing of the cost of maintaining it. In view of its exceedingly low usage by city residents it is difficult to justify the cost of the collection.

The main library performs high-level reference services. Are they worth the cost? Since the reference sections serve the entire region, perhaps there should be regional cost-sharing or limitation of service. To the degree that certain business make special use of the reference section, consideration should be given to user charges.

There should be a thorough review of the services of the main library and examination of the justification for each. Is it desirable, for instance, that the Oakland Library maintain a genealogical service? If there is sufficient demand, users of this special service might be assessed an appropriate charge.

Branches in High-income Areas Should Be Consolidated; Branches in Low-income Areas Should Be Maintained

It is important to have more branches in areas where people have low mobility. We therefore recommend that there be some consolidation of branches in higher socioeconomic areas where people are mobile and would appreciate a wider selection available at larger branches. At the same time, where most people walk, and where use by juveniles is high, there should be no decrease of branches in lower-income areas. The essence of this recommendation is that uniformly sized service areas throughout the city are not desirable. Oakland serves a variety of populations; hence different criteria for locating, stocking, and staffing branches should be used for different areas. When opportunities arise, as many branch buildings as possible should be rented rather than owned, to allow greater flexibility for adapting to future changes in clientele.

STRUCTURE OF THE LIBRARY

The Oakland Library System Should Decentralize Its Branch Operations Wherever the Majority of Users in a Particular Area Wish to Assume Responsibility

The rationale behind proposed decentralization should by now be evident. Oakland is not homogeneous with regard to income, reading tastes, ethnic origin, or cultural background. Areas served by the present branches differ significantly, and for some purposes should be treated as separate entities. The present lack of sustained effort to reach out to people in the areas served has roots in the existing centralized system. While this system might eventually adapt to the possibility of attracting new clientele, the groups that are not currently served would be much more likely to be attracted by people like themselves.

Let us begin by stating certain ground rules or assumptions upon which this proposal is based. The city does not have large sums of new money to spend on its library and is unlikely to obtain them. This proposal, like the others that have gone before, is capable of achievement within existing budgetary restraints. Any additional funds should come from the following sources: 1) maintenance of branches in high-income areas at the present level of expenditure, with only "cost of living" increases; 2) diversion of funds presently used to finance the main library, with substitution of user fees; 3) federal funds, for an innovative adventure of this kind.

Before discussing what should be decentralized, we should specify what should be left with the staff of the present central library: first, the main library and all pertinent functions and expenditures; second, handling of the forms and funds required for acquisition and cataloging of books; third, recruitment of senior librarians with the provision that local branches would have a number of alternatives and be able to suggest additional persons who would meet the usual criteria); fourth, disbursement of funds to branches, and establishment of auditing procedures and information reporting on cost and use of services.

People in mobile upper-income-area branches would be given an alternative: they could keep the existing branches, or they could allow the central library to consolidate them so that they could benefit from larger facilities with more specialized services. They should not be compelled to change, but they should be made to realize that funds would not be available to improve existing branches.

If the users in any existing branch wish to maintain the traditional relationship with the central library, they should be permitted to do so; but if they wish to have a voice in running their affairs, provisions would be made for an elected board. The members of the board should come exclusively from the area served; they should have power to select a senior librarian from among those certified and, with this librarian, to choose junior libarians who would be expected to come from the local area. Civil service regulations concerning junior librarians should allow ample latitude in appointment and should certainly not establish criteria more strict than supermarkets currently require for checkers. The board should have the power to allocate its funds among personnel, facilities, and materials subject to periodic auditing and required reports on cost, circulation, and effectiveness.

Economic and political costs of this experiment in decentralization would be small. The funds required are those now being spent or involve only small additions. Since most people are not concerned about libraries in other neighborhoods, there should be no conflict to set one neighborhood against another. Indeed, the low-temperature quality of branch libraries make them ideal candidates for decentralization. That a sufficient number of librarians are nearing retirement age (29 percent are over sixty years of age, as table 3.12 shows) would ease the transition. Decentralization, moreover, should enable city management to answer certain questions—such as, what mix of services will best serve to increase circulation?—by comparing results from different attempts to deal with the problems.

The greatest cost of change will be borne by existing library personnel. They can and must be protected, of course, in their security of employment; the combination of encouraging early retirement and making transfers easy should smooth the transition. Those who remain may feel that their traditional authority has been circumscribed and that they have lost the influence due

TABLE 3-12: Many Librarians are Nearing Retirement Age
Distribution of Professional Librarians (April 1969)

Age Group	Number	Percentage of Professionals
20–24	1	1.1
25–29	7	7.8
30–34	3	3.3
35–39	8	8.9
40–44	8	8.9
45–49	12	13.3
50–54	11	12.2
55–59	14	15.6
60–64	20	22.2
65–69	6	6.7
70 (mandatory retirement)		
N = 90		100.0

them as professionals who have given devoted service to the city; to some extent this would be unavoidable. Yet the librarians themselves know that life has changed and that they have not changed with it. Instead of harking back to a past that is no more, the present leadership of the library may see decentralization as an opportunity to help create new directions for urban libraries in America.

POSTSCRIPT

After these recommendations were made, the city manager and a new head of library operations instituted modest changes in the library system. One hundred thousand dollars was diverted from other activities to the purchase of books. As professional librarians began to retire, library aides or professionals at considerably lower salary levels replaced them, thus mitigating the grave imbalance between the resources devoted to professional librarians and to books. In 1970 the city manager organized a task force to investigate the library system and to recommend changes. The appearance of its interim report provides an opportunity to consider a broader range of alternatives to present library operations.

One alternative is to maintain the status quo—rejected in our study and also turned down by the city manager's task force. Both studies agree that there is too little circulation and general use of library facilities to justify the cost involved. The question is What approach should be taken to improve the use of resources?

The task force takes an essentially administrative view of the problem. Its emphasis is on building seven new library structures equidistant from current users, who are expected to drive them. Each new library would be able to have a larger collection of books, a complement of professionals, and a variety of services. Library workloads could be rationalized and made efficient by increasing the number of books circulated compared with the number of employees in the region. The cost per book circulated undoubtedly would decline. Presumably, circulation would increase as a result of new structures convenient to major arterials. Considerable attention is devoted to the suggestion that children, who account for perhaps half of library usage and who usually walk to the library, will be serviced at their neighborhood school. Apparently, though we are extremely skeptical, the city feels able to finance the building of new facilities and looks forward to increased efficiency over the years.

Yet, since little is known about how to increase effective use of the libraries, we think it wrong to institutionalize in concrete hypotheses whose validity no one can predict. It would be better to adopt at least a modified version of the decentralization recommendation in order to see if a different approach would work. If existing branches are too dilapidated to be fixed up, a finding not completely evident, new space can be rented at several points throughout the city. Efforts can be made to create community boards whose members would participate in hiring library personnel and work hard to reach citizens not now using library facilities. At worst, the experiment would fail. At best, something would have been learned about how to make libraries more effective, which is, after all, the main objective. We did not suggest consumer surveys because there seems little point in asking people why they do not attend a facility, when they may not know the answer. Faced with a forced choice on a questionnaire, they may feel compelled to say something. Who knows whether they would actually use libraries if certain changes are made, as they might say. It costs them nothing to answer and, if the tax implications are not pointed out in the survey, they may respond without considering costs. Nor is it likely they would be given alternative uses of city funds such as public safety. In the absence of a production function for libraries, that is, of an estimated relationship between different input and output in terms of use, the route to additional knowledge is through actual experience with a variety of alternatives.

4

A Comparative Analysis
of Outcomes

The preceding chapters, which described how three Oakland agencies distribute their resources among different sections of the city, provide us with material for a comparative analysis of outcomes. We focus on four questions in this final chapter: What are the patterns of resource distribution? Why do the agencies distribute resources in the ways they do? How are the agencies to be judged? How might outcomes be altered?

PATTERNS OF RESOURCE DISTRIBUTION

There is an adage that the rich get richer and the poor get poorer, but in our work we found a distribution pattern that favored both extremes. Some mechanisms were biased toward the rich. Other mechanisms favored the poor. We discovered no examples of mechanisms that favor the middle. But we are getting ahead of our story. Before proceeding, we should review the findings of the previous chapters.

Chapter 1 discussed the allocation of resources in Oakland's public elementary schools. We asked distributional questions: Do elementary schools with large percentages of minority students get more resources than elementary schools with small percentages of minority students? Do elementary schools in rich neighborhoods get more resources than elementary schools in poor neighborhoods?

Several different resources were analyzed. The first was teacher positions per student (class size). The distribution of teaching positions was actually the result of two sets of decisions: Oakland's allocation of positions financed from its own revenues, and the allocation of compensatory personnel financed from state and federal sources, including funds from the Elementary and Secondary Education Act (ESEA).

In 1969/70 the school system allocated its own positions relatively evenly among all elementary schools. Compensatory personnel (including teacher aides and teaching specialists) were concentrated in the poorest elementary schools. These schools also had the highest proportions of minority students but received compensatory programs on the basis of income rather than race. The resulting distribution of positions gave relatively more to low-income (and high-minority) schools than to other schools. In 1970/71 a new administration compensated further by reallocating the district's own positions. Class size was reduced, and thus schools in poor neighborhoods (not counting compensatory personnel) ended up with low teacher pupil ratios.

The second resource analyzed was teacher experience and degree attainment. Teachers with considerable experience and high degree levels generally taught in the upper-income, predominately white schools. This distribution resulted from past regulations governing transfers in the system. When a vacancy occurred in a school, a teacher in the system (i.e. one with experience) who requested a transfer into the vacancy was given priority over a new applicant. Most teachers prefer what they think is the easier job in predominantly white upper-income schools. When an opportunity became available, they transferred into these schools, leaving the new applicants to staff low-income schools. These transfers explain the finding of higher degree attainment for teachers in upper-income schools as well. Teachers with advanced degrees usually acquire them at night or in the summer while already on the job. Thus experience and degree level go hand in hand. Beginning in 1970. the new administration substantially reduced the number of transfers by not approving applications from teachers who were trying to escape low-income, black schools. It will take time, however, before this transfer policy has impact on the existing distribution of teacher experience.

The final resource analyzed was salary dollars per student, a rough aggregator of teacher qualification and class size. In 1969/70 the observed distribution of salary dollars versus neighborhood income level had a U shape. Children in upper-income, predominantly white schools received a relatively high level of salary dollars per student. The class sizes in these schools were average, but the experience and degree levels of the faculty were substantially above average. The high qualifications of their faculties resulted in high average salaries. Children in the low-income schools also received a high level of salary dollars per student. Their teachers possessed relatively low levels of experience and degree attainment, which resulted in relatively low salaries. But the low salaries were outweighed by small class sizes provided through compensatory programs. Schools between these two extremes—those neither rich enough to attract teachers with long experience nor poor enough to qualify for compensatory programs—received a relatively low level of salary dollars per student.

In 1970/71 the new policy of allocating Oakland's teachers equalized salary dollars per student in all schools before compensatory resources were considered. When compensatory personnel were added, the distribution had an L shape: high salary dollars per student in the poorest schools, lower, but equal salary dollars per student in all other schools.

In addition to these three resources—class size, teacher salaries and experience, and salary dollars per student—chapter 1 also described the distribution of supplies. The Oakland system itself had only a small supply budget, allocated evenly across the schools. In upper-income schools, parent groups supplemented the supply budget with direct contributions. In the poorest schools, the budget was augmented by supplies purchased with ESEA compensatory funds. Again, the schools between these extremes did not do as well, and a U-shaped relationship emerged.

In chapter 2 we discussed the allocation procedures of the street department. Again, our question was Do the upper-income neighborhoods receive more street resources than the lower-income neighborhoods? As with the libraries, there was a second dimension to this question: What is the allocation of resources between neighborhood streets and the select street system of major arterials?

We analyzed both street construction and resurfacing funds. The distribution of street construction funds favored major arterials over neighborhood streets. Figures were presented to show that two thirds of Oakland's streets (by mileage) were local and not in the select street system. But between 1960 and 1971, 94 percent of Oakland's street improvement expenditures were allocated to the select street system.

The rationale given for this allocation was two-fold. Much of the money for street reconstruction comes from the state apportionment of the gas tax revenues, funds that are earmarked for select streets. In addition, the professional standards of the street department engineers themselves favor such an allocation. Just as the libraries allocate acquisition funds to the branches with the highest circulation, the engineers allocate street improvement funds to those routes with the highest traffic flow—the select street system.

The limited new street construction in neighborhoods resembled the U-shaped distribution of school resources. The rich hill areas received new construction because they had no previous streets—the land was just being developed. Certain poor areas received new street projects under urban renewal projects funded by the federal government. Other areas of the city received few resources.

The allocation of street resurfacing expenditures among the neighborhoods tended to favor upper-income areas. Several criteria were used: degree of deterioration, high traffic volume, level of citizen complaints, and deferring the expenditure if the utility company expected to work on lines under the street within five years. These rules, especially the last two, favored upper-income neighborhoods, since they knew how to register complaints effectively and their utility lines, being newer, were less in need of repair.

Chapter 3 covered the allocation of services in libraries in a manner similar to our inquiry in education. Do libraries in wealthy neighborhoods, we asked, receive more or less resources than libraries in poor neighborhoods? Because of the structure of the library system, we added another dimension to this question: Do branch libraries get more or less resources than the central library? We concluded that the library allocated its funds in a way that left all users worse off than they need have been. Casual readers, however, were disadvantaged compared with users of specialized collections, and branch users in poor neighborhoods fared worst of all.

Compared with other big California cities, Oakland spent a relatively high proportion of its budget on personnel and a relatively low proportion on new acquisitions.[1] All users could have been better served if the system had reoriented some of its budget toward books. In fact, after the initial work on our study was done, a new head librarian made such a reallocation.

Users in the branches were hurt because the agency concentrated its resources in the main library. For the period we analyzed, the central library had 25 percent of the circulation but received 60 percent of all expenditures on personnel and acquisitions. Among the branches themselves, personnel were distributed relatively evenly.

Users in the poor branches were hurt most of all because of the way in which the library allocated its new acquisition funds. It distributed acquisition funds to the branches on the basis of circulation. The higher a branch's circulation, the more acquisition funds it received.

Branches in upper-income neighborhoods have books that suit their clients, and clients who like to read. As a result, their circulation was high, and so, under the allocation procedure, they received additional funds to keep their collections up to date. Branches in poor neighborhoods served clients with a low propensity for reading. Their lower demand was reinforced because these branch collections did not fit their needs. The low-income libraries surveyed, for example, did not have enough civil service examination manuals and black-history books. The circulation in these branches was low; consequently they could not get sufficient funds to improve collections to fill the demand.

The outlook of the library staff itself also promoted this re-

1. Table 3-3, p. 187: Oakland spends 79 percent of its budget on salaries and 6 percent on library materials. This compares with Los Angeles (76 percent, 14 percent), San Diego (66 percent, 13 percent) and San Francisco (67 percent, 20 percent). These figures differ relatively sharply. A comparison of school budgets, for example, showed that the percentages of expenditure going to teachers' salaries and supplies in Oakland were almost equal to those percentages for other districts in the state.

source pattern. It believed its job was to serve clients who walked through the door, to the extent that was possible, but *not* to publicize the library to potential clients in the neighborhood.

The resulting distribution of resources had a J shape. It favored the well-to-do, particularly those with scholarly interests who would use the specialized collections. To an extent this bias was offset by a federal grant which went to the Fruitvale Spanish-language library, but this offset was a small one.

THREE PATTERNS: THE MORE, THE MORE; COMPENSATION; AND RESULTANTS

From our findings, three patterns emerge as particularly important. One is what David Riesman appropriately calls "the more, the more." New library acquisition funds go to those who already read. Roads go only where the cars already are. Experienced teachers transfer to the well-to-do schools. It is as the scriptures say: "For to every one who has will more be given, and he will have abundance; but from him who has not even what he has will be taken away" (Matt. 25:29).

A second, opposite pattern is compensation. The poorest schools receive extra resources from the state and federal government. Streets in the poorest neighborhoods are repaved as part of an urban renewal project. A Chicano neighborhood, Fruitvale, gets funds for its own Spanish-language library.

With differing intensities, both of these patterns interact in each of our studies. Compensation affects the distribution pattern by altering its timing and amount. The Fruitvale library's compensatory resources were much smaller than the school district's. By 1970/71, the schools had undertaken compensatory programs to the point where the poor children received more resources than the rich. The more, the more dominated the libraries, however, as in the same year the library gave its branches in the poor neighborhoods less resources than its other branches.

A third pattern we shall call resultants: those patterns which no one intends. We may like some of the patterns we see. We may dislike others. But many of these patterns do not represent conscious policy choices. They are the result of a multitude of influences that interact in unforeseen ways: bureaucrats pursuing their own immediate objectives, federal and state legislators passing special programs, local agencies chronically short of money; the list is endless. Even in cases of straightforward discrimination there are often no villains: just a number of professionals, administering other people's intentions as well as their own, and unaware of the consequences of their actions. To examine the issue of discrimination, let us look again at the street engineers.

The broader social implications of emphasizing major street construction were beyond their realm of competence. They did not object to neighborhood improvements; they just did not think it was as important as moving traffic in and out. So far as we can tell, they did not consciously discriminate. If they turned down repair of streets in ghetto areas, they objected also to providing "frills" for Broadway merchants that did not enhance the flow of traffic. Traffic circulation was their master and they served it well.

How can we explain their apparent discrimination in favor of the richer dwellers of the hill areas? Hill dwellers were in a better position to benefit from the major streets favored by the street department. They received more of the limited paving funds, partly because they were better at making phone calls, partly because the street department let the utilities influence paving decisions. The individual procedures were all neutral. Only the outcome was discriminatory. And the citizen is hard put to understand why his street is in such bad condition.

The poor are not the only object of discrimination. How might one explain to the near-poor or working-class parent that his children are the worst off in terms of resources devoted to education? No one intends to disadvantage these children but it happens anyway. Children from upper-income families get experienced teachers, and parents supplement the schools' supply budget. The very poorest students receive substantial compensatory inputs from federal programs especially designated for that purpose. When the state required these funds to be concentrated, with each child receiving $300 of additional resources, the motivation was understandable. The state did not want the compensatory funds dissipated through the giving of just a little more to each poor student. But the overall shortage of funds meant the district had to reduce the number of students in the program. Those who were needy, but not the *most* needy, were hurt.

Restrictions on outside funds are responsible for more than

discrimination. They are also responsible for pure anomalies. Suppose an Oakland citizen learned that the school district was increasing the length of kindergarten sessions and proposing a decrease in the high school day. Suppose he learned that the district was reducing maintenance expenditures in regular schools and planning an elaborate rehabilitation of two dropout-prevention schools. In each case, he might reasonably conclude that these decisions represented the preferences of his school administrators: an increment of time spent in kindergarten was worth more than the extra high school period, the dropout-prevention schools were in more need of repair than other schools.

Nothing of the sort would be true. The school department wanted resources to distribute; the state gave a bonus for increasing the kindergarten day and it provided a restricted tax to fund the dropout-prevention schools. The reduction of the high school day and the cutting of general maintenance provided the district with badly needed money for other purposes. Naturally, a decision once made must be defended at least partially in terms of substantive merits. So the original confusion is compounded by efforts to rationalize a decision made on the basis of maximizing income by arguments about desirable educational policy that come from an entirely different realm.

We would like to say that if these patterns do not reflect local preferences, at least they combine state and federal preferences. Yet we know that this is often untrue. Outside money (for those agencies who can obtain it) comes from various sources. Each source dates from a different era and has a different set of rules attached. The original motivation behind any individual program is easy to understand. The federal government or the state legislature wants to specify a certain result—to give emphasis to arterial highways, to lengthen the kindergarten day. By making incentives sufficiently advantageous or penalties sufficiently onerous, they can and do get their way. They can put their passionate beliefs of the moment into legislation. But each program interacts with the others and conditions change. The result is that the seventh and eighth grade tax financed high expenditures for two grades in a time of financial crisis for the rest of the system, and restricted gas tax revenues expanded major arterial streets in an era of interest in ecology and of mass transit.

AN EXPLANATION

Our explanation of these patterns begins with the names we have given them—compensation, resultants, the more, the more—but to complete the explanation we must observe the government official. Our bureaucrat is, like all of us, concerned with his own welfare. He views his agency's policies as affecting that welfare. He is interested in the agency's clients primarily as they affect the agency and, through the agency, his own welfare. He cares about his profession, another aspect of the outside environment, as a source of guidance for internal conduct and as a means of furthering his mobility, thus increasing his welfare. While others may be directly concerned with the distribution of an agency's resources in the city, our bureaucrat is not. To him, the shape of the resource distribution is a by-product of pursuing his own objectives.

What are our bureaucrat's objectives? The bureaucrat wants to serve the public through a secure career with not too much personal conflict. He expects a stable, and perhaps advancing, income for the foreseeable future and gratification for meeting public needs. His personal goals cannot be reconciled unless his organization is stable. If it is not, neither his economic nor his psychic income may increase or one may have to be sacrificed to the other. His professional values connect service to the citizen with his own income. He does good by acting professionally, is rewarded by promotion, and receives a portion of the surplus the organization has accumulated.

We can think of our bureaucrat as seeking to advance himself in an extended organizational environment that includes not only the agency that employs him but the profession to which he belongs and the clientele he serves. The outstanding characteristic of this organizational environment is that it rewards conforming behavior in behalf of existing interests. The clients who exist want the bureaucrats to meet needs they have and not the needs of others who may not yet have formulated them. The profession necessarily hands down received wisdom. It encapsulates the experience of its members for getting along in organizations. It seeks to raise the status of the profession by lifting its standards. Since professionals might disagree about social goals, internal conflict is mitigated by focusing on how activities are to be carried out or on the quality of service to be made available. Precisely who gets how much of these products and services is not normally a professional concern. Organizations want people who are professionally competent, who will process the work, and who will adapt to the environment as it presents itself.

Complex organizations, with a formal hierarchy and a division of labor, seek to stabilize their environment. Uncertainty is shunned, and the internal maintenance needs of the organization tend to displace the purposes it was supposed to serve. That is the burden of virtually the entire literature on organizations from Weber to Crozier. Why?

The bureaucrat must make some sense of his environment. His organization exists to absorb, process, and reduce data to manageable form. Yet he must often act in the absence of theory specifying relationships between inputs and outputs or of criteria informing him of what is relevant. He deals with this uncertainty by vastly oversimplifying his conception of the environment, and by devising operational procedures that greatly decrease his need for information. He will accordingly limit this agency's concern to those clients who actually present demands— a small portion of all potential clients. Professionalizing personnel is another way to simplify and expedite; it helps internalize norms that tell officials what aspects of the environment are important, what types of information to collect, and how to respond.

The normal state of an organization, therefore, as observers everywhere testify, is caution. It gets along doing what it has always done. Before it does more, its bureaucrats, like other rational people, want to know whether they will benefit. Organizations exist and they already benefit their members. They have come to terms with their environment, terms that reflect existing relationships not future ones. So they deal with the presenting problems, as social workers say, and do not go looking for trouble. A bureaucrat will have his agency adopt formal rules and procedures that embody professional standards. With these rules, he will not be imposing the standards himself, but will merely be "going by the book." His universal experience has been set down by Herbert Kaufman:

Life in groups, especially in groups engaged in cooperative under-takings, is inconceivable without regularities of behavior, which is to say repetitive behavior. No group can stay together without such regularities; the absence of such regularities (if such a state can be imagined) would be the ultimate in disorganization. . . . Since *some* regularities are needed, and all required regularities have unpleasant features, why risk known imperfections for unknown ones? Why gam-ble an established imperfect order for possible disorder? The logic of collective life thus has a conservative thrust: it lends authority to the system as it stands.[2]

Our bureaucrat, then, will not be anxious to stimulate his environment. He will try to keep his relationships with it as quiet and as stable as possible. He will rely upon what we will call Adam Smith rules: When a customer makes a "request," take care of him in a professional manner; otherwise, leave him alone. We place the word "request" in quotes because we use it in the sense that high book circulation is a request to the libraries, and heavy traffic is a request to the street department. Adam Smith rules do not require our bureaucrat to have more contact with the public than he needs to advance his objectives. Together with professional standards Smithian rules also serve the organizational imperative to simplify decision-making and reduce uncertainty.

Now organizations might seek to shape their environments. Bureaucrats have long been accused of being empire builders. But the growth that is sought must be clearly understood. Is it growth that increases the resources of the organization in com-parison with the demands placed on it? That is good. Is it growth that increases clients and services without corresponding re-sources? That is bad. Advancement within an expanded organi-zation must not be pursued at the risk of collective impoverish-ment from which all members lose. Bigger is not necessarily bet-ter, and more may be monstrous unless there are excess resources left with which to reward loyal members.

Our bureaucrat could serve his security, income, and service objectives by helping his agency grow. The larger the agency's resources, the greater the possibilities for remunerative careers and for providing more service. But it may not be wise to maxi-

2. Herbert Kaufman, *The Limits of Organizational Change* (University, Alabama: University of Alabama Press, 1971), pp. 9–10.

mize the agency's growth and service unless its stability, and the bureaucrat's security, are also increased. So he will not spend every working moment looking for that extra dollar. Unless the environment appears munificent, he will not pursue growth at the expense of security. He will be content so long as the resources under the agency's control grow at a modest rate that he can control. The immediate source for these resources is the municipal government. But in Oakland municipal income has been sharply limited in recent years. Our bureaucrat will, therefore, supplement local revenues where possible with grants from state and federal sources so long as organizational benefits exceed costs. "Free" money is hard to turn down, but an outside grant may carry restrictions that reduce, rather than increase, his discretion and make his clientele grow faster than his resources.

How will our bureaucrat interact with the world outside—with his agency's clients? The answer will depend on the way in which our bureaucrat's clients can help or hinder him in obtaining his goals. Here the economic model of the firm provides us with a useful analogy.

Present-day economists have two, polar models of the firm. One is the "Galbraith" model. The other is what we will call the "Adam Smith" model. The difference between the two models is well stated by Professor Galbraith:

In virtually all economic analysis and instruction the initiative is assumed to lie with the consumer. In response to wants that originate within himself, or which are given to him by his environment, he buys goods and services in the market. . . . The flow of instruction is in one direction—from the individual to the market to the producer. . . . The unidirectional flow of instruction from consumer to market to producer may be denoted the Accepted Sequence.
We have seen this sequence does not hold. The mature corporation has readily at hand the means for controlling the prices at which it sells as well as those at which it buys. Similarly, it has means for managing what the consumer buys at the prices which it controls.[3]

The two conceptions of the firm differ in the tools the organizations use to achieve their objectives. The Adam Smith firm— Galbraith's "Accepted Sequence"—can only adjust its price. The

3. J. K. Galbraith, *The New Industrial State* (Boston: Houghton-Mifflin Company, 1967), pp. 211–212.

number of units demanded at any particular price—the consumer's demand curve—is an independent given. The Galbraith firm, on the other hand, has substantial influence over this demand. By doing marketing research, by making numerous adjustments in its product to suit consumer tastes, and by undertaking "manipulative" advertising, the firm plays a large role in determining the size of the demand which its product fills.

We can imagine a municipal agency looking like either the Galbraith or the Adam Smith model. Consider an antipoverty agency. It is new; its staff often has enthusiasm and zeal; its year-to-year funding is on shaky ground. To justify its existence, it has to demonstrate a clientele. For all these reasons, we can imagine the agency behaving like the Galbraith firm, spending large amounts of resources on the stimulation and organization of an active clientele to demand its services.

The agencies we describe, however, are all of the Adam Smith variety. They are not notably heroic. Bureaucrats are often shrinking violets who prefer adjustment to conflict with the environment.[4] Why should they struggle? Their appropriations do not, in general, depend upon the number of people they serve. Even though a bureaucrat wants his agency to grow, he does not see increasing his clientele as a means to that end. Hence he has no particular incentive to drum up more business.

To the contrary, more clients not only fail to help the agency to grow, they may cause the bureaucrat to do his job in an unprofessional way. At the least, a bureaucrat who tailors his services to a client's tastes may be forced to provide those services in an unprofessional manner. Libraries may be visited by unsavory characters who request the wrong sort of books. Moreover, new clients, like new students, mean new requirements for money, which is difficult to find in Oakland. Professionalism, in the garb of standards for service to existing clientele, makes it undesirable to take on more customers.

Professional standards, moreover, have an additional advantage of appearing to be fair. Hiring qualified librarians, moving traffic

4. See Arnold J. Meltsner, *The Politics of City Revenue* (Berkeley and Los Angeles University of California Press, 1971), pp. 86–131, and Anthony Downs, *Inside Bureaucracy* (Boston: Little, Brown and Co., 1967), pp. 216–217.

and setting equal class sizes all seem reasonable and appropriate.
They orient professionals to apparently worthy goals—quality
libraries and safe roads—that are within their realm of competence. The public should be well served. Yet somehow these be-
nevolent norms and the Adam Smith rules, which ought to help
everyone, end up helping some more than others.

Adam Smith rules, like many "neutral" decisions rules, are not
neutral. They have a class bias. In order to understand the bias
in the use of Adam Smith rules, we must understand that the rules
themselves stem from professional and organizational norms. The
professional norms set convenient standards for competence and
quality performance while the organizational norms provide a
means for the agency to adjust to its environment. Operationally,
the norms converge when the bureaucrat uses a rule to allocate
the city's resources, and the use of these rules encourages the
pattern of "the more, the more." Now that we know that the
bureaucrat is a twentieth century Adam Smith, let us reconsider
the behavior of our three agencies.

ADAM SMITH IN ACTION

How would our bureaucrat function in the libraries? To secure
his own career, he wants the library to grow. But in practice he
could do little about this desire. The municipal budget for libraries was fixed. There was little chance our bureaucrat could increase it either through appeals to the city council or through
obtaining outside funds (which were generally not available).
But the budget was also safe. There was not much chance the city
council would cut it because of lack of circulation.

Our bureaucrat would also want to do his job in the "right" or
professional way. In fact, the libraries were almost a pathological
case of such professionalization. The head librarian, an aggressive
personality, sought to impose professional standards by maximizing his internal discretion. His main interest became the hiring of
librarians with appropriately certified qualifications. The personnel, once in the system, would apply the same professional standards to decisions like the selection of proper books, the division
of resources between the central and branch libraries, and the
requirement for staff at branch libraries. The standards allowed

the library to keep up its specialized collections and keep out disturbing influences. Even in the branches, books of a "flighty" or temporary character were not allowed to enter the system, because the branch personnel were unlikely to order them and the supervisory personnel would not have approved the requests in any event. Personnel who imperfectly observed these norms were screened out.

The library's coping with its environment provides an excellent example of an Adam Smith rule: allocate new acquisition funds to those branches which have the highest circulations. The initiative lies with the customer, as library patrons "vote" with their cards. The more books they take out, the more money their branch receives.

We can imagine other rules. The library could have allocated its funds for new acquisitions on an equal per capita basis. Alternatively, it could have allocated the funds on the basis of circulation and unfulfilled requests. Under this system, the branches in poorer neighborhoods, with their unfulfilled requests for civil service manuals and black-history books, would have received better treatment. Branch libraries in poor neighborhoods would have done more in the way of advertising, letting the neighborhood know where the library was and what it had to offer.

But all of these strategies—"market research"—would have gone against the professional attitudes of the staff. From the time the libraries were first founded, librarians assumed that people either had the motivation to read or they hadn't. The people who used the library—people of quality—had it. These same people benefited from the professional standards applied to book selection: librarians value what people like themselves read. Among their peers, the top librarians no doubt took pride in their specialized collections and "quality books."

The library could rely so heavily on professional norms and Adam Smith rules because it was left alone. For many years, the library was an organizational isolate, free to be its own client. It could allocate resources by referring to national standards rather than to preferences of Oakland citizens, which were not strongly expressed. Nobody really bothered it, including its own commission of governing citizens.

The allocative biases of this laissez-faire procedure are clear: those who read get the most opportunity to read more. Those who read the least are obviously not interested and so are ignored.

How would our bureaucrat behave in the street department? He would find it easy to pursue his goal of agency growth. Unlike librarians, street engineers have access to substantial amounts of outside money on which their agency can expand. The most prominent of these sources is the state gas tax fund. Other funds include county road building revenues and federal urban renewal monies. The engineers also have a clear set of professional norms which they wish to impose upon their job. Simply stated, they want to move the largest number of cars at the fastest speed possible, subject to considerations of safety.

Hypothetically, outside funds and professional norms could have clashed. In fact they meshed. The major sources of street department monies—the gas tax revenues—completely coincides with professional norms. The legal restriction which limits them to use on the "select street system" insures that they be spent only on streets with heavy traffic. The same reasoning holds for the way in which the county distributes its gas tax funds. Only urban renewal funds, a minor exception, runs counter to the norms of the engineers. A good portion of the funds are for rebuilding streets in poor urban renewal areas where traffic will not be heavy after the renewal is completed.

Once again, Adam Smith is at work: put the money where the cars are. Traffic flow will be maximized by improving those roads that are already heavily traveled. Armed with this norm, the engineers can remain confident that they are making essentially professional decisions. They can look back to miles of physical accomplishment. They can point to impressive statistics about the number of vehicles moved. And in any case, their norms are reenforced by the restrictions placed upon the gas tax money. But this Adam Smith rule, too, has an allocational bias. Our conclusions must be based on traffic studies, which are sketchy at best. But they suggest that the effect of maximizing traffic flow in Oakland is to provide well-to-do commuters (including those who live outside Oakland) with routes from their homes to their offices. The poorer citizens are left with transportation that does not improve over time. By using this Adam Smith rule, the engineers can circumvent the question of who needs to get from one place to another. They simply take for granted that traffic is already in the right place. Those who already have the most mobility get further while those who have the least mobility get left behind.

Sometimes the poor do benefit because of Adam Smith. When a major facility, like the airport, was located in a poor area, the principle of "the more, the more" worked for the poor. New streets were built and old ones repaired to service those facilities. The downtown business section did not get the street modifications it wanted because its streets didn't have the necessary traffic. Once a neighborhood has something, for whatever reason, it gets more. The trick, apparently, is to get more earlier so that one can get more later.

The street department also allocated its resurfacing resources by using Adam Smith rules. One of these rules was simple: resurface those streets which caused the most complaints to the street department and the city council. Another rule was more involved. Because it was undesirable for a street to be resurfaced and then broken up again for utility work, the two activities had to be related in some way. The street department coordinated them by sending over a list of possible resurfacing projects to the public utilities. The utilities then crossed off those projects where they expected to work in the next five years. We call this an Adam Smith rule, for again the agency let the initiative for a decision lie with someone else.

Like the other Adam Smith rules, the resurfacing rules had a degree of allocational bias. Despite the talk about organizing the poor, the well-to-do neighborhood would generate more complaints than a similar street in a poor neighborhood. Similarly, the utility facilities in the poor areas were older and subject to more frequent breakdown. This made the utility company more anxious to replace them in the immediate future, making it unwise to resurface streets that would have to be torn up again. Giving the utilities a veto limited the amount of resurfacing that could be done in poor areas.

We have saved the schools for last because they are our most complex story. Hiring a new school superintendent between 1969/70 and 1970/71 marked a change from an administration that relied on Adam Smith rules to one that was explicitly concerned with the distribution of resources and designed allocation policies with that distribution in mind.

In the schools, our bureaucrat would have had ample opportunity to pursue a goal of agency expansion. Federal compensatory funds, state compensatory funds, and the numerous special programs and override taxes all provided sources of revenue for growth without increasing the number of students. Our bureaucrat also had professional norms he wanted to impose. But these norms were often overriden through the constraints imposed by various funding sources. In the middle 1960s, for instance, the school administration favored a variable class size ranging from thirty-four in elementary schools with high achievement level to twenty-seven in schools with low achievement levels. But these class sizes became centered around thirty (excluding compensatory programs) shortly after the state passed its class-size bonus regulation. The seventh and eighth grade override tax set up an incentive for the schools to spend substantially increased amounts on these grades while they were cutting back sharply on expenditures at all other levels.

Adam Smith rules were used in the allocation of supplies, teachers, and other personnel. If parents want to make direct contributions to the schools, let them. By the late 1960s, the district's own supply budget had shrunk to a low level. Parental allocations became important. The decision to let parents contribute to their children's schools meant that the distribution of supplies was being determined to a substantial degree not by the administration but by parental initiative. Teachers, as it were, allocated themselves. The policy of unrestricted transfers before 1970/71 created a situation where the assignments were determined largely by teacher preferences. Like most agencies, the schools also tried to take citizens into account. Parental protest caused the addition of a number of security guard positions in the later 1960s. They also led the district to use its own funds to replace a compensatory program for Spanish-language students cut back in 1969.

In 1970/71 a new administration came in and adopted policies specifically aimed at evening out the distribution of resources. It substantially reduced the number of transfers approved, and it adjusted the student/district-teacher ratios in poorer schools so that salary dollars per student (excluding compensatory personnel) were equal throughout the system. The distribution of supplies, however, remained unchanged.

JUDGING OUTCOMES

Having seen the effect of Adam Smith rules in determining patterns, such as the more, the more, we still require a convenient handle for addressing the totality of agency performance. Where there are several patterns of resource distribution, how should agencies be judged?

At the beginning of this book, we discussed the standard of responsiveness and concluded that a certain lag in responsiveness is an intrinsic feature of most local governments. We argued there that because of the costs and complexity of the issues, widespread citizen opinion on resource allocation within agencies was unlikely. Others could argue that the political process operates better than is readily apparent. By taking most allocations for granted and applying pressure to alter those elements that are deemed out of line, a few interested, active citizens secure resource allocations that are consistent with their preferences. Thus it would be surprising if present allocations differed radically from the citizen preferences which might be discerned.

This perceived harmony between citizen preferences and bureaucratic allocations, however, even if true would still be irrelevant for our purposes. First, we are working with patterns of resource distribution which are not self-evident to either citizen or bureaucrat. Second, citizen preferences are not likely to be as refined or on the same level as the allocation decisions bureaucrats have to make. Thus both citizen and bureaucrat can agree that more money should be spent on schools, but the operational question is how much and for what specific purposes. Finally, even if citizen preferences are articulated at a refined level and indicate a radical departure from present allocations, no government or agency could turn itself around overnight. Nor would it contemplate radical (that is, from 30 to 50 percent changes a year for, say, five years) reallocations. Whether citizens lack preferences on internal agency allocations or have opinions on departures too large to be feasible, it remains true that there is no citizen preference to serve as a criterion for judging agency allocations within margins normally considered by decision makers or studied by analysts. Therefore, we will concentrate here on the standards of efficiency and equity that allow us to make discriminating judgments.

EFFICIENCY

Our discussion of efficiency begins with a simple definition: an agency is inefficient if it can (but does not) produce more outputs for its existing budget. Are Oakland's agencies inefficient by this definition? By no means entirely, but in some areas they are, or at least were. Our answer depends, of course, on how we define an output. With that in mind, here are several examples of allocative inefficiencies.

Consider the libraries. One output of the library system is circulation. A key to circulation is a lively, up-to-date book stock. New books cost money which could be found by reallocating the existing budget. Our analysis of library staffing showed a significant overqualification of personnel. Many branch libraries had a staff of two or more professionals where one professional and a para-professional could have handled the work. High-salaried professionals were performing clerical tasks. If staffing policies were adjusted to the actual work load, the salary savings could be put toward new books.

The street department provides another example. We showed how the department's engineers downplay the use of cost information in decision-making. Costs are used as an engineering refinement after (but not before) most allocation decisions are made. Assume that the output of the street department is what the enginers state it to be: maximizing the flow of traffic. Implementing the goal raises a number of allocation questions: Is it cheaper to repave a street in an early state of deterioration, or should repaving wait until the deterioration is more advanced? Will traffic flow in the city be maximized by doing one large project (the Hegenberger Expressway, for example) or several smaller projects? Without heavy reliance on cost information, these questions have no answers.

So far, we have talked about inefficiency resulting from internal decisions. Inefficiencies can also be imposed from the outside.

The seventh and eighth grade tax and the four override taxes which finance employee health and pension contributions are examples. The first distorts allocations among grade levels. The second distorts bargaining settlements toward fringe benefits. School allocations would be improved if these monies were given to the district to use without restriction.[5]

The definition of efficiency we have been using concerns an increase in output—not who will receive the increase. That would be a question of distribution which is contained in the economist's criterion of Pareto-optimality. For the agencies we are concerned with, Pareto-optimality implies an allocation of resources such that nobody can be made better off without somebody else being made worse off. If there is a reallocation of resources so that one person could be made better off and nobody made worse off, the agency is said to be Parto-inefficient.

Suppose we apply Pareto-efficiency to the library and suppose we take technological and political factors as given. Libraries would be improved, in the earlier sense of getting more output out of their input, if less funds were spent on personnel in the central library and more on new books in the branch libraries. But in each of these reallocations, some people—existing personnel or users of the central library collection—would clearly lose. While many of the existing arrangements may not benefit the majority of people, they exist because somebody benefits from them in each instance. It is easy to talk about compensating the losers but difficult to imagine how this would be done. The overall output of the library system might, for instance, increase to the point where the professionals who were thrown out of work could be compensated for their loss of employment. In practice, however, there are no mechanisms for actually accomplishing this sort of compensation.

By this reasoning, the libraries and our other agencies are already Pareto-optimal. There is no easy way out, where no one ever gets hurt. There is little in chapters 1–3 to suggest Pareto-

5. Each of the programs serves a broad constituency. Removing their funding restrictions is different from removing the restrictions on, say, a compensatory education program which spends a large amount of money on a small constituency. In this first case, the recipients of benefits after reallocation will be about the same as the recipients before reallocation. In the second case, the recipients are likely to change drastically.

inefficiency, meaning that some citizens could be better off and no one made worse off. If there were enough for everyone, no matter what their desires, there would be no scarcity and no economics. Under Pareto-optimality, politics would also have ended as soon as it had begun. It would look like the Polish Diet, where every member had an absolute veto. Only if we keep efficiency and distribution as simultaneous, but separate, criteria can we approach politics as we know it: people bargaining over their expected gains and losses.

EQUITY

The second standard we shall apply to the distributions is one of equity. Like efficiency, equity has a number of specific meanings. In casual conversation, equity or fairness usually means whether rich citizens get more than poor, or white citizens more than black. When we try to develop equity as a norm, the issue becomes more complex. To illustrate our discussion, we shall use three possible standards of equity.

The first standard we will call *market equity*. Under market equity an agency distributes resources to citizens in proportion to the tax revenues they pay. The agency's function is to produce services but not to engage in any redistribution. The agency's allocation resembles what would occur if the service were provided in the private market—say education produced by private schools —except that in this "market" the municipal agency may hold a monopoly position.

Figures for 1970 show that a family making from $5,000 to $15,000 pays about 6 percent of its income in property taxes, while a family making from $16,000 to $25,000 pays about 5 percent.[6] Suppose a family making $5,000 income received one unit of a government service. The standard of market equity would specify that a family making $10,000 receive two units of the good, a family making $25,000 receive 4.2 units. Thus schools in poor neighborhoods would receive fewer dollars per student than schools in rich neighborhoods, and streets in poor neighborhoods would receive less repaving than streets in rich neighborhoods.

We will call a second equity standard *equal opportunity*. Here

6. These figures would be even more pronounced if retired people— people who have no current income—were excluded from the data.

the agency distributes an equal dollar amount of resources to each citizen regardless of what he has paid in taxes.[7] Each neighborhood receives the same amount of street repaving, all schools enjoy the same expenditure per child, each library has the same staffing and new acquisition allowance as every other in the city.[8]

Since property taxes are roughly proportional to income, equal expenditure per person implies a degree of redistribution. This redistribution is contained in the idea of equal opportunity and it can be justified in a number of ways. A community, for example, may feel that education is an important socializing agency and that all children should be exposed to the same education even if upper-income families bear a disproportionate share of the cost.

The third standard is known as *equal results;* when the agency distributes its resources, outcomes are equal for each citizen. For libraries, equal results means dividing resources among branches so that all have equal per capita circulation. Similarly, the street department allocates its funds in such a way that all neighborhoods have streets in equal condition, and the schools their funds so that all children finish with the same reading ability.

Equal results involves more redistribution than does equal opportunity. This is not surprising, since equal opportunity requires only that current inequalities be remedied, while equal results also requires that the effects of past inequalities be mitigated. Equal results in education means that a child has to be compensated for his parents' inferior education (transmitted to him in his preschool years) or even for his lack of parents. Equal results in streets implies that the state would have to change its apportionment formulas of the gas tax so that older cities with older streets could get more money, rather than continuing to distribute money on the basis of population.

The conflict between equal opportunity and equal results has

7. A basic foundation of equal opportunity in this country is the equal protection clause of the Constitution, which states in part: "nor (shall any state) deny to any person within its jurisdiction the equal protection of the law." This provision was applied to the level of municipal services in the recent decision of the Fifth Circuit Court of Appeals in *Hawkins* v. *Shaw.*

8. This description covers only the distribution among neighborhood facilities. It does not necessarily imply how resources should be divided between the neighborhood facilities on the one hand and a central facility (the main library) on the other.

been prominent in the civil rights movement.[9] When the civil rights movement first gained national attention in the late 1950s, its goal was equal opportunity. The movement wanted a man to be judged on the basis of his ability, not on his color, race or national origin. Within this goal was the belief that equal opportunity would produce equal results: if jobs were assigned on the basis of ability and not on the basis of criteria like race, for example, the proportion of blacks in any type of job would reflect their proportion in the society at large.

By the middle 1960s it became apparent that equal results would not automatically flow from equal opportunity. In education, children from poor families, including most Negro families, came to school performing at levels far lower than children from rich families.[10] If a school spent equal dollar amounts on all children throughout their education, the performance gap remained constant in relative terms and increased in absolute terms.

When the movement recognized that equal treatment did not make for equal results, its demands shifted. Some demands still focused on means to an end, like compensatory education programs. Other demands went directly to the ends themselves, as in the call for hiring by racial quotas to insure minority representation.

The concept of equal results raises a number of perplexing problems. Often it is not clear how the standard, even if adopted, could be enforced. It is impossible to accomplish objectives if one does not know how. If teachers know what school inputs lead to an improvement in reading, they can calculate how much it would cost to raise the poor readers to the level of the best. Given these costs, policy choices could then be made. The fact is, however, that the knowledge does not exist.

If equality of results in education cannot now be achieved by boosting the lower group up, it can be achieved by holding the higher group down. But who would suggest that the advantaged be held back deliberately in order to let the others catch up? Equal library circulation might be obtained by cutting down circulation (perhaps by letting the book stock become out of

9. See, for example, Nathan Glazer, "A Breakdown of Civil Rights Enforcement," *The Public Interest*, Spring 1971, pp. 106–115.

10. Cf. James Coleman et al., *Equality of Educational Opportunity* (also known as the Coleman Report), pp. 221–277.

date) in upper-income areas. Compensatory education is one thing; preventing children from realizing their potential is another. Problems are also created by the way in which equal results mesh with other goals. The push for minority quotas in hiring suggests that if employers searched only for the most qualified people, minorities would be underrepresented. Perhaps many of the best qualified people would have been overtrained for the job so that appropriate minority employment would represent no falloff in job performance. But in other areas performance and proportional hiring conflict. Despite these difficulties equal results has become one important standard by which to judge an agency's performance.

The equity standard a person chooses to measure plays a crucial role in his judgment of agency performance. Consider two parents looking at current allocations in the Oakland school system. A well-to-do parent might look at the present allocation of funds and suggest that, if anything, it overfavored poor neighborhoods. Student/teacher ratios are lowest in the low-income schools; these schools have specialists and extra supplies purchased with federal funds. By contrast, the richest schools have somewhat larger classes, fewer specialists, and practically no teacher aides. Any supplies they have beyond the small district allocation come through direct parental contributions. Thus the well-to-parent concludes that the system is biased in favor of the poor.

A poor, or minority, citizen might come to a much different conclusion. He might acknowledge that dollar expenditures per pupil were higher in the poorest schools; yet he might feel that expenditures are a poor measure of outcomes. He could argue that a more appropriate measure of outcomes would be reading ability on standardized tests, that as long as poor children are reading at lower levels than rich children (which is currently true) the allocation of resources favoring the low-income schools is insufficient.

The rich citizen uses equality of opportunity as his standard. The poor citizen is using equality of results as his standard. By applying different standards, these two parents can look at the same allocation and arrive at opposite conclusions as to how the agency is performing.

For the purpose of judging the performance of the three Oakland agencies, we summarize the three standards of equity in table 4-1. Market equity implies the least redistribution. Equal results implies the most.

Where do the agencies lie on this spectrum? The schools lie somewhere to the right of equal opportunity. The street department lies to the left of equal opportunity. The libraries lie somewhere to the left of the street department.

The rankings of the agencies in table 4-1 reflect the influences of compensation and Adam Smith rules. The more an agency has access to restricted funds for compensatory treatment, the more its allocations will approach equal results. The more an agency relies on Adam Smith rules to distribute its resources, the more its allocations will approach market equity.

The library is least redistributive because it was extreme on

TABLE 4-1: Three Standards of Equity for Judging Outcomes

	Market Equity	*Equal Opportunity*	*Equal Results*
	————————→ *Increasing Redistribution* ————————→		
Schools	The per child expenditure in each school should be proportional to the taxes paid by the neighborhood	Each child should receive equal dollar expenditure	Each child should receive enough expenditure so that all children read at the same level [1]
Libraries	The per resident expenditure in each branch should be proportional to the taxes paid by the neighborhood	Each branch should receive equal per capita expenditure	Each branch should receive enough expenditure so that circulation per capita is equal in all branches
Streets	The per resident expenditure on streets in each neighborhood should be proportional to the taxes paid by that neighborhood	Each neighborhood should receive an equal per capita (or per mile) expenditure	Each neighborhood should receive enough expenditure so that the condition of all neighborhood streets in the city is equal

[1] If not exactly the same level, at least an equal mean level for racial and income groups.

both counts. It had less access to compensatory funds than either of the other two agencies. It allocated its own budget through a combination of professional standards and Adam Smith rules which clearly favored the well-to-do.

Before 1970, the school system was a kind of paradox. It had access to money for large compensatory programs. This tended to shift its allocations toward equal results. But the district allocated its own resources through Adam Smith rules, including the rules for teacher assignments and supplies. These rules tended to move the allocation back toward market equity. Beginning in 1970, the new administration eliminated these rules as they applied to teacher assignments. The result was a definite shift of the allocations toward equal results.

ALTERING OUTCOMES

Before proceeding to answer our final question, how might outcomes be altered, let us briefly review where we have been. Our argument is shown in table 4-2, where we see that decision rules,

TABLE 4-2: Outcomes in Oakland

Stages of Government Activity	*Administrative Behavior*
Rules	Adam Smith rules
	Professional norms
	Federal and state funds
	Clientele requests
which lead to	Major vs. minor streets
Decisions	Central vs. branch libraries
	Parent contributions
analyzed as patterns of	Several distributions (U,J,L)
Outputs	The more, the more
	Compensation
	Resultants
to be evaluated as	Inefficient
Outcomes	Class bias
	Between market equity and equal opportunity
	Responsive to yesterday

such as Adam Smith behavior and constraints on federal and state funds, lead to allocation decisions that favor major streets, the central library, and experienced teachers for some but not other Oakland schools. From these decisions, we discerned a number of patterns of resource distribution (particularly the more, the more), which we then evaluated as outcomes. Oakland's outcomes, we concluded, were inefficient, had a class bias somewhere between the standards of market equity and equal opportunity, and were responsive to yesterday's demands. To alter outcomes, we must first know in what direction to proceed: so we state our preferences.

OUR PREFERENCES

Everyone lives in a world he never made. Bureaucrats have to deal with the world as they find it and not as others would wish it to be. The decision makers of today began their careers when public service meant doing an efficient job of handling the business that came to them. If they were asked why they did not seek equality of results, they could rightly say that it was not their business to remake society. They never had a mandate from the electorate or their administrative superiors to alter outcomes in favor of selected social groups. If some people use cars more than others or like to go to libraries, that is the way of the world; when income patterns and reading habits change, Adam Smith rules will favor new users as much as they did the old. These rules are fair for those citizens fortunate enough to make use of them. As society, in its mysterious ways, makes larger numbers of citizens more fortunate, they will then get a bonus in the shape of greater returns from municipal services.

This argument, however understandable in its time, is no longer acceptable. Oakland is a changing city. In 1940, less than 5 percent of its population were racial minorities. By 1970, the percentage had risen to 41 percent. While some minority residents are middle income, many are poor. They do not, in general, need libraries for scholarly research. This changing constituency should have an impact on our agencies, and ultimately, public goods have to serve the public. When that public changes radically, the goods must change too.

Where, then, along the range from market equity to equal results, should these agencies attempt to place themselves? In offering our answer, we should remember that agencies do different things and we cannot expect the same prescription to fit each of them.

The street department differs from libraries and schools in that the department supplies all the output the person receives. Unlike schools, which give a person part of his education while the home supplies the rest, the government is, for practical purposes, the sole supplier. If a neighborhood's streets are bad, it is because the department has let them become bad. This suggests that current department policy should be adjusted for past failures; something approaching equal results. Streets, however, are an adjunct to cars, a consumer good that is bought in the market. It would not be unreasonable, therefore, for the street department to assist citizens in proportion to their possession of cars. To the extent that cars are unequally distributed, the street department would favor the better off.

We have no easy answer for this conflict. But we can say that at a minimum the street department should compensate poor neighborhoods for past inequality and bring their streets up to the standards justified by their condition and traffic. This means allocating both repaving funds and some new construction funds on the basis of deterioration—not on the number of complaints or the plans of the utility company. There would not be full equal results, since allocations would ultimately be based on traffic, and car users would still be favored over nonusers or lesser-users, but the street department would not be inculcating any bias that did not already exist. The irony is that as aesthetic standards change, having streets that attract traffic is fast becoming a detriment. By the time the poor get treated equally, they may not want it.

If the citizens of poor neighborhoods do not want improved streets for increased traffic, then the money can be spent in other ways. A number of neighborhoods in Oakland, for example, could use sidewalks, curbs, and storm drains to prevent flooding of property during heavy rains. Usually such situations are handled by special assessment of the property owners, but with absentee owners and poor tenants such improvements are not forthcoming. With some changes to state and local law, the street department could start moving toward equal opportunity and at the same time take into account these citizen needs.

Securing equal results in libraries—equal circulation per citizen or size of neighborhood—is beyond anyone's present ability. The minimum requirement is equality of opportunity in access to books desired by different kinds of citizens. That would help assure that the libraries would tap the existing demand. Beyond that, all that can be asked are efforts to stimulate demand. If totally unsuccessful, the libraries could retreat to equality of opportunity. If partially successful, the libraries could push these efforts to the point where they begin to impair services to other citizens. Before we have to confront a situation in which more for one group means less for another, the libraries will have to be far more effective than they are today.

The schools are our simplest case, for their current allocation looks most like the allocation we desire. Our reasoning, however, requires more substantial explanation.

The promotion of discrimination within a school district, justified by a standard of market equity, is wrong. Even if education does not influence life chances as much as had been thought, it should not keep people down. Allowing market equity to prevail would perpetuate the disadvantageous socioeconomic position that students bring with them.

A policy directed toward equal results raises dilemmas of a different sort. A primary problem is the lack of knowledge; at this time no one knows how to improve significantly the performance of low achievers even if huge resources were made available. When we obtain this knowledge, we will be faced with a second problem; in a world of limited resources, what we give to low achievers we take from high achievers. How do we balance this allocation? Often this question carries racial overtones, but this need not be the case. Within any classroom, there is a substantial spread of abilities which is typically larger than the spread between the average ability of rich schools and the average ability of poor schools. How is a teacher to allocate her time in such a classroom? Is she to spend all her time with the poor readers and let the rich achievers fend for themselves? Is she to divide her time equally among all children? There are no easy answers to such questions.

If market equity and equal results are both suspect, this suggests a standard of equal opportunity—equal expenditure per child. Equal opportunity has strong intuitive appeal as being fair on its face. It is a value shared by many citizens. There is certainly no reason to do less. But might there just possibly be reason to do more?

How, to turn the question around, should we resolve our uncertainty about the effect of compensatory measures: by doing less, since there is no current evidence of improvement? Or by doing more in the hope that future evidence will provide the basis for more optimistic conclusions? We would do more if we thought it helped. A more cheerful element may be introduced: if we lack knowledge of how to help the worst-off, there is no evidence that the best-off are hurt by getting a little less. Thus we can afford to chance a little more than we might if anyone were being harmed.

Under conditions of risk, when a probability distribution of outcomes can be specified, we can make rational judgments relating proposed investments to likely returns. Under uncertainty, we have no such probabilities to go on. Rather than not act at all, we need a reasonable way of hedging our bets. Experimentation immediately comes to mind. Why throw a large sum away when new knowledge can be gained by spending lesser amounts through a series of experiments? We agree; but there is more to it than that. Good experiments are not exactly cheap and, since we lack good hypotheses, many of them have to be conducted. Now an experiment usually requires a sizable control group. The whole idea (recall Sinclair Lewis's *Arrowsmith*) is that the vast majority *do not get* the serum or the new educational technique. Thus experiments impose high political costs because, on their face, they are a means of continuing to deprive people who already have less. For most of them, experiments signify that they continue not to get what they have not had. That is why they so often say they are tired of being experimented on.

Not merely the structure but the time horizon of the experiments works against the deprived. The idea behind each longitudinal study is to determine whether varying the curriculum or class size produces lasting effects on reading or mathematical ability. The emphasis is on "lasting." Years have to go by before the results, if any, are known. In the meantime, from the perspective of the deprived, nothing is being done. Worse still, the existence of the experiment is used as a justification for not doing more until the evidence is in and analyzed.

Despite the vogue for experimentation, certain critical hypotheses cannot be tested, at least not right away or all at once. Suppose a tutorial reading program does not alter abilities over a three-to-five-year period. One hypothesis is that the theory or the practice of the program leaves a great deal to be desired. Another is that the subjects are recalcitrant; as the saying goes, nothing can be done with them. A third is that the program was not in operation for a long-enough period. A fourth is that more intense effort, more aid or hours per student, would have paid off. Some of these hypotheses may be tested simultanteously, varying aid versus hours, but others, the longer-time theory, only by letting the process work its way into the future. How long, then, must the deprived wait?

Experiments of several kinds have been and are now going on. A reasonable hedge against adversity would be to move the distribution of resources modestly beyond equality of opportunity. In this way, as experiments proceed, those who need help the most will be getting some, while the other students, so far as anyone knows, will not be harmed. Maybe we ask too much too soon of social policy. Perhaps each age group does get better; improvements may become visible to our crude instruments only after cumulating over several generations. It might be worth investing in this possibility against the current pessimism.

It seems that we are back again to the earlier distinction between outcomes and impacts. Outcomes can be determined; we can discover whether equality of opportunity is being approximated. But compensatory action requires a causal knowledge of impacts—how does policy ultimately affect citizens?—that few can discover. This book is about outcomes precisely because the impact of policy is so difficult to discern. If we had to talk about impacts, the most we could say is that we don't know.

There is also another lesson encapsulated within this one. Amidst the vagaries of the world it is well to do a little more than is required in the present just in case it turns out to be good policy in the future. Ultimately it may be the best-off who need the conviction they offered a little more than equal opportunity even if no one could get (or were sure they wanted) equal results. When in doubt, as the old politicians used to say, do right. And, we now add, do a little more.

Looking at the question of equality from the vantage point of level of government, there is good reason to choose a division of labor in which the locals move to equality of opportunity and the federals move toward compensation. The obligation of the local government is to afford each citizen genuine equality where the effects would be locally produced and felt. When local efforts are insufficient, it is desirable for the federal government to enhance the general quality of citizenry. That is what extra help is about.

There are many advantages in using the federal government as a mechanism for redistribution. Disparities in relation to taxes paid and benefits received, and inequalities in expenditures per citizen, are far more evident at the local level. The longer distance between the government and the taxpayer, as well as the increased difficulty of connecting taxes with specific programs, make redistribution more feasible at the federal level. No citizen, unless he is willing to leave the country, can escape the reach of the federal government. But he can move freely from one locality to another to escape conditions he considers onerous or unfair. It is difficult for a single city to engage in redistributive policies, which means taking resources from some citizens to give to others, unless other cities in its area do the same. Where the federal government could, at least in theory, take account of the anomalies among cities, no single municipality can do so. Of course, it is easy to urge the federal government to redistribute; it is another matter to accomplish it.

CITIZENS AND BUREAUCRATS

To alter outcomes it is necessary either to change the stimuli to which bureaucratic actors respond or to have them focus directly on how their actions affect citizens through the distribution of outputs. The more people have, we now know, the more they are likely to get. Pressure may be placed on professions to work against this trend. Although these changes are results of slow accretions and hence cannot be traced directly to specific events or announced on certain days, they are nonetheless important. These nascent tendencies may be thwarted or reinforced by the political climate in which municipal officials operate. Just as they responded to the old pressures of vehicular traffic and book orders, so officials can be expected to act appropriately toward new pressures if they are suitably motivated.

Bureaucratic stimuli can be changed in several areas. Work can be done to rationalize constraints on outside funding. The State of California has already relaxed some of the constraints which limit the rise of gas tax funds, but it can go further in providing more discretion to local officials. Anomalous override taxes like the seventh and eighth grade tax could be combined into the general fund. Although such funding reforms would not bring the millennium, they would offer administrators additional flexibility in making allocative decisions. It would then be easier to hold them responsible for what they have done, not what others have compelled them to do.

Bureaucratic stimuli can also be changed through better citizen political organization. Citizens are predictably concerned with small variances that affect their immediate vicinity. When they protest such variances, they are likely to be heard. The cost is little; the protesters are all neighbors; and the demands on the city council or the board of education are couched in terms of narrow appeals of immediate interest to the parties concerned. The school board (and the city council as well) [11] likes to meet visible citizen demands that are limited both in scope and in financial commitments. When they fail to do so, the reason is probably lack of funds or in the intersection of the citizen demands with some rule that would result in diminution of available monies.

Citizens who are most able to understand city procedures and to organize themselves are in the best position to take advantage of this opportunity to seek redress of grievances. If every citizen adversely affected were to seek opportunity to gain special treatment, the broad line of policy might be modified sufficiently to increase the general welfare.

Unfortunately, we know that only a relative few seek and use their opportunities. While the benefits gained are undoubtedly important to these few citizens, they do not drastically change the overall patterns of allocations. The street department, for instance, accommodates itself to these demands by altering its time schedule but not by changing its basic priorities. More substantial changes might be secured if citizens are related to a major institution, such as the Redevelopment Agency, that has sufficient

11. See the chapter on the city council in Jay Starling, *The Miracle of City Government* (Ph.D. dissertation, Political Science Dept., University of California, Berkeley, 1974).

muscle to alter allocation by virtue of its own activities. Institutions that can reduce costs by contributing funds to purchase right-of-way or that can impose costs by increasing traffic will get their way.

Agencies do know what is going on. They are aware of public demand. Their officials spend full time making decisions, collecting information, finding out what others are doing. The advantage of being an official appears in each of our studies. Take streets. The Federal Aviation Agency is able to get street work done near the Oakland Airport because its people know what is happening and because they can hint that traffic might be diverted to the rival airport in San Jose. County officials, who distribute part of the gas tax revenue, make their will felt by tugging on the purse strings. The Redevelopment Agency, acting through the city manager, claims additional land for new projects. This is possible only because the agency has a staff alert to this opportunity and the city manager has an interest in helping it out. Political organization helps both by increasing the responsiveness of elected officials and by creating or supporting new agencies.

We have seen examples where citizens' protests continue to prevent the closing down of small library branches. Parents persuaded school officials not to cut the sixth period out of the high school day and to retain an English-as-a-second-language program at a Chicano school even after federal funds for the program were cut. Citizens on Fifty-first Street, by playing the county against the city, were able first to prevent and then to expedite construction on their street as their requirements changed. Organizing citizens is not an easy job, but it pays dividends if only because it then becomes part of the course of least resistance to take them into account in providing government services.

Bureaucratic socialization is also important. Agency officials should be made aware of the way in which their outputs are distributed. Calling for changes in attitude might be dismissed as utopian. Yet in the last three years, we have seen movements in this direction. Beginning in 1970, the new school superintendent explicitly focused on the distribution of experienced teachers throughout the system. He drastically cut down transfers and reduced class sizes in schools with less experienced staff. When the new city manager and head librarian were presented with criticisms of their current allocations, they approved a budget which substantially increased expenditures on books while cutting back on staff. The street department is now engaged in discussions with the utilities, which will better synchronize their two schedules and will not cause the veto of so many repaving projects.

Since professional norms are so important in determining outcomes, those of us responsible for the education of these professionals may want to take a second look. Professional engineers do not have to be so single-minded about traffic circulation; they can be educated to understand that neighborhoods are important and that transportation involves more than roads. Both educators and librarians can be exposed to the assumptions about equality which will be part of their future work. Once we understand outcomes, there is less reason to leave them as unintended consequences.

Even if bureaucratic behavior changes, even if all the Adam Smith rules are abolished, it is unrealistic to expect agencies to undertake substantial compensatory allocations out of their own funds. All of our agencies are on tight budgets and they are beset by numerous demands. We have already seen that minor and modest (though not unimportant) changes can be made by citizens. Yet people who want drastic changes in allocations relating to streets or education could hardly do so at the local level alone. They would have to be organized at national and state levels as well so that the rules for distributing funds could be altered. No one can imagine such changes taking place overnight. Long years of preparation would be needed in which argument and fact were marshalled and political power mobilized to change officials or the values they bring to bear on these subjects. Few could predict with confidence the cumulative impact of proposed changes. No doubt each change brings with it a train of consequences that would be evaluated for their effects, and adaptation would be made on the basis of existing knowledge. Which is to say that we are not dealing with small local stuff, as it were, but with a society slowly altering fundamental notions of distributive justice.

DILEMMAS OF REDISTRIBUTION

We have been more concerned with what the government can do for the citizen than with what he ought to do for himself, to paraphrase President Kennedy. Placing the onus on government is understandable. This is, after all, a book about the activity of municipal agencies; citizens come in largely as they attempt to influence what government does, not as individuals who might wish to take responsibility for their own affairs. Let us, for a brief moment, therefore, change our focus to the citizen who has civic obligations as well as civil rights.

Every citizen ought to help himself as much as he can. It is wrong for him to place a special burden on the state if he can manage by himself. The state, in this respect, represents other people contributing their labors in the form of tax dollars for common purposes. Not only the rich but the poor support their fellows. How might our citizen help himself in regard to the services provided by the three agencies we have been discussing?

The maintenance and repair functions of the street department create no difficulties for our citizens. All are entitled to fair distribution of available effort, and the poor have been getting proportionately less. Citizens in the hills, who have higher incomes, get more and need it less; they should not get as much as they have been accustomed to in the past. The division of funds between arterial highways and city streets seems a better subject for general cultural change than for class divisions. Most citizens, including many poor ones, have cars and use the freeways. What is needed is not a reallocation to transfer advantages to some citizens but a consideration of whether most might not be better off by giving less emphasis to the automobile.

Libraries place a larger burden on the citizen than he has heretofore been willing to assume. Poor citizens could use libraries more than they do. The advantages of education and reading have been sufficiently publicized to make library use attractive. There is a point beyond which spending money to offer citizens inducements to do what is good for them anyway lacks an acceptable rationale. It is not only up to librarians to search out citizens but also up to potential users to come forward and make themselves known. Librarians, whatever their defects, are trying not to harm but to help. The Adam Smith rules that help branches whose patrons read many library books will also help others if they show initiative.

Poorer citizens who need the most help in schooling should get more. But schools do not know how to secure equal results in performance, much of which appears to have its roots in the home. Is it clear that all parents of poor students are doing what they can to reinforce learning in the home? Is it evident that the communities from which they come are mobilizing citizen self-help to aid poor students and to make them aware that good books and good performance go together? The errors of commission by public agencies should not be overlooked, but neither should the faults of omission by citizens.

The onus, to be sure, may be placed in the opposite direction. By what principle can inequality be justified? This profound question has agitated political philosophers from Rousseau to Rawls (indeed, long before them and no doubt long after).[12] Rousseau appears to answer the question by elevating the community, and Rawls by denigrating the individual. By submerging himself in community, by abdicating his sovereign will in favor of the general will expressed through the social contract, no man has an incentive to be more equal than others. A false individual liberty gives way to a true moral community.

To Rawls inequality appears accidental or at least not meritorious. No individual is to merit blame or praise for making use of his natural endowments or the advantages that have come to him through inheritance. He does what he does because of what he is. So, too, the least fortunate are what life has made them. Since men cannot be made equal in facing the vicissitudes of life, Rawls prefers to make use of inevitable inequality in behalf of the less equal. Thus his guiding principle is that no inequality in wealth, position, or status is justified unless it works to the benefit of those who have lost out. Talent is not to be rewarded so much as socialized in the interest of the poorer strata whose culture is impoverished through no fault of their own.

This is not the place and we are not the ones to make substantial contributions to this eternal debate. Here our sole concern is to point out some unexamined consequences of treating the individual as if he could not help himself. As a practical matter, the better-off (the more equal) are in little danger from this line of

12. See Rousseau's *Discourse on the Origin and Foundations of Inequality Among Men,* and John Rawls, *A Theory of Justice* (Cambridge: Harvard University Press, 1971).

argument. Their condition testifies to their accomplishment, or so it must seem in a society where subtle distinctions in thought are likely to be so subtle as to be invisible. It is the worse-off (the less equal) who are in danger of being considered an amorphous and inert mass, capable of no spontaneous or self-generating motion, fit to be acted upon but not to act in their own behalf. Things may be done (hopefully) for them or (regretfully) to them but not (independently) by them.

Having started down this slippery slope it is but a short distance to talk about the less equal as culturally impoverished. If their cultural blood, not merely their income, is poor, they must evidently receive transfusions from a richer source. The helping hand, the compensatory act, cannot be enough, for it requires a responsive clasp, not a dead weight. Now culture is the broadest of categories. Who is to say that many people with inferior income are not superior in other dimensions? Would poor Appalachian whites or urban blacks wish to think of themselves (or to have others refer to them) in this way? It seems odd to justify remedying inequalities by an argument more suited to rationalizing imperialism, for what do we have but a sophisticated version of the white man's burden. Perhaps we could afford to sacrifice a little equality for a lot more dignity.

Rawls's position could lead to perverse policy recommendations. No doubt his concern about the worse-off induces sympathy. But it also leads to an allocation rule in which less is given to the best-off, no matter how much they can use it, and more is given to the worst-off, no matter how little they can use it. We see no compelling rationale in justice or even charity for adopting a rule at once so arbitrary and counter to the dictates of good sense. It is a virtue of Rawls's trenchant argument, however, that we are made to face up to the consequences of our moral choices.

The dilemmas of redistribution are severe because we insist upon promising equal results, which we do not know how to achieve. But what is wrong with raising so high and noble a standard? Should not our reach exceed our grasp? There are dangers. If the poorest elements in the population find they are not much better off under the banner of equal results, they will reject efforts ostensibly made on their behalf. Observing dissatisfaction on the part of those receiving extra resources, the people who pay are likely to call it ingratitude. The political result would be disastrous: rising discontent on the part of both those who pay the costs and those who get the benefits. The have-littles will be plunged into conflict with have-nots (the working and lower-middle classes with the poor) because compensatory mechanisms fail to help the one, and do not stretch far enough to reach the other.

The problem of the near-poor needs to be considered. They are more easily helped because they have a bit more with which to begin. As they observe extra resources going to the very poor, who are most in need but least likely to be helped, they cannot help but wonder why they, who need less help but can use it better, are being left out. Their dissatisfaction with government is bound to rise. And so is government dissatisfaction with itself, for officials are asked to aid those least able and to sacrifice the more able, which leads to small visible results. Part of the secret of winning, as any football coach knows, lies in arranging an appropriate schedule. Governmental performance depends not only on its ability to solve problems but also on selecting problems it knows how to solve.

It sometimes appears easier for philosophers to assert appropriate criteria of distributive justice than it is for policy makers to to apply them. Changes in the distribution of income, for example, were accomplished in part by manipulating a complex tax structure with its transfer payments and hidden benefits. Redistribution required obfuscation. Perhaps caring but not knowing helped. As long as it appeared that someone else paid and somebody benefited, redistributive programs were acceptable. Now as redistributive programs become apparent failures with visible costs, one wonders whether they are still acceptable. What leads us to believe that citizens feel that altruism and equality have replaced achievement and status? And why should altruism replace achievement when no one knows how to make it do so?

Even when the government knows how to deliver, policy makers cannot simply act on a standard of equality that may do violence to the prevailing and often fragile consensus. At the level of expectations if not performance, equality of results interferes with the best of intentions because it is likely to clarify who wins, and who loses or pays. It implies some visibility of results, and therefore it cuts down on the ability of policy makers to finesse a conflict-ridden situation. Whatever the merits of different standards of equality, they did allow policy makers discretion to pursue a measure of redistribution.

Turmoil among the citizenry easily could be matched by consternation within the bureaucracy if it is expected to respond to inconsistent demands. Consider the trade-offs between experience and responsiveness among teachers. The schools may be criticized because their most experienced teachers, who pull down the highest salaries, gravitate from poor and black schools to those that are rich and white. At the same time, however, the schools are required to have teachers responsive to poor black students. Now such teachers by and large are younger and less experienced. One cannot usually have experienced *and* responsive teachers; insisting that the schools provide them will only lead to flight, withdrawal, or other neurotic behavior.

Another dilemma is that redistribution policies that aim toward equality invariably create inequality. They are certain to set off doctrinal disputes. They compromise other values such as equal treatment of all citizens, and by doing so they undermine the legitimacy of political institutions which were to be enhanced. Certainly universal application and equal treatment are central conditions to maintaining the approval of citizens. Yet securing equal results depends precisely on singling out groups for special treatment, not in handling all the same way. Thus the pipe dream of universally valid rules has to go. If the object in each area of policy is to provide special advantages for a specific minority, there will have to be a different rule for allocating resources for each.

When we pursue redistribution policies by providing services to some and not to others, we assume that officials can easily measure our progress toward equality. Certainly streets can be graded for their condition, and students can be tested for their reading achievement. Objective measures do exist, but will they suffice? Notions of what is fair and equal treatment may differ with the citizen and the occasion. Even if people agree to similar measures or criteria, they may still come to different conclusions because programs often have a differential impact. A substandard street may slow traffic for some citizens, and for others it may enhance the rustic character of the neighborhood. While equality of results may have sufficient clarity to cause political problems for policy makers, it does not have sufficient clarity and closure for bureaucrats to administer programs and allocate resources.

Suppose you want to advantage citizens in poor areas by having their streets repaved and repaired more often. For that purpose the criterion could be that funds are disbursed according to the number of citizens living in each district. Since the poor are numerous, they will do better than (or at least as well as) the rich, though not as well as the most numerous group in between. A per capita grant would also help the poor in regard to branch libraries. But the identical rule in regard to schools would leave the poor disadvantaged.

Suppose the criterion is "use." Allocating resources according to travel on the freeways and taking out books would not help the poor. Wealthier people prevail on those criteria. The poor would do better in education (because more of them use the schools) but not well enough, because compensatory devices are not allowed.

There is a real difference between Adam Smith rules that are neutral in content if not in consequence and rules deliberately skewed to alter outcomes. The economists' idea that every benefit has its associated costs must also be applied to bureaucracy. The more that distributive justice for certain groups becomes their aim, the less they will be able to manifest their traditional virtues. Rules that apply equally to all citizens will have to go. Responsiveness to political leaders will be lessened by commitment to clienteles. Favoritism will be not *de facto* but *de jure*. Due process will increasingly be sacrificed to desirable outcomes. And bureaucracy will become a more dangerous and problematic element in society.

Now we can see why students of public policy in recent times have come increasingly to prefer "income" solutions instead of meeting specific social problems head on. A "Karl Marx" bureaucracy might be worse than an "Adam Smith" one. If those that have get more, if prevailing allocations of resources in specific areas are difficult to change, increasing the income of poor people should have corresponding multiplier effects. Instead of trying directly to improve services for the poor, they can be placed in a better position to make use of the Adam Smith rules, which work for those who have more to begin with. We are sympathetic but not entirely, because government will have to make choices even on income. It will continue to provide services. There is no escape from either the empirical question—How do prevailing distributions affect citizens?—or the moral question—What should government do about it?

How far should government go in seeking to remedy inequalities? To say "as far as it can" is not a satisfactory answer. Suppose it took tens of millions to secure equality of result for a single individual. However much society values equality and the individual, the cost would undoubtedly be considered too great in view of alternative uses to which the money could be put. The example is absurd but not entirely. So long as equality is not "priceless," so long as there is some price beyond which government ought not to go, the problem is converted from one of absolute values to one of relative costs. Government should go as far as equality of opportunity. It should not go far beyond that unless compensatory spending will result in greater actual equality. When it knows how much a modicum of equality will cost, government will be able to make explicit trade-offs between the costs to some and the benefits to others, trade-offs including the support necessary to maintain the redistributions in which it is engaging. The question is not only one of economic rationality—which action will contribute most to national income—or of ethical rationality—which actions will best satisfy criteria of distributive justice; it also concerns political rationality—strengthening the respect in which government is held by increasing its ability to act effectively with the consent of the governed. Should equality of result, then, be pushed against the intense preferences of a substantial majority of citizens? The very statement of the question suggests that we would be better off putting it another way.

Perhaps a more modest interpretation of equal result would require only benefiting the poor more and keeping the rich where they are. The present position of the better-off would not be attacked, but as a richer society generates more resources these would be diverted to the worst-off. Such was our position, for example, in regard to libraries. Resources in the branches in the well-to-do neighborhoods would be maintained at current levels, while any increase would be channeled to branches serving the poorest people. An attempt would be made to gain knowledge through decentralization that would encourage a variety of approaches.

This approach smacks of tokenism. So what if a few more streets get paved in poor areas. So what if branch libraries have (and poorer residents read) a few more books. Suppose the reading ability of poor children does go up a little. If outcomes change only a little, does a progressive reallocation of resources over the years matter?

We should not overlook the desirability of ultimately making good on the traditional American idea (no matter how often it is violated) of equality of opportunity. There would be no need for hypocrisy if equality did not matter. Nor should we deride the symbolic value of making a visible and palpable effort on behalf of the least fortunate. To know that substantial efforts are being made may help to build social cohesion upon which the aspiration of a free society rests.

Appendix A

STATISTICAL TEST
OF HYPOTHESES OF DIFFERENCES IN
STUDENT/TEACHER RATIO, 1969/70

H_0: That schools in Group i have a larger ratio of students to total
teachers than do schools in Group j

H_1: That schools in Group i do not have a larger ratio of students
to total teachers than do schools in Group j

(A) Matrix of student's t statistics for schools classified by percent
minority

	0–10	11–50	51–90	91–100
0–10	—	.48	1.61	3.25
11–50		—	1.45	3.82
51–90			—	2.50
91–100				—

(B) Matrix of student's t statistics for schools classified by income
of surrounding census tract (1960 income data)

	9,000 & above	7,500–8,999	6,000–7,499	4,500–5,999	3,000–4,499
9,000 & above	—	.05	.12	2.94	6.29

7,500– 8,999	—	.23	3.48	8.73
6,000– 7,499		—	4.50	9.26
4,500– 5,999			—	3.83
3,000– 4,499				—

In each case, the coefficient t_{ij} refers to the hypothesis that Group i has *larger* student/teacher ratio than does Group j. For all tests, the critical value of t is approximately 2.0 (5%). A negative t statistic indicates that Group j is receiving more than Group i, the opposite of the null hypothesis.

STATISTICAL TEST OF HYPOTHESES OF DIFFERENCES IN STUDENT/TEACHER RATIO, 1970/71

H_0: That schools in Group i have a larger ratio of students to total teachers than do schools in Group j

H_1: That schools in Group i do not have a larger ratio of students to total teachers than do schools in Group j

(A) Matrix of student's t statistics for schools classified by percent minority

	0–10	11–50	51–90	91–100
0–10	—	.67	2.80	3.94
11–50		—	3.35	5.58
51–90			—	2.74
91–100				—

(B) Matrix of student's t statistics for schools classified by income of surrounding census tract (1960 income data)

	9,000 & above	7,500– 8,999	6,000– 7,499	4,500– 5,999	3,000– 4,499
9,000 & above	—	1.54	2.74	3.88	10.42

7,500–8,999	—	.99	3.26	11.40
6,000–7,499		—	4.18	11.56
4,500 5,999			—	2.22
3,000–4,499				—

In each case, the coefficient t_{ij} refers to the hypothesis that Group i has *larger* student/teacher ratio than does Group j. For all tests, the critical value of t is approximately 2.0 (5%). A negative t statistic indicates that Group j is receiving more than Group i, the opposite of the null hypothesis.

STATISTICAL TEST OF HYPOTHESES OF DIFFERENCES IN SALARY DOLLARS OF ALL TEACHERS/STUDENT RATIO (INCLUDES COMPENSATORY TEACHERS' SALARIES), 1969/70

H_0: That schools in Group i have a larger ratio of salary dollars per students than do schools in Group j

H_1: That schools in Group i do not have a larger ratio of salary dollars per students than do schools in Group j

(A) Matrix of student's t statistics for schools classified by percent minority

	0–10	11–50	51–90	91–100
0–10	—	— .22	.62	— 1.05
11–50		—	1.06	— 1.39
51–90			—	— 2.09
91–100				—

(B) Matrix of student's t statistics for schools classified by income of surrounding census tract (1960 income data)

	9,000 & above	7,500– 8,999	6,000– 7,499	4,500– 5,999	3,000– 4,499
9,000 & above	—	— .58	— 2.08	.46	— 3.50
7,500– 8,999		—	— 1.65	— .03	— 4.47
6,000– 7,499			—	— 1.66	— 6.70
4,500– 5,999				—	— 4.36
3,000– 4,499					—

In each case, the coefficient t_{ij} refers to the hypothesis that Group i has *larger* student/teacher ratio than does Group j. For all tests, the critical value of t is approximately 2.0 (5%). A negative t statistic indicates that Group j is receiving more than Group i, the opposite of the null hypothesis.

STATISTICAL TEST
OF HYPOTHESES OF DIFFERENCES IN
SALARY DOLLARS OF ALL TEACHERS/STUDENT RATIO
(INCLUDES COMPENSATORY TEACHERS' SALARIES),
1970/71

H_0: That schools in Group i have a larger ratio of salary dollars per students than do schools in Group j

H_1: That schools in Group i do not have a larger ratio of salary dollars per student than do schools in Group j

(A) Matrix of student's t statistics for schools classified by percent minority

	0–10	11–50	51–90	91–100
0–10	—	— .23	— .27	— 1.45
11–50		—	— .17	— 2.35
51–90			—	— 2.21
91–100				—

(B) Matrix of student's t statistics for schools classified by income of surrounding census tract (1960 income data)

	9,000 & above	7,500– 8,999	6,000– 7,499	4,500– 5,999	3,000– 4,499
9,000 & above	—	− 1.28	.34	− 1.25	− 8.32
7,500– 8,999		—	1.88	− 1.11	− 7.46
6,000– 7,499			—	2.11	− 10.915
4,500– 5,999				—	− .36
3,000– 4,499					—

In each case, the coefficient t_{ij} refers to the hypothesis that Group i has *larger* student/teacher ratio than does Group j. For all tests, the critical value of t is approximately 2.0 (5%). A negative t statistic indicates that Group j is receiving more than Group i, the opposite of the null hypothesis.

Appendix B

LIBRARY STANDARDS

Examination of all the sets of standards currently in use reveals many reasons why they should not be used to evaluate a library's effectiveness.[1] We will discuss the major shortcomings.

(1) Most standards surveyed are *not* performance standards; they do not relate specific requirements to specific goals. Nearly all are concerned with inputs rather than outputs. Nowhere do we find out what the library should be producing, only what the

1. The section on standards has been adapted from a report on the Oakland Library by Professor Michael Teitz and Rae Archibald. Over the years a number of standards for public library operations have been established. The first comprehensive set, *Post-War Standards for Public Libraries*, was published in 1943 and in many ways is still the best. Objectives, although vague, are explicitly stated, and standards, by comparison, are more explicit and more quantifiable than in later efforts. The next set of standards, *Public Library Service* (1956), reflects librarians' concern with the intangible aspects of library service and tries to define "quality." Most of the standards are expressed in terms of minimum achievement levels. Ten years later, many individual standards were altered in a revision, but there was no change in philosophy. Standards have also been promulgated by state groups. The official set, Public Library Service Standards for California, adopted by the California State Library Association in 1953, closely parallels the national standards. The latest effort, Public Library Service Equal to the Challenge in California, was prepared upon commission of the State Librarian by L. A. Martin and R. Bowler in 1965. It is essentially an expansion of the first—more of everything—and is generally considered to have superseded the officially adopted standards.

library should be using. The assumption is implicit that if a library has the prescribed number of books and personnel and amount of space, it is a "good" or "standard" library.

(2) Many of the standards include terms that are never defined or are defined in terms of themselves. Thus a library program of "adequate quantity" and "dynamic quality" is supposed to have "reasonable" financial support and "sufficient" book stock of "good" quality and "proper" proportions.

(3) Some of the standards are essentially descriptive—a large library would have this, a small library that. There is a complete loss of normative content. To say that a large library had nearly 100 percent of such-and-such while a small library had only 25 percent of this-and-that, however, is to say nothing about how much each *should* have.

(4) Most of the standards profess to prescribe minimum degrees of adequacy. By this token, more of everything is better. All sets of standards seem to imply, however, that these minimums are goals to be reached in the future. Thus a "reasonable degree of adequacy" is to be attained "one of these days." The standard-makers confuse statements of standards as norms of current good practice with statements of objectives to be realized in the future.

(5) The later sets of standards generally do not specify the goals of library service. Rather, the activities (preserving books, providing reference services, counseling readers, etc.) are just identified. The danger here is that librarians might believe that to describe activities is to state goals. Such a belief is essentially to deny that there are alternative paths to the same ends.

(6) Some standards prescribe outcomes in terms of service required by the community. A central library should have the amount of space necessary to provide the range of service "needed" by the community. But not once is the method of determining community need discussed. The implicit assumption is that if a standard prescribes a minimum book stock of 50,000 books, the community needs this many books. Standards based on such assumptions are tenuous at best; why not 25,000 or 100,000?

(7) If they were to meet some of the standards, librarians would have to perform nearly supernatural feats of prediction and analysis. It is asking a lot of a librarian to expect him to determine

"frequency of access in normal pursuit of activities." It may be intellectually satisfying to develop a conceptual scheme for the location of a library, but it is intellectually dishonest to prescribe this scheme as a standard if it is known that the professional librarian cannot follow it. More than a few of the standards, unfortunately, are useless to practicing librarians; some are so encompassing that the librarian can only muse about them.

(8) Finally, a comment must be made about the layman and the standards. National standards state that a layman could use the standards without further interpretation to evaluate the performance of a library. This is patently false. The standards are too vague, contradictory, and input-oriented to provide any layman with a suitable tool for evaluation. The standards do not adequately treat the outcomes of the system, and thus they provide sorry tools for a layman's evaluation process. To know that Oakland has a staff of 220 people in contrast to a standard of 193 is to know virtually nothing about the performance of the library system. The standards must be rewritten so that the library's performance, in addition to its amount of resources, can be evaluated.

If, in spite of our dissatisfaction with standards as an evaluating tool, we do compare the Oakland Library's operations with the prescribed standards, what do we find?

(1) The Oakland Library does not buy enough books annually. It purchased 10,000 fewer books in fiscal 1966 than required by the national per capita standard.

(2) Oakland does not allocate enough of its budget to the purchase of books. Oakland has consistently allocated between 6 and 7 percent of its budget to materials purchased even though the standards indicate that between 15 and 20 percent should be allocated for this.

(3) Oakland does not retire enough books from its system annually. It should have taken 20,000 more volumes off the shelf in fiscal 1966 than it did if it expected to operate according to the standard.

(4) Oakland employs too many professional librarians. Following one national benchmark, Oakland employs fifty-one more professional librarians than is recommended.

(5) Oakland has too many branches for a population of its

size. The branches each have too few books, serve too few people, and have too few seats.

Examining various aspects of the Oakland library system leads us to some similar conclusions, though methods of arriving at them are different. In spite of all our complaints about standards, we have to acknowledge that agreement with their conclusions is more than coincidence. After all, the standards are established by people who know a lot about libraries.

Yet there may often be good reasons for not meeting the standards. The large number of library branches in Oakland, for instance, may be an effective way to reach a larger proportion of the population. If this is true, such a structure should be permitted no matter what the standards recommend. There is no justification for aiming to meet any particular input standards; our aim is to find outputs that help achieve proper outcomes for the library system.

Index